the cinema of LARS VON TRIER

DIRECTORS' CUTS

the cinema of
LARS VON TRIER

authenticity and artifice

caroline bainbridge

WALLFLOWER PRESS LONDON & NEW YORK

First published in Great Britain in 2007 by
Wallflower Press
6 Market Place, London W1W 8AF
www.wallflowerpress.co.uk

A catalogue record for this book is available from the British Library

ISBN 978-1-905674-43-5 (paperback)
       978-1-905674-44-2 (hardback)

Book design by Rob Bowden Design

Printed and bound in Poland; produced by Polskabook

CONTENTS

ACKNOWLEDGEMENTS

This book has evolved over a number of years and parts of chapters three, six and seven consist of re-worked ideas based on 'Making Waves: Trauma and Ethics in the Work of Lars von Trier', which was published in the *Journal for Cultural Research* (2004), 8, 3, 129–41. Some of the material in chapters five and six draws on 'Just Looking?: Traumatic Affect, Film Form and Spectatorship' which was published in *Screen* (2004), 45, 4, 353–69.

I am grateful for the support and encouragement of many colleagues in the departments of Psychosocial Studies at the University of East London and Media and Cultural Studies at Roehampton University, especially Dr Paul Bowman, Dr Ben Cocking, Dr Andrea Esser, Dr Henrik Örnebring and Dr Paul Rixon. In particular, I would like to thank Dr Anita Biressi, Dr Deborah Jermyn and Dr Heather Nunn, all of whom have provided friendship, cocktails and a supportive ear on many occasions as well as commentary on various draft chapters. Special thanks are due to my dear friend and colleague Dr Candida Yates, whose enthusiasm and spirited approach to my work have sustained me more than she might realise; her insightful comments on the draft manuscript were frequently invaluable and I am much indebted to her for the generosity she has shown me. Professor Mette Hjort kindly let me have sight of her work in progress, for which I am very grateful. I must also extend many thanks to Yoram Allon at Wallflower Press for his unfailing generosity on this project and for his encouragement throughout. I would also like to thank Sarah, Trev and Archie Smith, Glenn Shadbolt, the Hamilton-Croft family, Jonty Hayes, Katharine Pincham, Dr Richard Carmichael and Dr Ashley Morgan for reminding me about life beyond the book and for keeping me entertained so often. Lastly, warmest thanks to my parents, Mary and Ed Bainbridge, and to my sister and brother-in-law, Nicki and Ed Chacksfield, all of whose love and belief in me mean the world. This book is for the bump, who emerged as Ewan Charles just as it was going to press!

PREFACE

The pursuit of authenticity through art is nothing new. However, as Denis Dutton (2003) has suggested, 'Whenever the term "authentic" is used in aesthetics, a good first question to ask is, *Authentic as opposed to what?*'. For Lars von Trier, the pursuit of authenticity in the art of cinema is to be understood in relation to the capacity of this art form to provide a means of escape from the tyranny of bourgeois cultural values and from the banality of the everyday. In a series of interviews about the provenance of his work, von Trier explains that 'When life gets too threatening, you have to create some sort of fantasy existence, a life where you can control the things you can't control in real life. That's a fairly good reason for creating fictions, I think' (Björkman 2003: 19). For von Trier, then, authenticity can be seen as something against which the experience of the individual can be gauged and defended, and in the context of which a worldview can be detected. The struggle for authenticity is a parallel one to the struggle for a sense of self. For von Trier, cinema is an archetypal medium through which to grapple with such struggles, and his work draws extensively on film history and the specificity of cinema as an art form seemingly in order to authenticate its suitability for the artistic pursuit of the 'real'.

This is interesting not least because von Trier's work in film is most often characterised as postmodern provocation. As a director whose work is grounded in the rather self-conscious referencing of films as diverse as *Mirror* (Andrei Tarkovsky, 1975) and *A Touch of Evil* (Orson Welles, 1958), and as an artist whose deliberate addition of 'von' to his family name has produced criticisms of arrogance and narcissism, von Trier seems to stand as an incarnation of artifice rather than authenticity. However, as this book explores, it is precisely this tension and von Trier's insistence on holding it in place that produces the specificity of his work.

The spread of von Trier's work is by now rather impressive. In the 27 years since the production of his first film school 16mm short, *Nocturne* (1980), von Trier has produced 23 pieces of work, incorporating three trilogies of feature films, several television series and television special events, music videos and artistic installations. He has also launched internationally significant developments in the context of cinema under the banners of the Dogme 95 and Advance Party projects and written and produced films made by other directors, such as Thomas Vinterberg. (A full filmography is included at the end of this volume, giving details of each of these projects.) As an artist, von Trier's work is not limited to the medium of film, and many of his most interesting cinematic projects overlay film with video and digital technologies. The question of cinematic authenticity, then, has gradually become eroded as his *oeuvre* has evolved.

At the same time, von Trier has repeatedly shown that cinema is important precisely because it does not deal with 'reality' and because of its extraordinary links to unconscious processes of fantasy and identification. The world of cinema is inherently one of artifice and contrivance, as von Trier's work makes explicit. It is the contention of this book that it is this opposition between authenticity and artifice that drives von Truer's creativity, fuelling his creativity and shoring up his work, creating new and important directions for the future of film in the twenty-first century. To this end, this book sets out to deal specifically with Lars von Trier's films and not with the full expanse of his work. For reasons of space and clarity, it has been necessary to delimit the scope of this study by exploring the key films of his back catalogue, the films which have enjoyed international theatrical release and which are now broadly available on DVD. However, it is important to acknowledge the ways in which many of the discussions that unfold in this book open up interesting channels for further exploration in relation to von Trier's early short films and his work in advertising, television drama, music video and art installations. (Jack Stevenson (2002) usefully charts the key forays made by von Trier outside the domain of internationally distributed cinema).

It is worth noting, however, that many of the key themes that emerge and persist in von Trier's earliest films set the scene for the work that follows. In *Befrielsesbilleder* (*Images of a Relief*, 1982), for example, the roots of *Forbrydelsens element* (*The Element of Crime*, 1984) and *Europa* (1991) are easily discerned as von Trier explores the discomforting scenario of Danes carrying out acts of vengeance against Nazi officers during the early days of liberation at the end of World War II. In *Medea* (1988), a television film adapted from a script by Carl Theodor Dreyer and released firstly in Denmark and later on VHS in France, strains of von Trier's concern with the feminine capacity for martyrdom are examined. Such themes come to dominate von Trier's later work as he couples these interests in betrayal, vengeance and salvation with his fascination with femininity and questions of goodness in the films of the 'Gold Heart' trilogy (*Breaking the Waves* (1996); *Idioterne* (*The Idiots*, 1998); *Dancer in the Dark* (2000)) and in the first two films of the 'U-S-A Land of Opportunity' trilogy (*Dogville* (2003); *Manderlay* (2005)).

This book sets out to show how these links can be made through an analysis of von Trier's technique and style and with reference to his extensive fascination with film as both a medium and an art form. By interrogating von Trier's relation to history and cultural values and by drawing on psychoanalytic theories to explore the seductions of his work, this study endeavours to suggest that authenticity has its roots in artifice for von Trier. This is, perhaps, most clearly suggested in his adoption of the 'von' at the heart of his professional name. In 'making a name for himself' (as Stig Björkman (2003: 2) suggests), von Trier creates a character for himself to embody. His provocative performances are wrought so as to best highlight the self-conscious posturing frequently alluded to in critical commentary. Underlying this masquerade, however, is a striking commitment to the pursuit of authenticity and a means of finding a mode for its expression. In making the films that he does, Lars von Trier is not merely making a name for himself; rather, it is possible to see his work as anchored in the search for an authentic sense of self, one that lies beneath the consummately composed veneer of provocation that caricatures his artistic sensibility.

CHAPTER ONE

From 'Enfant Terrible' to 'Punk Auteur': An Evolution of Technique and Style

It is well documented that Lars von Trier has no fixed style in his approach to film-making. In fact, the breadth of his work encompasses so many strains of cinematic technique and style that his *oeuvre* might be regarded as rather encyclopaedic, functioning as a kind of yardstick for key moments in the history of filmmaking in both Hollywood and art cinema. As Daniel Frampton (1993) has suggested, the plethora of cinematic references and quotations in von Trier's work pays testimony to the aesthetic achievements of many of cinema's greatest *auteurs*. Of course, the aim of this eclectic inter-textuality is not merely intended as homage – by signalling the key moments of his cinematic formation in this way, von Trier not only displays his extensive knowledge and appreciation of film, but also aligns himself with the magisterial qualities associated with the greatest moments of cinema history. The range of influences and references in von Trier's work is often astounding, but understanding his origins, sources and influences is essential to any project that interrogates his work. As von Trier himself has remarked, 'For me, stealing from the cinema is like using letters of the alphabet when you write' (Gruzinski 1997: 513). Von Trier's influences, however, are not merely cinematic; there are a number of references to literature, philosophy and music in his work too. This chapter sets out to trace the influences on von Trier in order to follow his trajectory from '*enfant terrible*' to 'punk *auteur*' (and back again).

A Man of the Arts

Lars von Trier's upbringing and family background were such that he was exposed to the arts from a very early age. As Jack Stevenson notes,

> The Trier household was a typical civil servant's home. It had books, art, a piano. The overall atmosphere was one of acquired progressiveness. A sense of liberalism and tolerance prevailed alongside a pronounced distaste for the sentimental or vulgar excesses of popular junk culture ... Lars unfailingly uses the term 'cultural radicalism' when he describes his upbringing ... Cultural radicals were a certain kind of people. They went in for jazz and classical music, not schmaltzy, popular ballads or Sunday morning sing-alongs. They preferred to take their vacations in Paris rather than driving the *autobahns* of Europe with a camping trailer, a popular pursuit of 'average' Danes in the late 1950s and early 60s. They would go to the theatre, to the opera and to films, but only *good* films. Their favourite painters included the likes of Asger Jorn and Picasso. One would never find kitsch exotica or mass-produced paintings of clowns, babies or cute puppies hanging on their walls. In regard to literature, well-known Danish authors like Hans Scherfig, Otto Gelsted and Hans Kirk were read by cultural radicals ... Solid Danish-design furniture was in, wall-to-wall carpeting and television was out. (2002: 7–8)

This experience left its mark on von Trier and is clearly discernible in his work. Von Trier himself references a number of non-cinematic key cultural figures in the formation of his artistic sensibilities.

Perhaps one of the most obvious non-cinematic influences on von Trier is the work of Richard Wagner. Von Trier had Wagner's music played during the making of *The Element of Crime* as part of his attempt to make the shoot into a kind of artistic 'happening' (Björkman 2003: 69), but the composer's influence can be seen in various aspects of von Trier's technique and style. As a composer, Wagner is well known for his orchestration and for his emphasis on counterpoint, the simultaneous sounding of separate musical lines. In von Trier's early work, the approach to style is heavily reminiscent of this mode of artistic structure, deploying techniques such as superimposition, back-projection, front-projection and the simultaneous visualisation of both colour and monotone images within the frame. Most clearly at play in *Europa* (aka *Zentropa*, 1991), the kind of cinematic counterpoint mobilised by von Trier echoes the technical innovations of Wagner, transposing his approach to opera into the realm of the cinematic.

For Wagner, opera was to be understood as 'musical drama' in which the musical form is inseparable from the operatic performance and narrative, the one enhancing the other (see Tanner 1995). Traces of this influence can be seen clearly in von Trier's 'Europa' trilogy – *The Element of Crime*, *Epidemic* (1997) and *Europa* – in which the sometimes alienating form and style are designed to inflect the narrative, characterisation and performance, but this also remains visible in some of the later work. In

Fig. 1 This image from *Europa* illustrates von Trier's innovative use of back-projection

Dancer in the Dark, for instance, the opening of the film is labelled as an 'overture' by von Trier in the screenplay accompanying the film (2000: 1). For Wagner, the operatic overture carries important emphasis as it encapsulates and communicates the essence of the emotional and narrative drama of a piece. This emphasis on emotional expression is also central to von Trier's *oeuvre* as a whole, perhaps being most easily discerned in the films of the 'Gold Heart' trilogy – *Breaking the Waves*, *The Idiots* and *Dancer in the Dark* – which make extensive use of hand-held camera-work that emulates a documentary style and seemingly heightens the emotionality of the narrative as a result (see Bainbridge *et al.* 2004a).

Wagner, of course, was a friend and mentor to Friedrich Nietzsche, whose philosophy has also had some influence on von Trier. A key concern for Nietzsche in his philosophical writings was the question of morality and the relationship between good and evil. He was profoundly fascinated by the death of the dominance of religion as a formative influence in the thought underpinning European culture and consistently sought to ponder the effects of science and knowledge on modalities of thinking. Time and again, Nietzsche returned to questions of religious belief and the relationship of this to the institution of the Church, arguing that the Church promoted the transvaluation of key religious beliefs, reframing the values associated with them and thereby demeaning the value of spiritual commitment and fervour. Nietzsche is also very well known for his discussion of the cosmological value of the 'eternal return' of all life events. Drawing on the work of Heinrich Heine and Arthur Schopenhauer, Nietzsche believed that one of the greatest maxims by which anyone could live was premised in the notion that all events would always be repeated exactly as they had already happened, carrying the very same emotional effects and burdens. For Nietzsche, the wish for an eternal return of all events amounts to an affirmation of life, despite the deep-rooted possibility of a kind of fatalism implicit in this way of thinking (see Alderman 1977).

These ideas are re-played in certain ways within von Trier's work and are seen especially in the moral fables that underpin it, perhaps most obviously in the 'Gold Heart' trilogy. In *Breaking the Waves*, for instance, these concerns are at the very heart of the narrative and are centred on Bess (Emily Watson) and her motivations in acting against the rules of the Church to which she belongs in pursuit of her desire for the romantic beginnings of life with Jan (Stellan Skarsgård) to be returned to her after his accident. Nietzsche's concept of *amor fati* (a love of fate) enables the subject to move beyond a state of endurance with regard to the eternal return and into a position of actively wishing for this, regardless of the pain and anguish it might entail. This profoundly echoes the love that Bess seeks to express for Jan throughout von Trier's film, highlighting many of his own religious and philosophical convictions and attitudes and drawing attention to the ways in which cinematic stories allow for the exploration of fundamental emotional and intellectual terrains of value in a world in which notions of the spirit have long been hailed as 'dead' or 'dying'. That von Trier places 'goodness' at the heart of the film's thematic context also indicates the extent of the influence of Nietzsche in this regard.

Breaking the Waves also draws on another key influence on von Trier in that it seems to refer to August Strindberg's *Miss Julie* (1888), a play in which an aristocratic young woman embarks on a lustful relationship with a servant, thereby defying social conventions of class and gender. This inevitably leads to her social downfall and the play culminates in her suicide. Strindberg's play foregrounds the dramatic tensions that are produced by the use of realism and by the endeavour to create characters whose psychological motivations are made explicit. The play is renowned for its frank portrayal of sexuality and lust and for its schematic interrogation of social mores and conventions. Like von Trier, Strindberg has been accused of misogyny in this work – various critics have labelled *Breaking the Waves* and the other films in the 'Gold Heart' trilogy as sadistic and misogynistic (Winters 1996; Scallan & Garin 1997; Romney 2004). Strindberg was intrigued by social and cultural hypocrisy around expectations of gendered behaviour and sexual morality, however, and it is not difficult to see how these themes are also explored in von Trier's trilogy of films. Strindberg was also committed to both Naturalism (a movement premised on social Darwinist ideas of 'the survival of the fittest') and Expressionism (a movement that values the evocation of subjective states of mind rather than objective observations of them), both of which are key stylistic approaches in von Trier's work. Von Trier himself signals his fascination with Strindberg, which partly stems from the playwright's experience of madness. Moreover, the fact that Strindberg not only wrote plays but also painted appeals to von Trier as he aligns this multifaceted approach to artistic creativity with a kind of romanticism (Björkman 2003: 28). Echoes of this influence are seen in the imagery used to mark the end of the chapters in *Breaking the Waves* (Björkman 2003: 197).

It was through the influence of Strindberg and also of Edvard Munch, whose key paintings von Trier has described as 'remarkable schizophrenic works' (Björkman 2003: 28), that von Trier himself felt driven to take up painting and to explore his visual sensibilities in media other than film. For him, 'artists are meant to have it bad, because it makes the results so much better!' (ibid.). As with Bess in *Breaking the Waves*, Karen (Bodil Jørgensen) in *The Idiots* and Selma (Björk) in *Dancer in the Dark*, Munch's depictions of women tended to focus on frailty, innocence and suffering. Munch, of course, was a key influence in the development of German Expressionism,

Fig. 2 The intertitles marking the 'chapters' of *Breaking the Waves* are replete with romantic imagery

an artistic movement which has had a profound influence on cinema in general and on von Trier in particular, as we shall see below.

Of central importance in von Trier's work is the influence of the playwright and poet Bertolt Brecht. A key figure in Weimar Germany and a deeply political artist, Brecht formulated innovative theatrical strategies and techniques in an effort to reformulate the political effectiveness of art and culture. Brecht's innovations around 'epic theatre' and the '*Verfremdungseffekt*' ('the alienation technique') were consciously developed to provoke audiences into reflection on what they watch when they attend the theatre. Instead of being encouraged to identify unconsciously with protagonists and dramatic events, spectators are required to become stirred up by what they see, responding in ways that question mainstream cultural practices and the ideological values that underpin them. Brecht wrote a number of '*Lehrstücke*' ('teaching plays') which were specifically designed to instil political sensibilities in the workers. Brecht was profoundly influenced by Marxism and by communism and his work was always very highly politically charged, leading to a period of exile during Hitler's rule during the 1930s. Brecht's techniques of estrangement and alienation included having characters speak stage directions and the use of placards to disrupt the tendency of spectators to become too focused on the narrative drive of a play. Brecht made great use of aphorisms and sought to place the responsibility for viewing practices and pleasures firmly on the shoulders of his spectators.

While von Trier's work does not overtly deploy such radical political positioning, the influence of Brecht's approach to theatre is seen throughout his work. At times, the technological mastery of the 'Europa' trilogy is so overwhelming that it is almost impossible to take pleasure in the narratives that unfold and the protagonists of these films are themselves profoundly alienated individuals. In *Europa*, for example, Leo Kessler (Jean Marc Barr) arrives in Germany as a somewhat naïve idealist, but he is quickly recruited to 'The Werewolves', a terrorist organisation, and his association with this group eventually leads to his demise. In *Epidemic*, Dr Mesmer (Lars von Trier) sets out on a single-handed mission to stop the plague from spreading, unwittingly spreading it as he goes. In *The Element of Crime*, Fisher (Michael Elphick) gets caught up in the mystery of Harry Grey to the extent that he actually takes on the guise of the murderer, committing the very crime he initially set out to understand. The overarching concern of the films in this trilogy with life in Germany also points to the influence of Brecht, and the tendency toward the alienation of the spectator and the intention of blurring the boundaries between art and everyday life are of key significance throughout this part of von Trier's career. Similarly, the drive toward alienation is seen in the shift toward hand-held camera and the attendant disruptions of cinematic convention that are seen in the 'Gold Heart' trilogy.

More recently, both *Dogville* and *Manderlay* are explicitly Brechtian in form and structure, with their highly theatrical content and the paring-down of set design and cinema-specific considerations of location and modes of representation. In these films, von Trier also follows Brecht's suggestions around the usefulness of historicisation in order better to draw attention to contemporary social issues and contexts. *Dogville*, for instance, is set in the 1930s and yet its thematic content and the closing credit sequence are highly pertinent to contemporary life and to ideological and social concerns about globalisation. Related anxieties about 'outsiders', discourses of immigration and the experience of exploitation, vengeance and social responsibility are all clearly evident themes. In setting these films in the United States, von Trier does appear to be making some kind of politicised commentary on contemporary global values as they are mediated through American cinema. In this regard, it is worth signalling another source of influence which stems from von Trier's admiration of Franz Kafka's unfinished novel, *Amerika* (1927), which was also set in the United States and written by a man who had never been there. Von Trier is often keen to draw this parallel in the face of criticism of films such as *Dancer in the Dark* and *Dogville* (Calhoun 2005; Holden 2006).

Fig. 3 *Dogville* (and later *Manderlay*) make use of theatrical set design and staging that recall the work of Bertolt Brecht

Von Trier's non-cinematic references are not restricted to 'high' culture, however. His work also draws on popular cultural moments, both historical and contemporary. For example, the Marquis de Sade's *Justine* (1797) provides considerable inspiration for the female characters of the 'Gold Heart' trilogy, especially for Bess in *Breaking the Waves*. De Sade's philosophy of freedom unrestrained by ethics or law is also mirrored in the substance of Stoffer's (Jens Albinus) social project in *The Idiots*. Von Trier has plans to adapt *Justine* for film – its melodramatic qualities sit neatly with the broad spectrum of narrative concerns in his work (Thomsen 2003: 110). More broadly, von Trier's humour is influenced by the kind of absurdist comedy seen at play in *Monty Python's Flying Circus* (BBC, 1969–74). Again, the imagery in the interludes in *Breaking the Waves* is illustrative of this influence, recalling the seemingly disconnected thematic qualities of Terry Gilliam's animations placed in-between sketches, and, in their use of pop music, emulating something of the popular cultural concerns of the 1970s in a northern European context.

For von Trier, another key figure of fascination who enjoyed popular cultural prominence during the 1970s, in particular, is David Bowie. Describing the ways in which Bowie constructed 'a complete mythology around himself', von Trier comments that the myth was as important as his music (Björkman 2003: 167). One of the key sources of fascination for von Trier was the perpetual self-reinvention paraded by Bowie throughout the 1970s and 1980s (Roman 2003: 140). The parallels with von Trier's own shaping of his image are clear. The drive toward 'the shock of the new' applies not only to his films but also to von Trier himself, with the result that he has courted a great deal of personal attention and media controversy. The chameleon personality is a trait that can be seen as a kind of homage to David Bowie, and the frequent use of his music in von Trier's films underscores Bowie's importance to him.[1]

In a more contemporary vein, von Trier has now purportedly abandoned cinema, preferring to spend his time engaged in video games. The importance of play in the visual cultural realm of this iconoclast of cinema is heightened here. The move towards this playful reputation, however, has been a gradual one. In his earliest work, von Trier approached his projects with a deeply-ingrained seriousness, seeking to reference film history and to demonstrate the extent of his knowledge and perspicacity as a director, and to build an image of himself as a serious player on the stage of world cinema.

Film History Repeating Itself

For von Trier, as already noted, cinema is a resource to be plundered. It was in his earliest work at film school and in the films of the 'Europa' trilogy that we see detailed homage to the great directors and films of cinema history, in moments that encompass textual, formal and technical references and quotations.

In making the 'Europa' trilogy, von Trier's primary point of reference is the German Expressionist tradition and the Hollywood *film noir* movement it inspired.[2] The German Expressionist tradition in film has its origins in Weimar Germany (1919–33), a period in which emotional responses to the social upheaval that followed on from defeat in World War I began to make themselves felt in contemporary art. Bourgeois cultural values and aspirations to eloquent forms of unattainable beauty began to be roundly rejected in favour of a new mode of aesthetics that was driven predominantly by intensities of emotion.[3] Realism came to be abandoned with new themes of death and decay emerging in the context of a nightmarish vision of society in the aftermath of military defeat.[4] The post-war period saw an upturn in the fortunes of the German film industry, with Universum Film AG (UFA) developing its own unique style of filmmaking designed to embed mood into its film products in order to distinguish them from Hollywood fare. UFA would go on to turn out a number of key players on the Expressionist scene, producing films such as *The Cabinet of Dr Caligari* (Robert Wiene, 1920), *Nosferatu* (F. W. Murnau, 1922), *Metropolis* (Fritz Lang, 1927) and *M* (Fritz Lang, 1931). With an emphasis on exaggerated *mise-en-scène* and highly intellectual, anti-realist and emotive themes, German Expressionist cinema made great play of light and shadow, of scenery and performance, and of fear and horror. With the advent of Nazism in Germany, many of the key directors associated with the movement fled to the US, taking with them their techniques and styles, which would eventually find their way into Hollywood thanks to the *film noir* style which arose in the aftermath of World War II. In this context, crime became a key theme of the narratives that were produced and the circulation of ideas between the US and Europe became very closely ingrained as a result.

As a film student in the late 1970s and early 1980s, von Trier would have been well aware of the context of these film historical developments. He was also able to experiment and play with the stylistic, technical and formal constructions that this period of film history leaves as its legacy. The extent of this influence on von Trier's work is seen in his graduation film *Images of a Relief*, a film set in the last few days of World War II and depicting the aftermath of the liberation of Denmark. The key themes of the film focus on revenge, torture and the highly emotive violence that accompanies the responses of Danish citizens to informers and German soldiers. The Nazi officer at the centre of the narrative ends up being brutally murdered in an ambush in the woods; von Trier's film takes a risk in depicting a sympathetic portrait of a Nazi official, and its refusal to set up a moralistic judgement at its heart, singles it out as provocative in the extreme. It is interesting to note von Trier's upbringing in a liberal family setting in relation to this film. As Stevenson notes,

> To make a film set during the war was in and of itself nothing special – there were many Danish films set during this period. But to show sympathy (as many saw it) for a Nazi officer seemed odd, not least in light of his parents' experiences during the War.[5] [Von Trier] knew full well that the film would provoke discomfort in audiences who found themselves in sympathy with the German officer, but he rejected charges that the film had a fascistic viewpoint. (2002: 28)

The trope of crime and the Expressionist style are integral to von Trier's first feature film, *The Element of Crime*, and the Expressionistic form of this film is easy to discern. Graham Fuller notes that it 'restores *film noir* to the Germans who engendered it'

(1992: 29), while von Trier has described this work as a latterday *film noir*, stating that it is 'based on Expressionism and is the bastard child of a mating between American and European cinema' (Larsen 1984: 39). In fact, in this film, the inter-textual referencing to films and other modes of artistic practice is so liberal that one critic has commented that it is 'so calculatedly derivative that it is impossible to see the *homme* for the *hommages*' (French 1985: 21). Amongst the points of reference are such films as *Casablanca* (Michael Curtiz, 1942); *The Third Man* (Carol Reed, 1949); *Confidential Report* (Orson Welles, 1955); *A Touch of Evil*; *The Trial* (Orson Welles, 1962); *Stalker* (Andrei Tarkovsky, 1979); *Alphaville* (Jean-Luc Godard, 1965) and *Blade Runner* (Ridley Scott, 1982). The film also pays homage to a number of directors including Sergei Eisenstein, Erich von Stroheim, Luis Buñuel and Luc Besson. *The Element of Crime* encompasses many aspects of narrative strategy and *mise-en-scène*, from the trope of the hard-boiled detective to the low-light cinematography, from the narrative conceit of moving back through time and space to the watery, apocalyptic imagery that pervades the story. As a result, von Trier's film bears testimony to his immersion in cinema as an industry, revealing him to be well-schooled in the most significant texts and styles and able to carry off his own interpretation of them. As critics were keen to note,[6] the end result was rather bewildering and there was not much sense of any depth of characterisation, garnering him the label of a 'precious *enfant terrible*' (Smith 2000: 22). The influence of Wagner, whose music von Trier had famously played on the shoot, is writ large in the operatic scale of the project he had undertaken.

These modes of approach and the criticisms to which they led were to continue in relation to the other films in this trilogy, *Epidemic* and *Europa*. In these films, von Trier continues to make great play with cinematic techniques and conventions. In *Epidemic*, for example, the narrative consists of a film-within-a-film structure and can be read as a commentary on contemporary filmmaking practices, especially with regard to issues of funding, dramaturgy and script-writing. The film-within-the-film's narrative references Roman Polanski's *Dance of the Vampires* (1967) in its exploration of the spread of infection, and the use of hypnosis in both this narrative and the narrative frame is reminiscent of the work of Werner Herzog, who hypnotised the entire cast of *Heart of Glass* (1976). In its extensive and highly detailed attention to complex cinematic techniques ranging from back-projection to front-projection, super-imposition, dissolves, and the layering of film over film, *Europa* indicates von Trier's desire to be seen as a consummate master of the cinema in his own right. Rosalind Galt provides a usefully concise description of the key technical achievements of this film:

> What is most striking about *Zentropa's*[7] form is its layering of discrete images, whereby a technologically sophisticated form of matte effect is used to combine several superimposed and/or back-projected images in a single frame. This layering takes place in almost every shot in the film. Colour is combined with black-and-white, 16mm with 35mm, and wide angle with telephoto lenses. Thus, the image in the foreground usually has a different quality from that in the background. Furthermore, layers are frequently manipulated. In addition to black-and-white and colour film, colourisation is used, so that part of

Fig. 4 This image from *Europa* recalls Charles Laughton's *Night of the Hunter* and signals von Trier's interest in iconic Hollywood films

> the image is sepia-toned or highlighted in red. The layers are also frequently projections, the quality of the back-projected image made visible by the flickering and degradation of the film. But it is not only a matter of foreground versus background. Von Trier describes layering up to seven images, each shot with a different lens and different kind of film. (2005: 11)

Furthermore, as Fuller notes, *Europa* is a kind of 'guilt trip, by rail, through the eternal night of the Allied Occupation of Germany following the fall of the Third Reich. It's also a journey into the illusory heart of cinema itself' (1992: 29). In almost every shot in this film, Expressionism makes itself felt. In the scene in the railway yard, with a group of Zentropa workers towing the train, we are reminded of scenes from *Metropolis*. Echoes of Welles's *The Trial* are felt in the scene when von Trier, playing the Jew, absolves Max Hartmann (Jørgen Reenberg) of any associations with the Nazi past of Germany. The film as a whole is reminiscent of *Casablanca*, not least in the way it satirises America's involvements in European politics. There are references, too, to films such as *Citizen Kane* (Orson Welles, 1941), *The Night of the Hunter* (Charles Laughton, 1955) and *Vertigo* (Alfred Hitchcock, 1958), all of which are key examples in the mythology of Hollywood cinema. The film makes explicit reference to a number of post-war films set in Germany which were shot on location in the ruins of Berlin and Frankfurt. Perhaps most obviously, *Europa* has parallels with *Berlin Express* (Jacques Tourneur, 1948), a film which also has an American protagonist and in which the action unfolds on board a train, with the plot centring on assassination and Nazi sympathisers. There are other explicit cinematic quotations present here, from films such as *Germany Year Zero* (Roberto Rossellini, 1948) and *A Foreign Affair* (Billy Wilder, 1948).

The focus on the American protagonist as the flawed and tragic hero in von Trier's film is indicative of the director's fascination with the notion of America and its influence in Europe (at both the cinematic and socio-political levels). Whereas Galt suggests that this film 'stages Europeanness as a textual problem, and it does so by constructing a relationship between the spectacular and the geopolitical, a relationship that works to overlay 1945 with 1991 and to map the cinematic spaces onto or into the psychic space of Europe' (2005: 1), there is much here to suggest that von Trier's self-confessed obsession with America as a kind of 'bad object' asserts itself at this early point in his career and that this is the main political thrust of the narrative. Von Trier cites Kafka's unfinished *Amerika* as a key source of inspiration for this film, highlighting the fascination with the philosophical and geopolitical dominance of the United States across the world at both the micro- and macro-levels. This fascination continues in his films *Dancer in the Dark*, *Dogville*, *Manderlay* and the yet to be completed *Wasington* (sic). In this context, it is important to signal the close imbrication of film history with geopolitics for von Trier – film becomes a terrain for philosophical musing in this approach.

This movement between Europe and the United States and their film traditions was also undertaken by Alfred Hitchcock, with whom von Trier shares a number of parallels. The 'Europa' trilogy seeks to replicate motifs of suspense and the intrigue of the unconscious[8] and von Trier certainly borrows from Hitchcock's work in his technical accomplishments; *Vertigo* was a key source of inspiration for the use of back-projection in *Europa* (Andrews 2003a: 82). As Michael Tapper suggests,

> The Alfred Hitchcock connection is emphasised on several occasions by moments of suspense, so-called red herrings, and, of course, by the use of Bernard Herrmann's music from *Vertigo*. Herrmann's score is also interesting in relation to von Trier's recurrent fascination for the music of Richard Wagner, since it is a paraphrase of none other than Wagner, in this case the opera *Tristan und Isolde*. (1990: 78)

Hitchcock's obsession with voyeurism is another trope with which von Trier self-consciously plays throughout his work (Larsen 1984: 44). The closing scene of *Dancer in the Dark* and the structure of *Dogville* are particularly pertinent in this regard. Indeed, these films also highlight another similarity between Hitchcock and von Trier, which is their infamously manipulative and somewhat sadistic attitude toward working with actresses on their films. As Glen Garrett suggests,

> Hitchcock has often been described as a misogynist, and certainly, some of the characters portrayed [were] killed by Hitchcock, and others suffered various horrible fates. And yet, what's also true about the women in Hitchcock films is they're typically the object of very strong sympathy from the audience. (1999)

As with Hitchcock, von Trier is frequently labelled as a misogynistic director, although he himself believes that the women he portrays are 'idealists' (Koplev 2003: 197) and that the female characters of the 'Gold Heart' trilogy, especially, are supposed to be strong (Smith 2000: 25). The international press makes frequent reference to his 'emotionally pornographic' relationship with Björk during the filming of *Dancer in the Dark* (Scott 2000; Rockwell 2001) or to the fact that Nicole Kidman claimed that he beat her up emotionally (Morrow 2004; Billen 2006) and there are clear echoes here of Hitchcock's strained and obsessive relationship with actresses such as Tippi Hedren, Ingrid Bergman, Janet Leigh and Eva Marie Saint. Von Trier has commented that he admires the fact that Hitchcock was 'such a pig' (Larsen 1984: 45) and this has contributed to debates around whether or not it is possible to see von Trier's work as feminist in any form as well as around whether feminist commentaries are even relevant to his work (see chapter six for further discussion of this). What is interesting, here, is the way in which both Hitchcock and von Trier place their characters in the grip of (highly gendered) human dilemmas in order to scrutinise better their psychological effects. Suffering, idealism and the pleasures and anxieties associated with such experiences are central to the work of both directors, and they both set out to manipulate film form to reflect and heighten these narrative tropes, to enormously successful and well-documented effect.

The influence of Orson Welles in this context is also striking. Like von Trier, Welles took a Wagnerian, highly operatic approach to his films, highlighting the human dilemmas at the hearts of his stories and using camera technique and composition to heighten their emotive qualities. In Welles' work, there is a focus on mood that is linked to the depiction of darkness and light that is reminiscent of the *chiaroscuro* effects seen in the work of directors such as G. W. Pabst and Fritz Lang (Cowie 1973: 13). These aspects of the *mise-en-scène* underscore the fascination with the oppositional drives of madness and compulsion on one hand and pathos on the other. Welles deploys humour to off-set the depth of the human dilemmas he depicts, another point with which von Trier's work often resonates. Welles' characters are often singularly and catastrophically flawed, obeying no discernible moral code and perishing as a result of their pursuits. Von Trier's 'Europa' trilogy echoes a great many of these themes and concerns, with its focus on the futility of the actions of the anti-hero and its often bleak yet darkly humorous take on the human condition. As he has stated, 'I feel a lot of sympathy towards humanists and all the humiliations they have to suffer. At the same time, I don't think it's unreasonable that they have to suffer the things that they have to go through' (Björkman 2003: 143).

Like Welles, von Trier is also deeply influenced by the work of Ingmar Bergman – a frequently referenced director in von Trier's many interviews.[9] Von Trier has suggested that he feels 'religious' in response to Bergman's films (Berthelius & Narbonne 2003: 55), enjoying something of a love-hate relationship with him and his work (Tapper 2003: 75). This is interesting, as many of the themes of Bergman's work that find echoes in that of von Trier can also be aligned with the fascination of the human condition and the quest for spiritual insight and fulfilment. Bergman's work often involves journeys, made by characters who are in pursuit of a deeper understanding of their own subjectivity and experiences. Visions of God, death and endless game-playing are ever-present in Bergman's work, as are deep-rooted considerations of emotional cruelty and intense passion. Everyday life with its somewhat transient sensibility is often juxtaposed with the most profound elements of what it means to be a human being: love is scrutinised in all its forms and death provides an object of meditation in a number of his films. The aim of Bergman's narratives is often to prompt self-confrontation in order to invoke radical changes in his characters' attitudes to life. Such themes resonate through von Trier's work in both the 'Europa' and 'Gold Heart' trilogies, though the latter is perhaps more idealistically-inflected in its treatment of some of these themes.

Like Bergman, von Trier produces a number of woman-centred films, exploring, as Bergman does, the emotional drive of female characters such as Karen in *The Idiots* and Selma in *Dancer in the Dark*. He also forges intense relationships with actresses ranging from Björk (who remains adamant that she will never converse with von Trier again) and Nicole Kidman (with whom he was reputed to walk in the woods during the filming of *Dogville* so that they could scream at each other to release the tension that built between them as a result of von Trier's demands on set). For von Trier, Bergman is a key point of reference in his own formation as a Scandinavian film director and, it seems, in terms of his sensibilities around life and its emotional enigmas.

It is the question of emotional experience and its visual depiction that draws von Trier to the work of film director Andrei Tarkovsky. For von Trier, Tarkovsky is a master of cinema, whose work depicts timeless and elemental imagery (Michelsen 2003: 7). He describes himself as having 'an almost holy relationship' with Tarkovsky (Berthelius & Narbonne 2003: 55), describing his first encounter with *Mirror* (1975) as 'a revelation'. Tarkovsky's films are profoundly autobiographical and deeply personal – tropes which do not make themselves felt very obviously in von Trier's work. But in their concerns with the intensities of emotion and in their scrutiny of psychological truths and the inter-relation of anxiety and happiness, the resonances with von Trier's work are clear. In addition, Tarkovsky's fascination with water imagery is also deeply meaningful to von Trier, who, making a direct link to Tarkovsky's work, has commented that 'Water is comforting. Whenever I have to travel, I always want to be near water. It would be very uncomfortable to be somewhere where there was no water for miles' (Björkman 2003: 14). More specifically, *Images of a Relief* and *The Element of Crime* draw directly on Tarkovsky's work at the aesthetic and technical levels in their use of the colour tinting of film. *The Element of Crime* also owes a great debt to Tarkovsky's *Stalker* (1979), in which the protagonist scrutinises the meaning of faith in a totalitarian state that resembles a wasteland. Similarly, von Trier seems to quote Tarkovsky's 'floating women' motif at the end of *Breaking the Waves* when we see the bells pealing in the heavens for Bess's soul. Concerns with spirituality, suffering and anguish mark the narratives of von Trier's work as much as they do those of Tarkovsky.

These questions of spirituality, suffering and anguish owe the clearest debt of all to the influence of Carl Theodor Dreyer. It is this director to whom von Trier pays homage most frequently and whom he idealises above all others. The marks of Dreyer's influence on von Trier are seen throughout his work as a whole, as he employed Dreyer's cinematographer, Henning Bendtsen, on *Epidemic* and *Europa*. The clearest tribute comes in the work that begins with his TV adaptation of Dreyer's script for *Medea* and continues through the 'Gold Heart' and 'U-S-A – Land of Opportunities'[10] trilogies. The use of female protagonists in all of these films is central to understanding the influence of Dreyer on von Trier, and it is this question to which we shall now turn.

Throughout the history of his engagement with film, von Trier has repeatedly cited the work of Carl Theodor Dreyer as the source of greatest influence in his approach to cinema. Von Trier has infamously claimed that 'There have been two Danish directors – Carl Theodor Dreyer and me' (Matheson 1985; Lumholdt 2003: xviii). Describing Dreyer as an 'honest' director, von Trier has claimed not to be influenced by the man but rather by his style of directing which he sees as very calculated and rather rebellious in its refusal of the contemporary cinematic vogue (Björkman & Nyman 1995: 101). Making what have been described as 'impeccably solemn, serious and passionately humanitarian spiritual odysseys' (Milne 1971: 12), Carl Theodor Dreyer is perhaps best known for his in-depth exploration of the relationship between good and evil and his meditations on religion, faith and the question of what is to be understood as 'God'. Sexuality and sensuality are also key themes in Dreyer's films, with the importance of love between men and women also playing a central role in works such as *Ordet* (*The Word*, 1955). Dreyer's *oeuvre* concerns itself with rather abstract but nevertheless universal themes such as justice, faith and the need for love in the quest for a rewarding life. As Tom Milne suggests, in Dreyer's narratives the story is usually set in the past and often concerns an intimate group of people – a family, or a village, or a prisoner of faith and her judges. The action is usually restricted spatially and the narrative arc usually involves a lone figure who gradually becomes separated from the group as a result of cruelty.

The similarities with von Trier's work here are numerous – in all of his films, many of these themes are replicated, albeit in the context of a diverse range of sensibilities and cinematic styles. In addition, Dreyer has a particular propensity for working with actresses, especially in order to explore a sense of suffering. For von Trier, this directly influences the formation of his adaptation of Dreyer's script for *Medea*, and both the 'Gold Heart' and 'U-S-A – Land of Opportunities' trilogies. A concern with supernatural possibilities (seen, for example, when the bells ring at the end of *Breaking the Waves*), also points to his homage to Dreyer, as is his recently over-riding obsession with the status of women as deeply mysterious and potent. Themes of self-sacrifice, fidelity, belief, joy, purity, suffering, martyrdom and love are at the heart of the narrative structures of von Trier's work since the mid-1990s. Indeed, the working title for *Breaking the Waves* was 'Amor Omnia' ('love is everything'), a direct quotation from the closing scene of Dreyer's *Gertrud* (1964).

The trope of the miracle became personally important to von Trier in the context of his conversion to Catholicism, and his search for a 'credible miracle' in films such as *Breaking the Waves* and *Dancer in the Dark* can be understood in this context. Von Trier's mode of religious belief is described as 'humanist' and he attributes this to the influence of Dreyer's view of religion – throughout his films, religion and the organisation of religion are frequently attacked, but the idea of God is not (Björkman 2003: 168). This approach to religion is explored in most depth in *Breaking the Waves*, especially in the context of the film's explicit rejection of strict Presbyterian values. Towards the end of this film, when Bess, who has been expelled from the Church, appears in the congregation and ignores the rule that stipulates that women must remain silent in the congregation, she refutes the concepts underpinning the Church's advocation of belief in the Word and the Law by saying 'You can't love the Word. You can only love a person.' This re-working of the religious theme of love and what it means in terms of making religion bear some personal value, is the central moral of the tale for von Trier (Björkman 2003: 176).

Dreyer's influence is most obviously seen in von Trier's adaptation of Dreyer's unrealised *Medea* script, the only film von Trier has made which he has not himself written. The script indicates that Dreyer was intending to make this film in colour, and von Trier has commented that he found this fascinating (Tapper 2003: 78), influencing his decision to shoot the film on video, transfer it to film and then back again to video in order to achieve 'an almost archaic character, like an old silent film' (ibid.) in homage to Dreyer's work. The theme of sacrifice that runs through Dreyer's work and seen very explicitly in the adaptation of *Medea* becomes fundamental to much of von Trier's exploration of femininity, goodness and martyrdom. Bess sacrifices herself in order to ensure Jan's recovery in *Breaking the Waves*, and there has been a great deal written on the theme of martyrdom in relation to this film (Heath 1998; Keefer & Linafelt 1998; Makarushka 1998; Watkins 1999; Mercadente 2001; Bekkenkamp & Sherwood 2003; Penner & Stichele Vander 2003). Selma's self-sacrifice in *Dancer in the Dark* echoes Medea's sacrifice of her children and von Trier plays with these ideas further in *Dogville*:

> So what can we say about sacrifice? I can't stop myself thinking at least ten times a day about how pointless life is. You make your entrance and then bow and disappear again ... But someone who sacrifices himself or herself is at least giving their existence some kind of meaning – if you can see a meaning in doing something for others, for an idea, a belief. The characters in these films are struggling to bring meaning to their time on earth. It must feel easier to die if you are doing it for something you believe in. (Björkman 2003: 221)

The principle of sacrifice can also be seen to be at work in Dreyer's method of working. Von Trier makes a great deal of the fact that Dreyer worked very slowly, producing scripts of some 500 pages in length and slowly cutting and re-working them, whittling them down to twenty or so pages in order to produce pared-down and very sparse dialogue that strove to get to the essence of the ideas with which the narrative was concerned (Smith 2000: 24). On *Breaking the Waves*, von Trier sought to work in just such a way, taking many years to produce the script and re-working it in several well-documented ways (Björkman 2003: 164).

Von Trier's fascination with his predecessor's method of working is also important in understanding the importance to which he attaches the experience of working with professionals who worked on Dreyer's films. In *Medea*, von Trier used two of Dreyer's actors, Preben Lerdorff-Rye and Baard Owe (whom he also used in *Riget* (*The Kingdom*, 1994)), and in the 'Europa' trilogy, he used Dreyer's cinematographer,

Henning Bendtsen, and Henning Bahs, with whom Dreyer had also collaborated as scenographer on *Europa*. Henning Bendtsen played an important role in von Trier's first trilogy of feature films, acting as cinematographer and cameraman on *Epidemic* and overseeing lighting on *Europa*. Von Trier was reportedly aspiring to the look of simplicity and sobriety in *Ordet* and *Gertrud* (Björkman 2003: 108) in this work, and was delighted that Bendtsen made use of the same camera and lighting equipment that he had used with Dreyer (Ciment & Rouyer 2003: 62). He has commented on the value he placed on Bendtsen working against his ideas (Geijerstam 2003: 66), describing his style as 'impressionistic' and delighting in the 'disharmony' of their approaches to film. It was also Bendtsen who gave von Trier the tuxedo that had belonged to Dreyer which he wore at Cannes and in the preamble scenes of the televised version of *The Kingdom* with great pride. Thematically, too, the 'Europa' trilogy builds on Dreyer's fascination with hypnosis. Dreyer's reported uses of hypnosis on *La Passion de Jeanne d'Arc* (1928) and *Gertrud* provides the impetus for von Trier's explorations of the effects of hypnosis in each of the three films that make up this trilogy, at the level of character, narrative, enunciative address to the spectator and commentary on the pleasures and potential terrors of film as a medium (seen especially in *Epidemic*). The effect of Dreyer on von Trier's work, then, has been substantial and on-going. Whereas von Trier has often been quick to dismiss the over-arching importance of influences such as Bergman and Tarkovsky by disparaging certain elements of their work, with Dreyer, the homage seems all-encompassing and the extent to which this is signalled throughout von Trier's work is remarkable.

Post-New Wave: Dogme 95 and the Digital Revolution

Von Trier played a central role in the establishment of the 'movement' known as Dogme 95 and his input and impact mark a key turning point in his approach to his filmmaking and attitude to cinema. Chapter five scrutinises this movement in much more depth, but it is interesting to signal the origins and influences underpinning this pivotal moment in von Trier's work.

Dogme 95 was launched in Paris at a special conference on the future of cinema on the eve of its second century. Distributing the manifesto and the rules making up the 'Vow of Chastity' to which the Dogme 95 'brethren' would adhere by throwing a sheaf of red leaflets into the audience, von Trier adopted a particularly provocative stance, courting media attention and overtly attempting to place Danish cinema at the heart of European film initiatives. Much has been written on the international significance of Dogme 95, and also on its Danish specificity (Bondebjerg 2003; Hjort 2003a and 2003b), but the origins of this movement are profoundly European, drawing on a tradition and history of cultural manifestos[11] and on a range of cinematic movements known as the 'new wave'.

The 'new wave' is an umbrella term used to describe a flurry of cinematic initiatives which took place in the European context predominantly during the period between the 1950s and 1970s. (Subsequent 'new waves' across a broader world context of cinematic production have also been identified, such as the Japanese new wave; the

Hong Kong new wave, and so forth). The idea of the 'new wave' (or '*la nouvelle vague*') originated in France when a number of filmmakers including Jean-Luc Godard, François Truffaut, Claude Chabrol, Eric Rohmer and Jacques Rivette began to query the canonisation of classical cinema and to explore alternative approaches to cinematic technique in their own work. Citing the work of both Hollywood and European directors as key points of reference,[12] and establishing a journal in which to explore their ideas (*Cahiers du Cinéma*), the pioneers of *la nouvelle vague* seized on technological innovations to fuel their experiments with cinematic technique and form. Mobility, lightweight equipment, experimentation with editing techniques, jump cuts and lengthy tracking shots all became significant in the work that these directors produced (see, for example, Truffaut's *Les Quatre Cents Coups* (*The Four Hundred Blows*, 1959) and Godard's *À bout de souffle* (*Breathless*, 1960).

The parallels with Dogme 95 become immediately apparent. Launched at the forefront of the digital revolution in image- and sound-based technologies, Dogme 95 heralded the beginning of the age of digital cinema and drew worldwide attention to the possibilities opened up by cheaper and more accessible technologies. Dogme 95 amounted to a kind of democratisation of filmmaking, attempting to put creativity at the forefront of new considerations about the meaning of cinema and setting itself up as the source of guidelines for a refusal of the creeping commercialisation of cinema. In this regard, too, Dogme 95 has its parallels with *la nouvelle vague*. Just as the French critics of the 1960s sought to de-sanctify the dominant approach to what counted as 'Art', Dogme 95 seeks to move beyond the seemingly unshakeable financial and commercial restrictions and sensibilities of the international film industry. However, the critics at the heart of the French new wave also eventually established a hotly-debated yet key tenet of film theory, with the development of the '*auteur*' theory, which played against the apparently revolutionary idealism of the proponents of the new wave in that it reified directors such as Hitchcock and Renoir, seeking out their cinematic 'signatures' and lauding these as crucial to any understanding of the artistic value of cinema. As the Dogme 95 manifesto makes clear, this move toward reifying the *auteur* can be seen as having undermined the radical sensibilities of the new wave movement: 'The auteur concept was bourgeois romanticism from the very start and thereby … false!'[13] Just as Truffaut, some forty years earlier, had criticised the tendencies of French cinema, Dogme 95 extended this critique to cinema as an industry driven by the commodification of culture, arguably seeking to make room for more artistic approaches. As von Trier has commented,

> It's impossible to deny that Dogme 95 is largely inspired by the New Wave.
> It was a fantastic shot in the arm. Maybe we won't be able to do the same,
> but we might be able to provide some sort of preventive vaccine. (Björkman
> 2003: 203)

Dogme 95, then, simultaneously pays homage to the French new wave and refutes its effects on the cinema of the late twentieth century. Citing the French new wave as the sole source of newly defined 'certain tendencies', however, somewhat belies the influence of other avenues of new wave cinema that rippled across Europe and around the world. There are traits in common with the American Underground cinema of John Cassavetes, Andy Warhol and others, and also a specific sensibility that draws on the 'swinging London' films of the 1960s.[14] In addition, the films of the German new wave, including those of Werner Herzog, Wim Wenders and Rainer Werner Fassbinder, are other important points of reference to the Dogme 95 brethren. Stevenson usefully charts these influences in some detail (2003: 25–49) signalling highly mediated debates around whether or not Dogme 95 could be seen as anything other than iconoclastic provocation, whether it is 'a fake or constructed wave' (2003: 43). Drawing attention to the fundamental ways in which the very idea of a 'new wave enables self-promotion', Stevenson usefully articulates the importance of Dogme 95 'in giving a massive boost to the entire Danish film industry' and suggests that 'thanks to von Trier's clout, in the Danish film world and his financial muscle as co-owner of Zentropa studio, it has become positively mainstream' (2003: 49).

While much of the commentary on the Dogme 95 manifesto signals the ostensibly politicised roots of the movement, there are also many paradoxical observations that von Trier, in particular, is not interested in making political films. Interviews with von Trier draw attention to the ways in which he insists that Dogme 95 is not a protest movement, but, rather one designed to make suggestions (Björkman 2003: 202). Seeing the impetus of the movement as one towards opening up a terrain for debate (2003: 218), von Trier associates the rules associated with Dogme 95 with his obsession with control:

> 'Control is a key thing in my production and in my life, that's for sure', he agrees. The idea for the Dogme film aesthetic, he says, emerges from a desire to submit to the authority and rules he did not have as a child. Von Trier's upbringing in a free-form, hippy-Marxist setting, which he describes tartly as 'humanistic, cultural-leftist', left him feeling untethered and deeply fearful. (Roman 2003: 137)

This tendency towards working in a collaborative way has recently allowed von Trier to work very closely with another of his acknowledged influences, Danish director Jørgen Leth, to produce a new film based on a re-working of Leth's first film, *Det perfekte menneske* (*The Perfect Human*, 1967). *De fem benspænd* (*The Five Obstructions*, 2003) is a collaborative venture between Leth and von Trier, working in the documentary style. Von Trier's project in this work with Leth is to introduce five restrictions or obstructions which Leth must observe in the re-making of his film on five separate counts.

The relationship between the two men is crucial to the project, with Leth having been a former tutor and mentor of von Trier. Leth is a documentary filmmaker and one who has never formally been admitted to the so-called Dogme 95 'brethren'. Nevertheless, he has had impact on the movement, not least in its reincarnated form of 'Dogumentary'.[15] As a filmmaker at the forefront of the ABC Cinema underground Danish film collective, Leth participated in the kinds of activities associated with new wave filmmaking and underground cooperatives, forging new modes of engagement with film structure and film language and attempting to work around the techno-logical constraints of the filmmaking apparatus (Stevenson 2003: 201–8). The marks of influence on von Trier quickly become apparent, and it is fascinating that the two directors sought to collaborate on the documentary re-working of the Dogme 95 rules and on its first product, the re-working of Leth's own film. Tropes of game-playing, story-telling and the complexity of notions of truth and fiction abound here, concerns that run through the whole body of von Trier's work and are brought into focus by the Dogme 95 experiments, as chapter five will explore.

Genre Blending

By now, it will have become clear that von Trier's work's is not able to be pigeon-holed neatly. The breadth of his work demonstrates a stark propensity for a kind of disruptive playfulness around the conventions of cinema and its language. Just as in the Dogme 95 movement where von Trier worked to assert an innovative cinematic style and approach, other films in his *oeuvre* make great play with genre and generic conventions. From the re-visiting of *film noir* conventions seen in the 'Europa' trilogy, through the deeply melodramatic 'Gold Heart' trilogy to the highly theatrical recent films making up parts one and two of the 'U-S-A – Land of Opportunities' trilogy, von Trier has consistently manipulated generic expectations, to the extent that this can be seen as something of an authorial signature running through his work. Von Trier does not work within the bounds of convention. Instead, he works to uproot convention and its place within the film-industrial context, to re-work it and to re-formulate the possibilities of cinema as a result.

This play with genre is also seen in television pieces such as *The Kingdom* where von Trier blends stock soap opera narrative structure with ghost stories, horror, detec-tive stories and comedy. Von Trier explicitly cites *Homicide: Life on the Streets* (NBC, 1993–99) as an important influence on his style in *The Kingdom*, and the generic play, together with the scale of the narrative, makes for very idiosyncratic and challenging television, which has, nevertheless, enjoyed popular global appeal.

As already seen, in the 'Europa' trilogy, von Trier's generic points of reference run the whole gamut of Expressionism, encompassing both stylistic elements of *film noir* and tropes of Weimar cinema, together with those from the work of many great Holly-wood directors. Von Trier deploys stylistic and technical expertise to illustrate his own technical mastery of cinema and his highly informed understanding of cinema history. For example, the use of blinds and window-shades to cast shadows is reminiscent of *film noir* and there are numerous nods to mythologised statements by directors such as Welles (who saw the cinema as 'a giant train-set'). What emerges most forcefully from the pieces in this trilogy is the importance of excess in the approach von Trier takes up in his attempts to b(l)end genres, and it therefore seems fitting that the second of his trilogies is overtly marked by structures of melodrama.

Melodrama is a genre associated with 'the woman's film',[16] and von Trier main-tains this generic convention in marking his 'Gold Heart' trilogy of films as feminine. With their somewhat beleaguered female protagonists, at first glance, the films appear to be archetypal examples of cinematic melodrama with all its conventions of narrative focused on love and romance, sentiment, domestic- and family-driven drama, psychosexual confusion, fantasy, repression and bourgeois ideology. However, unlike most directors of melodrama, von Trier has been singled out for a particularly sadistic rendition of these concerns, especially in *Breaking the Waves*. What is more, none of the films can specifically be labelled as melodramas as they each break with the generic conventions in important ways and/or make forays into other genres, confusing the boundaries of generic convention and problematising the tendency of the film industry to catalogue films according to their generic styles. *Breaking the Waves*, for example, is overtly melodramatic in its narrative content, themes and structure. It is also profoundly excessive in its rendition of its story and in its enunciation of the film's subject positions. Yet the film is shot on video and marked stylistically by an insipid bleakness. While this does reflect narrative concerns, it also seems to refuse the melodramatic convention for an excessive *mise-en-scène*. It is as though the convention of melodramatic stylistic excess is displaced in this work onto the narrative, which is certainly very intense and deeply provocative. Von Trier also makes short forays into the domain of the pop video and conventions of literature in this film, with his use of 'chapter headings' accompanied by 1970s pop songs. In some ways, this is testimony to the origins of melodrama as a cultural form in the context of popular theatrical culture and its association with popular music, but this is certainly breaking the boundaries of cinematic melodramatic convention. These ideas are explored further in chapter six.

In the subsequent films of the trilogy, von Trier brings together discordant cinematic genres to even greater effect. In *The Idiots*, melodrama and bleak *mise-en-scène* are blended with documentary footage, the status of which is never quite clear. This has the effect of blurring the boundaries between truth and fiction to the point that it becomes difficult to establish whether the 'talking head' sequences in the film are interviews with the films' actors or rather the characters they play. I have argued elsewhere that the deployment of a documentary style in the context of this film is fundamental to von Trier's play with spectatorship and pleasure (Bainbridge 2004a) and it is interesting to note the ways in which the blurring of generic conventions is central to the way in which von Trier is perceived as exploiting both his actors and his audience. Chapter seven returns to these ideas in more detail.

Von Trier's propensity for and fascination with excess is seen most clearly in *Dancer in the Dark*, a film on which one hundred video cameras were simultaneously used to film Selma's fantasy sequences, making the technical and stylistic realisation of the film rather melodramatic in itself. This film, of course, is also a musical, albeit a highly melodramatic one that deploys the staples of mainstream cinematic devices, such as the courtroom drama, throughout. Like the melodrama, musicals are concerned with everyday life and emotion, but they are centred much more on issues of community and ways of expressing sensibilities and sensitivities through music, song and dance. Von Trier cites a number of key musicals that influenced his work on this film including *An American in Paris* (Vincente Minnelli, 1951), *Singin' in the Rain* (Stanly Donen & Gene Kelly, 1952), *West Side Story* (Jerome Robbins & Robert Wise, 1961) and *Cabaret* (Bob Fosse, 1972) (Björkman 2003: 223), and, of course, the film explicitly references *The Sound of Music* (Robert Wise, 1965) as Selma's personal favourite.

However, von Trier does not wholeheartedly take up the technique of the backstage musical; instead, he takes the musical form and tries to render it into something rather distinctively operatic in structure and form. The musical numbers in the film are illustrative of Selma's fantasy world rather than real, lived experiences that act as a commentary on life in the American community in which she lives and works. Von Trier uses the musical form to speculate on the political subtexts of the film, signalling the importance of the psychological experience of the everyday for the individual who does not fit into the norms and standards of everyday life in the United States. The film can be seen as a commentary on issues of immigration and identity, especially given that its setting is an overtly-mythologised America, a country to which von Trier has never travelled, but which is well-known to cinema-goers around the world as a result of the output and distribution of American films.

The emergent concern with politics seen in the overlaying of the politics of immigration onto the 'Americana' of the film musical grows ever more heightened in von Trier's later work in the 'U-S-A – Land of Opportunities' trilogy. Both *Dogville* and *Manderlay* concern themselves with everyday life and ideological and community values in twentieth-century America. The form of these films moves beyond the tendency to blend genres, however, in that they deploy a distinctly theatrical style, eschewing cinematic conventions around *mise-en-scène*, and concentrating on a very pared-down, literary style of cultural politics. The techniques are Brechtian rather than cinematic and von Trier deploys this manoeuvre in order to attempt to draw film back to the importance of theatricality. Citing the Royal Shakespeare Company's production of *Nicholas Nickleby* in 1980 as a key influence in this work,[17] von Trier suggests that he is setting out to return to the obviously stylised qualities of such work as it has been forgotten in the context of cinema (Kapla 2003: 208).

What is fascinating in the evolution of von Trier's work is the way in which it has increasingly moved away from an over-arching concern with the need for technical accomplishment and stylistic flourishes toward a more palpably affective mode of film-making that is marked by a commitment to innovate, stimulate and reinvigorate. Von Trier has been described in many ways ranging from the claim that he is a 'precious *enfant terrible*' of European cinema (Smith 2000: 22), through accusations of misogyny and sadism to being seen as a 'punk *auteur*' (Arroyo 2000: 16). As he himself makes clear, what is most striking about his work is that he is over-archingly responsible for it.[18] He comments that 'I've always placed great importance on being able to see on a film that I've made that it's been made by me' (Björkman 1996b: 13), and goes on to suggest that his own marks of authorship centre on the importance that every image should contain an idea and on the fact that every cut is carefully thought out.

Von Trier is a consummate purveyor of directorial, production and distribution processes and he is a 'media-savvy' director with a proclivity toward self-promotion and playfully sensationalist agendas that seem to be constantly shifting and evolving. Far from being 'The Man Who Would Give Up Control' (Knudsen 2003), von Trier sets out to construct himself firmly in the framework of ideas about authorship opened up by *la nouvelle vague*. His desire for control feeds into all aspects of the filmmaking process, from the production company he owns and partially funds (Zentropa) to the example of his move into digital filmmaking and his ideas about improvisation with actors, the speedy production of scripts, and the need for the director to take the camera into his own hands. Von Trier is something of an enigma in contemporary filmmaking, but a very visible one and it is clear that he has set himself up as the '*agent provoc-auteur*' of contemporary filmmaking.

PART ONE

The 'Europa' Trilogy

CHAPTER TWO

Visions of History

The 'Europa' trilogy of feature films was made after Lars von Trier's graduation from film school and consists of the films which first brought him to the attention of European critics and cinema-goers. Each of the films comprising the trilogy is marked by a concern with film aesthetics, technical mastery, cinema history and the failures (but also the possibilities) of idealism. Each also makes use of strategies and techniques familiar to us from German Expressionism before settling into something more of a *film noir* mode. In this context, then, it is not surprising that the films all deal with issues around masculinity as a category of gender which is intimately bound up with ideas of history. The style adopted by von Trier makes interesting play with the tendencies of *film noir* to foreground issues of masculinity and history.[1]

Time is a key theme for von Trier in this trilogy and there is a particular concern with the idea of the past. While *Europa* clearly demarcates itself as set in Germany in 1945, both *The Element of Crime* and *Epidemic* strive toward a dystopian notion of the future, yet the versions of the future set out here demand an interrogation of the past. In *The Element of Crime*, Fisher (Michael Elphick) needs to traverse the history of the serial killer, Harry Grey, in order to discern 'the element of crime' for himself; in *Epidemic*, the vision of a future outbreak of the plague is deeply rooted in the mythological and historical accounts of various plague periods in Europe. Questions of the future, then, are shot through with a keen scrutiny of the past, of history and its inflections of power and politics. Von Trier playfully deploys his fascination with film history to underscore the key thematic moments of this work.

Film History and Origins of the 'Europa' Trilogy

As we have seen, von Trier's influences are many and varied and are, perhaps, most easily discernible in this trilogy of films in terms of aesthetics and film history. As discussed in chapter one, much of this early trilogy of work has its roots in German Expressionism and *film noir* and the influence of these movements on von Trier is seen in both the aesthetic and thematic components of the films. *The Element of Crime* is described by von Trier as a '*film noir* in colour' (Björkman 2003: 71). With its saturated hues of yellow and red, the film is often rather nightmarish in quality, recalling the psychological uneasiness at the heart of Expressionism and pointing to the dystopian confusions of the film's plot and characterisation. *Epidemic*, with its film-within-a-film structure, is a markedly mythologising film. Shot in black-and-white throughout, this film weaves together societal discourses of panic, knowledge and power with concerns about the supernatural and an apocalyptic vision of the ideological underpinnings of a world in which power is unconditionally reified at the expense of notions of the spirit. There are indications here of von Trier's interest in the writings of Nietzsche and Strindberg, and his fascination with madness and disease also underlies this film's narrative. It is interesting that this film is shot through with the conundrum of film-making and that von Trier himself plays one of the protagonists. The close imbrication of cinema, society and history is spelt out in this film with extraordinary results. Finally, *Europa*, the most technically consummate of the three films, is in some ways an ode to Expressionism as a cinematic style. It is here that von Trier most clearly deploys technique in the service of narrative. The film's technical prowess works to emphasise and often delineate the expressionistic concerns at the heart of the narrative.

The discursive inscription of the trilogy lends itself to a Foucauldian reading. Von Trier is keen to disestablish many of the assumptions and conventions of film-viewing in this work and he does this in a number of ways. Firstly, he takes the mode of *film noir*, wrenching it from its association with the post-World War II context of the United States and firmly returning it to its German place of origin and influence. The heavily stylised look of each film is greatly indebted to the expressionistic mode of film-making. Debts to Hitchcock, a director also heavily influenced by Expressionism, are also very apparent. The dazzling array of inter-textual reference points and cinematic techniques suggests that von Trier is playing with the expectations of his audience, placing a demand for recognition of heritage and origins squarely as the responsibility of the viewer. The knowing inter-textuality across the trilogy might be interpreted in this way, although the attempt to construct these films as 'masterpieces' clearly lends itself to a critique of highly invested masculinism. Von Trier's provocative and slippery claims to the importance of mastery in cinematic production are foregrounded through this manipulation of technique and interpretation.

The trilogy is structured as an archaeology of film history in terms of its interrogation of both social and cinematic discourses and their relation to (culturally specific) power. How, then, do these films forge links between film history and world history? How do the formal properties of the films help to offset the mythologising tendencies of cinema against global industrial and geopolitical contexts of production and consumption? And how can von Trier's work in this trilogy be read as a specifically European mode of cinema?

Cinematic Mythologies: Inter-Textuality and the Question of Meta-Cinema

Commentary on the films that make up the 'Europa' trilogy is often littered with references to specific filmic 'quotations' which are seen as evidence of von Trier's 'inter-textuality' (see, for example, Kennedy 1991; Gruzinski 1997; Galt 2005). The extraordinary attention to the technical production of the images that make up von Trier's films is also a preferred topic in critical responses to the work, with critics frequently alluding to his consummate expertise as a director and his far-reaching knowledge of cinema. The work of von Trier in this trilogy, then, is read as a signifier of a certain cinematic knowingness and expertise, which grounds the work in a mode of meta-cinema designed to signal how these films become a place for commentary on the status of film at both the artistic and industrial levels.

In this regard, the work of Roland Barthes (1972) is useful in terms of setting the scene against which von Trier's work can be seen as mythologising around what we understand by cinema. Barthes suggests that the mythologies that emerge from signifying systems within any given cultural context illustrate the complexity of the cultural values attributed to signs and their role in the formation of class-based ideological assumptions. Arguing that mythologies arise around the second-order processes of connotation, Barthes shows that mythologised forms of cultural value come to be naturalised and accepted as 'truthful'. Semiotics is intended to expose the ways in which these processes are at play in sign systems and Barthes provides useful examples in his analyses of Italian food and the fashion system (amongst other things) to illustrate his ideas. For example, this can be seen in his striking analysis of the ways in which discourses and values around race, patriotism, military supremacy and national identity are compounded in the image on the front cover of *Paris Match* magazine showing a young black solider saluting in deference to what is assumed to be the French flag (1972: 116). What Barthes demonstrates is that 'myth has, in fact, a double function: it points out and it notifies, it makes us understand something and it imposes it on us' (1972: 117). Elements of mythologies are bound to the systems of representation inside which they function but they are also altered by them.

Nevertheless, myth is illusory, a trait it shares with cinema. Indeed, cinema has come to occupy a very particular cultural position as a direct result of its mythological status. Many film theorists and critics have commented upon how Hollywood cinema in particular has become a mode of myth-making, a 'dream factory' which proffers and circulates images rooted in the dominant ideological domain. Cinema has come to function as an archetypal signifying system, an apparatus through which cultural values are not only re-presented but also re-formulated according to shifts in cultural, historical and ideological value systems.

In constructing his films with explicit reference to cinema history, then, von Trier taps into its mythological structure, the better to symbolise his own grasp of its significance. Yet the deployment of the mythologies of cinema is also important because of the levels of 'inter-textuality' that come to characterise von Trier's films as a result. As chapter one made clear, von Trier's influences are wide-ranging and he does not draw on a limited repertoire of cinematic images. Instead, as we see in the 'Europa' trilogy, von Trier references an array of directors, styles and genres encompassing classical Hollywood (Orson Welles, Alfred Hitchcock, *film noir*, Marlene Dietrich); Italian neo-realism (Roberto Rossellini, Federico Fellini); German Expressionism and New German Cinema (Fritz Lang, UFA, Werner Herzog, Rainer Werner Fassbinder, Margarethe von Trotta); and European art cinema (Ingmar Bergman, Carl Theodor Dreyer, Andrei Tarkovsky, Jean-Luc Godard).

The layers of inter-textuality running through the 'Europa' trilogy are rather complex, then. Inter-textuality works alongside mythology to produce cultural signifiers of the highly mediated environment of everyday reality. As Scott Lash has suggested, 'We are living in a society in which our *perception* is directed almost as often to representations as it is to "reality"' (1990: 24). Part of the pleasure of inter-textuality is related to the way it interpellates the spectator, acknowledging the cultural capital with which s/he is invested. However, it also constructs pleasure through its construction of a critical distance. In re-presenting elements of other texts that exist outside the text itself, the inter-textual object places itself against a backdrop of specific moments of mythologies, thereby casting itself with reference to it. Of course, this has an alienating effect too, enabling us to manufacture a distance from the object which is central to any critical capacity to discern its meaning.[2] The inter-textual film, then, is shot through with questions of authenticity (which, in turn, is central to discourses of postmodernism), and this is important in understanding its political effectiveness.[3]

In the 'Europa' trilogy, the question of authenticity is central to the filmic narratives. Von Trier casts this question in different ways in each of the films. In *The Element of Crime*, for example, Fisher is in pursuit of what should be understood as 'crime'. In his dogged investigation of Osbourne's (Esmond Knight) hypotheses around criminality and his insistence on pursuing Harry Grey, the murderer, Fisher idealises notions of truth and sets out on a journey that ends in his demise. His alienation is made explicit from the film's opening scene in which we see Fisher being hypnotised in Cairo and in which his longing for Europe seems fundamental to his sense of subjectivity. In *Epidemic*, the question of authenticity runs through the film-within-the-film, centring on Dr Mesmer's (Lars von Trier) insistence on the reality of the plague. Authenticity and its impossibility are also embedded in the narrative structure of the framing film, as von Trier and his fellow script-writer (Niels Vørsel) struggle to produce a script in five days in order to meet the deadline imposed on them by their producer and end up infected by the fictional plague at the heart of the film they write. The boundaries of truth, reality and fiction become blurred here, highlighting the complex relationship of the illusions of cinema and its pro-filmic event to realism and its flipside, fantasy. In *Europa*, of course, authenticity is a central conceit of the plot which articulates many ethical and moral concerns. For example, there is a scene in which the complicit

Fig. 5 In *Europa*, Lars von Trier plays a Jew who testifies to the friendship of Max Hartmann (Jørgen Reenberg), thereby exonerating him from associations with the Nazi regime

silences of the Americans as they accepted the dominant practice of having Jewish people testify to the friendship of known Nazis in order to salvage the heritage of German industry in the reconstruction programme in post-war Germany. The authenticity of Leo Kessler's (Jean Marc Barr) motivations is also in question throughout the film as he moves from a rather ill-informed position of naïve idealism to that of unwitting participant in terrorist excesses.

Implicit throughout these narratives is a commentary on the geopolitical subjectivities at stake in the pursuit of authenticity. It is striking that each of the films in this trilogy refers to an iconic notion of 'Germany' as the heart of Europe. 'Germany' becomes a key mythology running through this trilogy, as the next section will explore.

Key Mythologies

Throughout the 'Europa' trilogy, von Trier draws on a number of mythological constructs to elaborate a sense of 'Germany'. In *The Element of Crime*, the film opens with scenes set in Cairo, as the protagonist is hypnotised and encouraged to return to Europe for the first time in thirteen years in an attempt to resolve his headaches. 'Europe' here is represented by Germany (signified through the iconic use of the German language), invoking the idea that Germany is somehow at the heart of the continent, inscribed as its focal point. In *Epidemic* and *Europa*, Germany is the explicit setting for the narratives, with the latter film clearly signalling at the outset that the story takes place in Germany in the 'Year Zero'. In each of the films making up the trilogy, von Trier returns to a trope set up in his film school graduation picture, *Images of a Relief*, as he makes his characters list the names of several key German cities, one after the other. He has commented that this is because

> when you see or hear the names of these cities, they summon up images. It's
> a very visual thing, talking about cities, because a lot of cities have some sort

of soul attached to them, whether or not you've actually been there. Cities are like people. (Björkman 2003: 47–8)

Similarly, von Trier has argued that, for Danes, Germany is what can be seen when they look down at Europe and he repeatedly highlights the historical importance of the country for a vision of how the world works.

'Germany', then, has a number of connotations in von Trier's work. Firstly, he draws on its geographical size and position in relation to other, smaller northern European countries. Germany is cast in terms of its might and in relation to its roots at the heart of the Austro-Hungarian Empire. Von Trier's interest in the place occupied by Germany is inflected through a general knowledge of its history. In more recent historical contexts, of course, Germany needs to be understood in terms of its roles in the world wars that dominated the first half of the twentieth century. From the outset of his career, von Trier's interest in Germany has related to the experience of defeat at the end of World War II. Germany becomes the site of failed attempts at power-mongering and acts as a geopolitical symbol of the dynamics of power and capital.

However, Germany is not only to be understood in relation to geopolitical and historical contexts. As a site of film history, it is one of the most influential countries outside the United States. As a film scholar, von Trier's rendition of Germany at the heart of Europe draws on the cinematic traditions and styles associated with Expressionism, the birth of *film noir*, uses of propaganda films and the construction of film as art. It also points to the representation of Germany in any number of cinematic contexts encompassing war films and 'ruin' films as well as art-house cinema. The focus on Germany can also not easily be separated from the contemporary cultural and geopolitical context of the films' production given the important developments around the European Union and the changing shape of European identity.

The construction of 'Germany' in von Trier's films, then, is complex and it seems to act as a condensation point, encapsulating a number of inter-related perspectives on the function of the country at the symbolic and iconic levels. It is particularly interesting that much of the symbolic power of Germany as a cinematic construct is articulated through reference to film history in von Trier's work and his rendition of Germany is carefully inscribed in terms of this. For example, the images of Germany we see in *Europa* owe a very great deal to the images of Germany seen in the 'ruin' films produced by Hollywood in the period following World War II. Chapter one traced some of these origins, citing films such as *Berlin Express, Germany Year Zero* and *A Foreign Affair*. As Rosalind Galt has suggested in relation to *Europa*,

the historical and geographical setting for *Zentropa* [*Europa*] is not merely a foreign one; rather the location is a space as overdetermined in international film history as in European politics ... These 1940s (ruin) films provide some of film history's most iconic images of Germany ... To refer to these films is to invoke Germany as projected by others onto a divided and uncertain space. *Zentropa* repeats this work of projection by dint of its status as another non-German film representing Germany in 1945, but it also textualises and elaborates this work through extensive visual and narrative references. (2005)[4]

It is possible to go further here to indicate the ways in which each of the films in this trilogy owes a debt to cinematic visions of Germany. The setting of *The Element of Crime* with its watery apocalyptic vision of the desolate spaces of Europe is distinctively marked out as expressionistic and *noir* in flavour. It draws on the heritage of the films produced by UFA during the 1920s and 1930s, sketching links between the Hollywood re-visioning of Expressionism as *noir* and the work of directors such as Fritz Lang and F. W. Murnau amongst others. In *Epidemic*, the literary structure of the film (which is split into chapters) evokes a Kafkaesque style associated with the links between Germany and the United States which echoes the cross-cultural seeds of *film noir*. It also draws heavily on the Wagnerian operatic tradition. There are markers, too, of the influence of Rainer Werner Fassbinder and Wim Wenders. There is an important contrast between the slick and polished style of the film-within-the-film and the framing film, which feels grainy, hand-held and *ad hoc* in style, marking it out as indebted to the New German Cinema 'underground' films.

The emphasis on the cinematic in von Trier's treatment of 'Germany' as a mythology in these films also signals film itself as another important mythology at

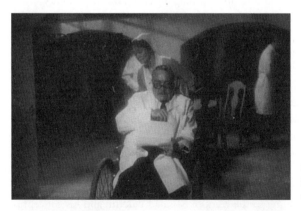

Fig. 6 The film-within-the-film in *Epidemic* is shot in 35mm and has a slick, polished look

Fig. 7 By contrast, the framing of *Epidemic* is shot in 16mm, providing a raw, grainy, hand-held look that heightens the immediacy of its style

the heart of the work. The complex layers of inter-textuality allude to the roots of many iconic moments and movements within cinema, as already seen. Similarly, in von Trier's nods to other domains of culture such as drama, music and literature, the roots of cinema itself are charted through the iconicity of the reference points he exploits. Cinema itself is signalled as mythological and mythologising in its own right in this way. The 'Europa' trilogy puts this to work in order to highlight the important overlap between Germany and the United States in terms of the history of cinema as a mainstream global industry. Once again, the trilogy seems to act as an archaeology of myth here, constructing a palimpsest of references points that are littered throughout the films in a way that creates a rich seam for cinematic analysis at both the formal and narrative levels.

In its focus on the specifically *noir* mode and on its intersection with themes of dereliction, loss and a vision of history that is distilled through images of plague, war and human fallibility, the trilogy also sets itself up as a refraction of the psyche. The masculinity of this trilogy (which von Trier proclaims in numerous manifestos relating to the films included in it and also in a range of interviews) is linked to the mythological questions around idealism and subjectivity in the context of twentieth-century history. The inter-linking of these aspects of the dominant mythological conditions of ideological and cultural value are condensed into the figure of Germany, a country which becomes a terrain on which the films' protagonists test out the validity of the cultural mythologies in which they find themselves bound up.

The 'Europa' trilogy of films connotes a complex set of associations to what Germany signifies within the European and global cultural, political and historical arenas, then, and von Trier self-consciously plays with this to frame his own work in relation to these values. As he has stated, 'I'm obsessed with Germany. For Denmark, it's a very big neighbour. Germany is a symbol. It is Europe' (Audé 1991: 40). What is interesting is the way in which this concern with Germany and its legacy is played out not simply through processes of narrative evocation and formal conceits around inter-textuality. Instead, it is useful to consider the intersection of film-form, story and style in any attempt to grapple with von Trier's play with ideas of history and nation. The next section considers this in relation to the spatio-temporal qualities of the films in the trilogy by turning to the work of Mikhail Bakhtin and his concept of 'the chronotope'.

Cinema as Chronotope: Inter-Textuality, Politics and the Psyche

As the previous discussion has begun to signal, von Trier's approach to the films of the 'Europa' trilogy is marked by close attention to the ways in which film form and technical style can be used to augment the narrative thematic. For von Trier, the idea of history is not to be understood in any simplistic terms. Instead, he articulates the significance of the spaces and times through a complex layering of film structure, plot, story, characterisation and technical style. As already seen, much of this is evoked through inter-textuality and the symbolisation of certain dominant mythologies. The trilogy gives particular attention to the mythologies associated with Germany as a geopolitical, cinematic and cultural formation. How, then, does von Trier play with these ideas to produce a mode of cinema that invites political analysis? It seems that it is in the relationship of time and space to discourses of narrative and cultural value that these films can best be read.

Writing in relation to literature, Russian theorist Mikhail Bakhtin has suggested that he will 'give the name chronotope (literally "time space") to the intrinsic connectedness of temporal and spatial relationships that are artistically expressed in literature' (1982: 84). For Bakhtin, the concept of the chronotope illustrates the 'inseparability of space and time'. He also claims quite clearly that it is 'a formally constitutive category of literature' (ibid.). The chronotope is used by Bakhtin to define both genre and the way in which 'man' is represented within literature. He locates within the chronotope the place in which all narrative meaning has its origin. The chronotope, in short, determines the representability of events. Bound up within the process of giving materiality to time in space, the chronotope fuses together space and time so that they are inseparable. In Bakhtin's words, 'time thickens, takes on flesh, becomes artistically visible; likewise, space becomes charged and responsive to the movements of time, plot and history' (ibid.). Developing this work, Robert Stam has signalled the particular quality of the chronotope as inherently cinematic, showing that the chronotope is ideally suited to the analysis of film. Film, for Stam, forms the ideal textual site for the chronotope because

> whereas literature plays itself out within a virtual, lexical space, the cinematic chronotope is quite literal, splayed out concretely across a screen with specific dimensions and unfolding in literal time (usually 24 frames a second), quite apart from the fictive time/space specific films might construct. (1989: 11)

Sue Vice (1997) observes that the chronotope functions in three different but inter-related ways: it allows external history to be represented within the text; it constructs the film's own images of space and time; and it plays a role within the film's own formal construction. This latter definition of the chronotope is particularly useful when applied to the layers of inter-textuality seen in von Trier's 'Europa' trilogy, as it highlights the way the films' uses of images of space and time are interwoven with the use of cinematic quotations and the importance of all of this for an understanding of what the films communicate about their own contemporary setting. In what follows, the notion of the chronotope will be used to analyse the filmic construction of the key mythologies pervading these films, namely the tropes of Germany, cinema and the (male) psyche.

As already discussed, notions of 'Germany' in this trilogy function mytho-logically throughout. Germany appears to stand for a certain vision of European culture and history (defined through world events and cinematic reference points). The history of Germany is seen in the thematic concerns of the films, and the films express this history through the use of metaphor, film form and narrative conceits. In *Epidemic*, for instance, Germany provides the space for an interlude in the narrative of the framing film, when the filmmakers travel there as part of their script development work. However, as a chronotopic construct, Germany figures in this film in much more symbolic terms.

The story of the film-within-the-film is premised on the experience of plague epidemics, which travelled through medieval Europe along the trade routes. In defining the space of Germany in terms of shots of its industrial landscape and in naming key industrial towns as the scriptwriters make their car journey into the country, the framing film echoes something of the narrative trajectory of the film within it. Near the opening of the framing film, there is a sequence in which a medical historian talks the filmmakers through this history of the plagues in Europe, signalling the ways in which the plague was often dealt with according to religious belief systems and practices. In the black plague of 1348, for instance, it was widely held that the source of the infection originated in a Jewish plot to poison the public water wells as a means of insurrection against the Roman Catholic Church. During this period, many Jews were tortured into false confessions and into incriminating others and the records of these confessions were transmitted through Switzerland and Germany, resulting in the widespread butchering of the Jewish population and a culture of incrimination and blame-mongering (Halsall 1998).

It is interesting to note here the parallels with historical events around World War II and the Nazi persecution of the Jews. *Epidemic* makes this link in a distinctively chronotopic way in its foregrounding of Udo's (Udo Kier) story about the experience of his mother during the cluster bomb attacks on Germany. As the filmmakers build their story about the plague, visiting the German industrial trade towns that contributed toward its spread through the continent, Udo recounts a tale of other historical events which unfolded in the context of the very same persecution of Jews and the iconicity of these historical moments become intertwined in the film's deployment of time and space. The complexity of the structure of *Epidemic*, with its film-within-a-film structure, also heightens the chronotopic effect here, allowing narrative spaces and times to become so inter-referential that they eventually supersede their boundaries at the end of the film, when the plague of the fiction infects the scriptwriters in the 'real' world. The representation of history within the text quite literally becomes the history of the filmic text as a whole, drawing attention to the fundamentally chronotopic quality of cinema.

The use of a list of German cities is also present in the other films in the trilogy. In *The Element of Crime* and in *Europa*, the lists echo a naming of places von Trier regards as 'mythological' and particularly 'Teutonic' (Björkman 2003: 48). The city names are iconic of the spaces and places important to the filmic narratives, but they also evoke a sense of Germany as a vast geographical space, a space that must be traversed, not only with reference to its spatial coordinates but also with reference to its history. Part of Germany's historical chronotope is articulated through the cinematic inter-textuality of the films, as von Trier links the catechismal quality of the places named within the films to the references he makes to well-known moments of cinema history.

In *Europa*, this is seen most clearly at the level of film form. The sheer complexity of von Trier's technical prowess is designed to layer spaces upon places and times so that the relationship of the characters to the spaces they occupy is constantly thrown into relief.⁵ The materiality of the film as an object is foregrounded in the many sequences such as these that run through the text. With its nods to cinematic history, and its over-laying of this history onto a more geopolitical level through its referencing of the *noir* and ruin films as well as broader sweep of European art-house cinema, *Europa* presents a complex chronotope of cinema itself. The spatio-temporal indexicality of cinema as a marker of cultural values and dominant worldviews is made clear here. Von Trier's film serves as a kind of commentary on the power of cinema to construct itself as a historical record at both the narrative and formal levels. The chronotopic quality of the film as text turns it into something of a meta-text in this regard, commenting on the way cinema becomes part of the machinery of mythology, contributing to the prom-ulgation and perpetuation of culturally-inscribed and historically-bound assumptions at the heart of dominant symbolic and ideological practices.

Many aspects of *Europa* tap into the notion of the chronotope. The movement through the German landscape by train is a useful example here because it brings together a space that is not bound to geopolitical considerations (the train and its tracks) but in a context in which the metaphorical and metonymical significance of the train is irrevocably tied to moments implicit in the historical specificity of the film's narrative (the train as an icon of the Nazi persecution of the Jews during World War II; the train as an emblem of cinema, following Orson Welles' declaration that cinema is like a giant train-set; the overnight train journey as a marker of the geographical expanse of the spaces of Germany in particular and Europe in general; and the train as iconic of a kind of non-place that exists beyond time and thus conjures up associations with the psychological spaces of the mind which are so central to the formation of the very ideas of individual and nation with which the film plays).

The chronotope of the psyche is also a theme that runs through each of the films in this trilogy, and is important in constructing the atmosphere of apocalyptic doom that characterises each of the narratives. The notion of the psyche as chronotopic is bound up with several elements of the films, spanning their deployment of space and location as well as their uses of time and memory. As von Trier has frequently acknowledged, much of this trilogy is to be read alongside the trope of hypnosis that informs it. In *The Element of Crime*, the opening scene, set in Cairo, introduces the protagonist, Fisher, as he is hypnotised by an Egyptian man who is trying to help with the problem of his headaches. In *Epidemic*, hypnosis is used in both components of the film and actually provides the narrative device through which one strand of story is able to insinuate itself into the other during the film's closing scenes. In *Europa*, the spectator is made aware of the hypnotic quality of film as a medium through the opening voice-over, in which Max von Sydow directly addresses the audience, lulling the spectators into a state of openness to the film's ideas. (Chapter three will go on to deal with the impor-tance of hypnosis in relation to the materiality of these texts and their narratives.) It is important to note here, however, that hypnosis is a marker of the chronotope of the psyche because of the way it displaces and condenses senses of space and time, drawing together strands of the narrative in ever more meaningful ways.

Hypnosis is fundamentally connected to notions of the unconscious and it provided the roots and origins of Sigmund Freud's work on the nature of the mind and its instinctual drives (Freud & Breuer 1991). In each of the films in the 'Europa' trilogy, metaphors for the mind abound in the cavernous underground spaces seen in the medical headquarters of the new government in *Epidemic* and the labyrinthine hotel, sewerage channels and wasteland spaces of *The Element of Crime*. In *Europa*, as already noted, the train interiors and railway tracks conjure up visions of unnamed territories, expanses of space across which time can be lost and/or compressed. The sense of time in these films is indiscriminate, with much of the action being shot at night. This lends an air of the dream-state to these films, opening up what critics frequently describe as a 'nightmarish' sensibility in the films. In addition, each of the protagonists is motivated by rather an aimless sense of guilt and obligation. The fundamental humanistic endeavour undertaken in each of the films ends up in a hopeless mire of death and decay, suggesting a rather bleak outlook on the capacity of the individual to transcend the doom-laden atmosphere of the time-spaces they inhabit.

The importance of hypnosis in the formation of the chronotope of the psyche running through these films relates to the temporal suspension that is evoked by their quality of timelessness. While the historical chronotope abounds in relation to the films' depictions of Germany and Europe, hypnosis enables the timescapes of the psyche to move seamlessly across epochs. Each of the films scrutinises links between generations and sets up its protagonists as heirs of some kind to the legacy of their predecessors. The hypnotic element of the films is important because it enables an elision of the temporal and spatial distances between the generations concerned and it also allows for an overlap between the historical contexts and legacies of each period. Thus, in *Epidemic*, the legacy of the plague finds its way into the domain of contemporary Europe, invoking something of the legacy of persecution that remains in the contemporary historical context. In *Europa*, von Trier explicitly presents an anti-American reading of the political machinations at play after World War II. He draws attention to the American complicity in silence around the practices of former Nazi officers, highlighting the hypocrisies of American democracy, and the legacy of this seeps into the hypnotic state invoked through the voice-over and the inter-textual references to other films. This results in the formation of a certain sensitivity to the psychological motivations underpinning the narratives of these films and to the question of human fallibility that runs through them. The particular nature of the psyche as it is presented in this work is broadly framed as masculine by von Trier, and there is something fundamental to the gendered nature of the mind as it is deployed in this work that intersects with the historical focus of the work and with the ethical inscriptions it provides for us, as the next chapter will discuss.

The idea of the chronotope, then, is a useful one because it sketches von Trier's complex and technically-detailed work in this trilogy, and constructs a very specific perspective on the way culture and ideology are at work within texts and within the framework of their consumption. The films in this trilogy are deeply inscribed with questions of political motivations and sensibilities – these are key issues that are discernible in von Trier's early work, as discussed in the introduction, and they also persist in more recent work, albeit on less 'masterly' terms. The intersection between film form, narrative content and cultural and historical contexts is fascinating in its illumination of the function of cinema as art. As the next section will discuss in relation to the 'Europa' trilogy, it is important to draw the focus back to the broader European context of the work, which is especially visible in the label that has been used to name this trilogy and to consider the impact of the contemporary European context for the significance of this body of work.

Von Trier the 'Euro Paean'[6]

The question of 'Europe' in von Trier's work cannot be separated out from the cultural events unfolding across the continent during the 1980s and 1990s as von Trier made the films in this trilogy. The shape and face of Europe began to shift immeasurably in this period, which saw the fall of the Berlin Wall and the consequent end of the Cold War as well as the establishment of the European Union through the Maastricht treaty of 1992. The sense of what is signified by 'Europe' was at the heart of the political and cultural context in this period, and the relationship with America was also ever-shifting as the balance of world power was re-negotiated.

The fall of the Berlin Wall and the end of the Cold War which had dominated the Western cultural arena since the end of World War II is interesting in understanding the emphasis accorded to Germany by von Trier in this period. As already seen, for von Trier, Germany has functioned as a kind of microcosm for Europe, signalling the way the country functions as a metaphor for the circulation of ideological and geo-political values. As a signifier of oppositional worldviews and the juxtaposition of capital against communism, the Germany of the period preceding the fall of the Berlin Wall provides a trope for von Trier of the discursive construction of cultural inscription and sensibilities. In *The Element of Crime*, for instance, the space of Europe, represented through a series of Germanic inflections, is murky and oppressive, secretive and darkly threatening. The overtones of espionage, control and fear of reprisals running through the film are redolent of the cultural sensibilities around repressive state apparatuses and their relative positions of authority and power. Despite the fact that the narrative unfolds in the English language, the police force is referred to by the German noun *Polizei*, and the deployment of costume and other aspects of the *mise-en-scène* are designed to heighten the stifling atmosphere associated with the oppressive regimes of power most frequently aligned with the communist political position, especially in images originating in the western European capitalist context.

Of interest here is the way von Trier draws on the *film noir* style in this work. Thematically, many of the *film noir* narratives emerging from Hollywood can be read symptomatically in relation to the perceived threat of communism and cultural values associated with eastern Europe. In turning to this set of discursive contexts, von Trier, a child of a leftist politically-active family and an erstwhile member of the Communist Party, can be seen as taking up a provocative position intended to upturn the familiar assumptions of mainstream cinema. In *The Element of Crime* and *Europa*, von Trier continues to pursue the question of sympathy for the aggressor, which was first set out in his graduation film, *Images of a Relief*. Arguing in *Epidemic* that 'film should be like a stone in your shoe', von Trier sets out to antagonise and to disrupt hitherto relatively

Fig. 8 The importance of 'Germany' as a symbol is seen in the use of a German police car in
The Element of Crime as an indexical sign for the film's setting

safe cinematic values and he does so with reference to a notion of 'Europe' that is
aligned with a certain set of cultural values.

For von Trier, Europe stands in opposition to America, a nation which symbolises
appropriative and materialistic social and political values and which von Trier appears
to perceive as rather unwholesome. In his re-rendering of the sensibility of *noir*, he
seems to highlight the ways in which Europe differs from the United States but is
also irrevocably bound up with it and with the attitudes it embodies.[7] For example, as
mentioned earlier, in the films of the 'Europa' trilogy, von Trier makes regular use of
lists of German city names. He has suggested that this is because there is something of
a 'Teutonic cultural quality' to such cities which evokes a certain 'depressing *film noir*
feel' more usually aligned with 'the mystical content in all the American cities that the
film noir genre is anchored to' (Björkman 2003: 48).

The mystical origins of the *noir* sensibility then, are also to be found at the heart of
Europe, for von Trier, and are explicitly rooted in the state of Germany. The Germany
of the cultural period in which von Trier made these films is a complex condensation of
political oppositions, embodying a range of (often contradictory) cultural and ideological values. Germany comes to function as a site of political awareness in this respect,
as the tropes of the complex political inscriptions operating inside a divided country
become symbols of a worldview which is corroborated as complex and uneasily disen-
tangled from sensibilities and sensitivities around ideological freedom and idealism.
(Chapter three will go on to explore these ideas in greater depth.)

By the time *Europa* was made, the political context of Europe had shifted. The
fall of the Berlin Wall in 1989 had marked the beginning of the *perestroika* period in
eastern Europe and had opened up space in which the reunification of Germany began
to parallel that drive toward a more integrated European Union. The question of what
was to be understood as 'Europe' became a hot topic of debate across many social,

political, ideological and economic contexts and this continues to date (Pinder 2001; Reid 2004; Brooker & North 2005a and 2005b). *Europa* was released in 1991, a year before the Maastricht Treaty establishing the new terms of the European Union was signed and implemented. The context of the release of this film, then, is interesting in terms of the way it signifies an emergent mythology of what Europe might be seen to be. Galt has argued compellingly that this film 'inscribes the ambivalent relationship between Germany now and Germany in 1945, but it also maps a fractured European space from which to look' (2005: 17). Discussing the collaborative European sources of funding for the film, she also suggests that *Europa*

> constructs history as a double bind; it looks back on a history that it also needs to debunk. There is no single Europe at the moment of reunification, and there was no single Europe before partition. What centres the historical image is this knowledge that it is necessary to return the postwar past despite its inevitable disappointments. [*Europa*] structures the impossibility of creating a truly European image, but in staging the collocation of the continent's disjunctive historical spaces, it begins to imagine the stakes in the idea of a Europe outside the dominant Western discourse. (2005: 18)

It is interesting to chart the evolution of this position through all three films in this trilogy and to cite the way von Trier draws upon a distinctively mythologising discourse to raise questions around what it means to be European. Each film grapples with this in terms of notions of history as already noted, but they also make extensive use of the metaphor of the psyche to draw attention to the ways in which perceived histories are anchored in fantasies of subjectivity and power. Much of the work in the 'Europa' trilogy of films depends on the articulation of the fantasies at the heart of identity and its representation through a distinctly poetic approach to film form and *mise-en-scène* which is reminiscent of the Modernist agenda to demonstrate the attractions of myth through a process of de-realising historical events.

In von Trier's trilogy, cinematic technique calls attention to the formal construction of the films as texts and thus to their narrativity. Throughout, von Trier mixes factual events with images of fantasy and these images are complicated by formal experimentation in the use of flashbacks, colour saturation, front- and rear-projection and super-imposition. For example, it is never quite clear in *The Element of Crime* whether Fisher's deeply subjective experiences in the hotel with Kim (Me Me Lai) are real events or dream images. Scenes such as the sexual encounter between these two characters on the bonnet of a car are inflected with Fisher's feelings and emotional distress around the case of Harry Grey and his experience of intense headaches. Bound up with the consumption of a drug to *relieve* the pain, Fisher begins to *re-live* the pain of Harry Grey's investigation, with the result that the investigation becomes a metaphor for the medical investigation of Fisher's symptoms. The framing scenes of the film are important here, as the hypnotism of Fisher helps to inflect these scenes with a status of uncertainty for the viewer. The often vexed question of the relation of reality to fantasy is ever-present in this film.

The use of hypnosis as a mechanism by which the films in the trilogy might be understood is important in grappling with inter-relationship between fantasy and history that marks the films' treatment of historical moments.[8] This, in turn, is important for understanding the way the films come to comment on the contemporary experience of what it means to be a European.

History, Fantasy and Europe

Vivian Sobchack has suggested that history must always be understood as meta-history and that historiography is about arranging and telling stories rather than delivering any kind of objective truth (1996: 4). From this perspective, then, our relationship to history is always a narrativised one. This is similar to the relationship of subjects to fantasy, which, in order to find expression, must always be put into words and thereby rendered through what Freud calls 'conditions of representability' in order to be accessible as a story. Like history, fantasy is always re-conveyed and therefore re-worked in any attempt to depict it. Von Trier's use of hypnosis to explore the implications of narrative for an understanding of history is useful in this regard. As Sobchack has suggested,

> If history 'happens', it happens only in the present, in the temporal space between the past and the future. But 'the persistence of history' suggests a temporal connection and spread that confers on 'history' ... a magnitude and significance that emerges from historiographic reflection and makes out of that present unshaped material something that deeply matters. (1996: 14)

The sense of history throughout the trilogy is, as already seen, closely connected to the thematic of Germany in the films. This is important in understanding the way von Trier calls upon our understanding of history to shape a vision of what is understood as the contemporary cultural position of an evolving Europe. The history of Germany (as an icon of Europe) and its effect on how a sense of 'Europeanness' might emerge is inscribed throughout the films in the trilogy. This suggests that the representation of history functions as a kind of symptom of the cultural traumas that define the incipient formation of 'European' identity.

In their extensive referencing of World War II and the effects of the experience of defeat, the elements of history with which von Trier engages can be described as moments of cultural trauma in European history. Yet, as E. Ann Kaplan has noted,

> In what senses is it possible to speak of 'cultural' trauma? What analogies might be possible between forms of individual and cultural trauma? Could we say that in a culture as an individual the impact of an overwhelming event cannot be absorbed and is split off? That it returns in fictions apparently unrelated to that event, yet insisting on its remembrance, insisting on keeping the event present? (2001: 202)

It is in this context that von Trier's use of the trope of hypnosis becomes interesting. As we have already seen, the trope of hypnosis plays an important part in shaping the filmic treatment of space and time in this trilogy. The chronotopic analysis of the psyche remains important here, as hypnosis is a way of exploring repressed memories of the past and their effect on the way the subject in the present is affected by them. In this trilogy, the repressed memories at stake are complex, relating as they do to the often complex and traumatic nature of war and its unwholesome acts. Through hypnosis, there is an opportunity to re-stage the complexity of these events with a view to working through them and thereby to finding ways of living with them. With its strangely hypnotic quality (emphasised by von Trier in *Europa* especially), cinema offers a way of positioning the spectator as a cultural witness to historical events which are often rather unthinkable and not easily articulated. In the context of issues around European identity which seem to be at the heart of von Trier's trilogy, it is as though the message is that the silences around war are fundamental because of their effect on the constitution of Europe as a geopolitical space.

A key facet of hypnosis as a means of unearthing repressed events or memories from the past is the principle of *nachträglichkeit*, or deferred action. This is used to explain the importance of how human beings perpetually revise past experiences to invest them with new significance in the context of present issues relating to identity.[9] The evolving and shifting sensibility of what is to be understood as 'Europe' in the cultural context surrounding the release of von Trier's films can usefully be illuminated by reference to such ideas. The nature of cinema is such that the exploration of fantasy and history is easily subsumed within the formal practices of the art form, especially with regard to the study of events that can be seen as particularly traumatic (see Elsaesser 2001; Kaplan 2001; Radstone 2001; Turim 2001). Indeed, as Kaplan suggests, 'independent cinematic techniques show paralysis, repetition, circularity – all aspects of the non-representability of trauma and yet of the search to figure its pain' (2001: 204). The use of hypnosis as a defining trope in von Trier's 'Europa' trilogy highlights the need to examine the painful (and often inadequately acknowledged) past underlying the struggle to establish a new 'European' sensibility in the context of historical and polit-ical events during the late 1980s and early 1990s. By drawing attention to the legacy of the war and of war-time national identities, von Trier's films begin to speak something of the silences that complicate the struggle to assert a new sense of cohesion emerging from events such as the development of the European Union and the fall of the Berlin Wall. Hypnosis, then, becomes a useful structure through which to acknowledge the struggle implicit in these developments. As Maureen Turim argues,

> Postwar tranquillity that might be put aside or bury a past that had not been worked through (can) be slashed not only by a call to remember, but also concomitantly by a call to make the connections between the past and atroci-ties in the present. (2001: 207)

This is precisely what is at play in the psychoanalytic deployment of hypnosis, and one might argue that von Trier's work makes good play of this in its articulation of the power of cinema to address these fundamental aspects of (supra-)national history and identity.

The deployment of formal experimentation across the films works together with their narrative structure to mythologise key moments of historical trauma for Europe but it does so in a way that presents these very moments of trauma as ineluctable in the formation of new sensibilities around the formation of any 'European' identity. Following Fredric Jameson, Haydn White (1996) argues that such an approach can be read as fundamentally Modernist in style in that events are 'de-realised' in such a way that the historicity of events is rejected and replaced with an over-arching awareness of their mythological importance. Highlighting the way in which traumatic events can neither be forgotten nor adequately remembered, White suggests that

> Modernist techniques of representation provide the possibility of de-fetish-ising both events and the fantasy accounts of them which deny the threat they pose, in the very process of pretending to represent them realistically. This de-fetishising can then clear the way for that process of mourning which alone can relieve the 'burden of history' and make a more, if not totally, realistic perception of current problems possible. (1996: 32)

In articulating the hidden moments of cultural trauma underpinning the emergent formation of European identity through the trope of hypnosis, then, von Trier's films express some of the complexity of the different mourning processes that need to find room for expression in the evolution of a European future. In its clever re-staging of strategies of representation familiar to us from post-war cinema, the 'Europa' trilogy constitutes a very adept exploration of the ways in which cinema can address larger issues of identity and history through form as well as narrative. The apparent postmod-ernism of the multiplicitous layering of film quotations and stylistic excesses arguably masks a modernist sensibility in the sense that it 'de-realises' the historical events and re-presents them provocatively. Throughout the trilogy, this is anchored very clearly in the iconic function attributed to Germany as a geopolitical construct.

The position of von Trier's work within the context of European cinema is also interesting in this regard. *The Element of Crime* was selected for competition at the Cannes Film Festival in 1984 and marked the end of a somewhat fallow period for Danish cinema. The film was awarded the technical prize and, as a result, von Trier quickly garnered European critical attention. Indeed, this film was extremely well received in France, as Stevenson has noted (2002: 39–40). It is interesting that the low-budget *Epidemic* fared relatively weakly, despite playing in the 'Un Certain Regard' section of the 1987 Cannes festival. Once again, the film was best received by the French press while it achieved little positive coverage in Denmark itself. It was with *Europa* that von Trier's status as an *auteur* began to be considered and the film won both the technical prize and the Prix du Jury at Cannes in 1991, going on to screen in foreign territories around the world.[10]

The idea of 'Europe', then, is configured in terms of both geopolitical and cine-matic mythologies in counter-point to the United States and with distinct reference to Germany as the philosophical heart of Europe. The question of what is perceived as cinema runs through this work and is important in considering the place of power and ethics. The question of ethics is closely bound up with idealism and the importance of this in relation to the narrative drives in each of the films in the 'Europa' trilogy. The next chapter considers these themes in more detail.

CHAPTER THREE

Ethics, Idealism and Identity

As we saw in chapter two, themes of nation and geopolitical perspectives on history are important in formulating an understanding of Lars von Trier's work in the 'Europa' trilogy. However, at a more micro-textual level, there is also an important concern with notions of power and ethics and the place of the individual within it running through these films. The politics of identity and questions about how human nature works to position us within society are very significant in this work and this shows the extent to which von Trier is fascinated by debates about humanism. The question of what is to be understood by identity is at the heart of these films. Von Trier sketches his analysis of identity in relation to the struggle to establish an appropriate relationship to the tenets of good rather than those of evil, but his films also demonstrate that this apparently moral dynamic is not a simple one. Ethics are overlaid in very complex terms with notions of identity and cultural values and this trilogy of films scrutinises the problems that this presents in relation to human nature.

The films foreground issues of ethics and morality through their examination of power relations and the effects of power on the construction of identity. Particular emphasis is given to the exploration of masculinity in these films, with von Trier even suggesting that this trilogy is fundamentally a masculine one. The tendency toward idealism and its failure is overlaid with an analysis of how men are able to shape their sense of identity in relation to the complex structures of power that are spread across ideological terrains such as religion, the bourgeois sensibility and social structures of authority. Discourses of crime, mental illness, terrorism and sickness come to dominate, creating the sense that the perspective on human nature with which we are presented in this work is a fundamentally dystopian one. This chapter will consider these themes in relation to the pursuit of ethics and its framing as a distinctively gendered component of human nature. It will also consider how the films comprising the 'Europa' trilogy present a dystopian view of such ideological structures as the family. The politics of identity in this body of work is inscribed in a rather pessimistic sensibility that is anchored in the cinematic and historical contexts explored in chapter two.

Picturing Ideology and Power

It is well documented that von Trier was brought up in a very liberal, 'culturally radical' context and that this experience is one that has impacted extensively on his life and work.[1] Von Trier himself has suggested that his lack of a sense of authority led to the rebellious streak which underpinned his perfectionist attitudes to his early work (and the attitudes to his actors that this entailed). It is also at the heart of his recent attempts to foster a film community in Denmark, a project which has its roots in the establishment of the Dogme 95 brotherhood.[2] Von Trier's life and work can be characterised in terms of a distanced concern with the realm of the political and also by a determination to refuse conformity.[3] Inevitably, this experience inflects von Trier's relationship to ideology and to its depiction in his work.

Aligning himself with a tendency to question and refuse prescribed ideological positions, von Trier states,

> I have little use for niceties and good intentions. I'd like to see all kinds of films, including Nazi films, as long as they have something to say. I belong to the school of thought that believes that people are able to draw their own conclusions. (Hjort & Bondebjerg 2001: 217)

For von Trier, 'humanist pieties' are closely bound up with prescribed social and ideological values, and his films grapple with the effects of this on the individual. This is connected to the inscription of power in society and can be understood with reference to issues of ideology and hegemony, as discussed by theorists such as Louis Althusser and Antonio Gramsci.

Althusser suggests that ideology is 'a system (with its own logic and rigour) of representations (images, myths, ideas or concepts)' and that social and interpersonal practices shape the ways in which individuals relate to the real conditions of their lived existence (1969: 231). Ideology, then, defines the individual's sense of society and their relationship to its social formations. It is internalised as an element of the subject, though it is also important in evoking the idea of 'the other', with reference to whom the subject defines her/himself. Althusser stresses the unconsciousness of the processes at play in the work of ideology, and highlights the fact that symptoms of ideology must be read off representations not simply through what they overtly articulate, but also with reference to their silences. Althusser goes further to suggest that ideology also operates through the system of material practices that are constituted through ideological and repressive state apparatuses. Ideological state apparatuses such as the family and the education system work to instil within the individual certain sets of cultural and ideological values. This is how ideology interpellates the individual, hailing her/him as one of its subjects. These values are policed and reinforced through the system of repressive state apparatuses such as the police force and the military. For Althusser, this is how ideology perpetuates itself and we are constantly hailed as its subjects as a result of the internalised fear of reprisals should we fail to observe the material practices sanctioned as *bona fide* articulations of ideological positions.

Althusser's definition of ideology, however, leaves little space for the notion of conflict with the values inherent in the ideological social formation. It assumes a consensual relationship to the materiality of ideology. Gramsci's (1971) formulation of hegemony is useful in articulating more conflictual aspects of social experience. For Gramsci, ideology needs to be understood as a component of hegemony. Hegemony operates as a continuous process through which the balance of power is perpetually maintained. Gramsci suggests that hegemony operates because the dominant powerful class 'leads' rather than 'rules'. Values that are subordinate to those articulated from a position of power are nevertheless bound into the systems of power and thereby contained. Conflict or divergence from the 'norm' exists, yet it is managed through an on-going process of negotiation. As a result, conflict is often contained within the parameters of dominant practices – it finds outlets for expression but hegemony operates to allow its expression in such a way as to maintain the *status quo*. Practices of resistance and incorporation help to ensure that power remains in its place, but power is not simply imposed on the subjects of hegemony. These ideas about the operation of power and its effects on the formation of individual identity are useful in thinking through the representation of the struggle with idealism and ethical relationships to power explored in von Trier's films.

In the 'Europa' trilogy, concerns with ideological and hegemonic processes tend to dominate in the construction of the filmic narratives and this is seen through the conceptualisation of 'the other' with reference to which the protagonists of the films are characterised. Running through these films is an over-arching concern with the experience of the other and the effects of this on the formation of identity. In each of the films making up this trilogy, the central protagonist finds himself taking on the guise of the other, often against his will. For example, in *The Element of Crime*, Fisher becomes so ingrained in the logic of crime as it is carried out by Harry Grey that he becomes the murderer himself. In *Epidemic*, the filmmakers' dramaturgy centres on the outbreak of a plague and they themselves end up contracting the disease as their story-world collides with their lived reality. In *Europa*, Leo Kessler is blackmailed into carrying out a terrorist bomb attack despite his moral disgust at such activities. This is important for understanding how von Trier depicts the effects of ideology and hegemony on the experience of the individual and for understanding how this plays out in his narratives to highlight the constructedness of apparently 'naturalised' hegemonic values.

From the very outset, von Trier's work has demonstrated a particular concern with the sensibilities of the other in the grand scheme of history and the perceived moral high ground with which this is associated. His graduation film, *Images of a Relief*, is set in the final days of World War II, shortly after Denmark was liberated, and explores themes of responsibility and retribution in the context of the activities of a Nazi soldier. The film unhesitatingly constructs sympathy for the Nazi officer making for rather provocative and discomforting viewing. It deals with the ambivalences that circulate around binaristic models of good and evil, setting out to demonstrate that the grey area in between is fraught with complexity and moral fascination. For von Trier, it is precisely this fascination which bolsters his interest in the experience of defeat and the otherness that ensues from it. Issues of guilt cannot be separated out from processes of disavowal and questions of morality. These themes are extensively elaborated in the 'Europa' trilogy of films. In this work, the key narrative thread centres on an idealist whose project fails as he allows himself to be sucked into acts that betray his idealistic motivations. Questions of morality, power and identity become central to this endeavour, as we shall see.

This interest in the inter-relationship between morality, power and identity is made manifest in a number of ways. For example, *Europa* grapples with the truthfulness of historical accounts of the motivations of the Americans in post-World War II Germany and with the German experience of defeat. The trilogy as a whole contemplates the inter-relation of morality, religion and ethics and foregrounds the contradictions of desire and moral certainty in ways that signal the slipperiness of attempts to represent the formation of identity in any clear-cut monolithic sense. Von Trier's work here concerns itself with the politics of identity in the contemporary global context. It encompasses debates around gendered identity and cultural difference and his work articulates many crucial concerns and questions around what it means to be a meaningful human being. What are the effects of societal and cultural constructs on the formation of a sense of identity for the individual subject? This is a fundamental question running through the 'Europa' trilogy.

Questions of Identity

As a trilogy of films, the 'Europa' trilogy deals with questions of nation and cultural politics very overtly, as the last chapter explored. While *The Element of Crime* and *Epidemic* occupy nondescript contemporary periods, *Europa* is over-archingly concerned with notions of history and national identity in the context of post-World War II Germany. Yet each of the films also deals in the mythologies that circulate around questions of identity and culture, scrutinising the relationship of one generation to another and examining the ways in which youthful idealism is gradually corrupted by the mechanisms of power and cultural politics that dominate in each narrative context. Whether this is in relation to criminality (as in *The Element of Crime*), medicine and health (*Epidemic*) or terror and fascism (*Europa*) seems unimportant; the trilogy exposes the unsettling possibility that idealism is always misplaced, bearing little cultural value in a world that seems rather bleak and devoid of humanity.

In *The Element of Crime*, Fisher's faith in the system of justice is undermined at a number of levels. In many ways, he becomes the archetypal *noir* anti-hero, a lone detective who comes up against the paradoxes of desire and honour in pursuit of the ideal of 'truth'. For Fisher, the corruption of Commissioner Kramer (Jerold Wells) is connected to the failure to pursue the purity of Osborne's crime detection system. Unwittingly, he sets out to overturn Kramer's cynicism but becomes so personally bound up with his investigation that he himself is corrupted by it, committing the last of the Lotto murders. His idealism is undermined at the end of the film when he colludes with Kramer in allowing Osborne's suicide to establish Osborne as the killer rather than Fisher himself. The paradox of Fisher's idealism and its corruption is overtly connected throughout the film to questions of justice and power. Numerous scenes involving the judicial system and various aspects of the investigation of crime such as the post-mortem examination signal the ways in which good and evil are enshrined in the ideological values established by the state. Hegemonic formations of power operate through the deployment of such systems and work to ensure that notions of justice and recrimination are defined in relation to the relevant ideological positions. Fisher, with his somewhat naïve investment in the possibility of a pure mode of detection leading to the implementation of a 'pure' form of justice, learns through experience that individualism does not hold much force in relation to the systematised processes of hegemonic power. It is in relation to these that the binarism of 'good' versus 'evil' is enshrined. The greater social 'good' is served by ideological and repressive apparatuses which are shaped with reference to a prescribed system of morality that, in turn, upholds values which allow the locus of power to remain intact.

The narrative structures of both *Epidemic* and *Europa* also shore up the apparent inescapability of such processes by foregrounding apparently opposing ideological conflicts and gradually breaking them down to the point where the essence of hegemonic power becomes irreducible. In *Europa*, for example, Leo Kessler's liberalist agenda is characterised throughout with reference to capitalism and imperialism and this is in counterpoint to the baldly anaesthetised terrorist imperative of the Werewolves who embody a set of values more frequently aligned with Fascism. Through a naïve sensibility premised in romantic love, Kessler fails to see through the manipulations of his emotional world by Katharina Hartmann (Barbara Sukowa) and he becomes irrevocably caught up in the enigmatic uncertainties around what it is possible to justify in the name of love and freedom.

For each of the protagonists in these films, identity is something that is in crisis. For Fisher, the crisis is rather an Oedipal one and is bound up with his flight from Osborne, his former teacher. In returning to Europe in an effort finally to understand 'The Element of Crime', Fisher is established as a kind of prodigal son whose return to the father is mapped existentially, inscribed as the pursuit of both ontological and epistemological meaning. In *Epidemic*, Dr Mesmer acts as a lone proselytiser, seeking to resist the domination of hegemonic forces by deploying his training to work against them. Despite the warnings made to him by the council of medics who become the acting government in the film within the film, Dr Mesmer embarks on his misinformed mission and ends up spreading the plague as a result. This is a case of individ-

Fig. 9 Dr Mesmer (Lars von Trier) unwittingly spreads the plague in *Epidemic*

ualism as the locus of resistance gone badly wrong. The tale of Dr Mesmer reinforces the inevitable inscription of the subject within the framework of ideology and the film within the film acts as a kind of parable for this. In *Europa*, Kessler's identity crisis is bound up with a tendency to idealise the possibility of benevolent cooperation and congenial attempts to integrate opposing ideological positions in the name of peace. Kessler's desire to understand the place of the other and to evangelise is bound up with unbearable guilt around the silences of war and the terror that is perpetrated in the name of 'good'. His idealism is, in the end, displaced through cynicism and punished through death.

Von Trier has suggested that he believes in 'the unalienable right of the individual to shape his own life' (Schwander 2003: 23), yet each of the films in this trilogy throws into sharp relief the problems that accompany the project of individualism. The place of the individual is, in the end, shaped with reference to hegemony and an ideologically-defined system of morality and ethics. As Althusser's work insists, the individual is interpellated by ideology, and thereby inscribed as a subject of its systems. The 'Europa' trilogy scrutinises the workings of this and symbolises the mythologising tendencies at play in hegemonic systems and their inevitable inscription of identity in a space that does not allow much room for manoeuvre.

Another key marker of this trilogy is its attention to form and stylisation, and the formal elements of the films are important in terms of constructing an analysis of the politics of identity and power. *The Element of Crime* is a *film noir* shot in colour and its saturated hues of colour set up an apocalyptic vision of contemporary Europe and its vicissitudes. The film is overlaid with macabre sensibilities around death and murder, truth and integrity, and good and evil. As with any film in the *noir* style, *The Element of Crime* concerns itself with the futility of idealism and the inherent weaknesses of man in the face of power and knowledge, and the *mise-en-scène* establishes this neatly. Referencing the work of Andrei Tarkovsky in *Mirror* and *Stalker* and neo-apocalyptic

Fig. 10 Images of water add to the apocalyptic atmosphere that dominates in *The Element of Crime*

films such as *Blade Runner*, this film leaves little room for anything other than despair in relation to its resigned acceptance of the apocalyptic underworld it depicts.

By contrast, *Epidemic* is a stark and pared-down piece of filmmaking which sustains an elaborate film-within-a-film structure my means of careful experimentation and minimal intervention. The framing narrative concerns the struggles of would-be directors to raise funding for a film script and is heavily ironic and self-reflexive. The film-within-a-film eventually comes to collide with the real world, as its unwitting hero spreads the plague beyond the bounds of fiction, extending it into the 'real world' of the framing narrative. The metaphorical implications are clear: film has the capacity to infect and destroy; its insidious relationship with creativity and capitalism lends it catastrophic potential and the joke is on the spectator who seeks pleasure in the work. Here, von Trier appears to send up the notion of the *auteur*, but he does so by simultaneously casting aspersions about the nature of the film industry and its relationship to entertainment. Once again, power is at the heart of this 'meta-film' and its inter-relation with money is clearly demarcated. The film appears rather pessimistic and defies expectations, formulating itself as an essay on the apparently bleak prospects for cinema in the contemporary age. It also highlights the proclivity of the audience for neat and unencumbered films which do not challenge but rather sustain the dry and somewhat meaningless pursuit of cinema for the sake of entertainment.[4]

By contrast to the earlier films of the trilogy, *Europa* is pure cinema. With its highly-wrought narrative strategies and techniques, it deploys expertise in the service of narrative to produce a film that is highly stylised and very slick. As already seen, von Trier makes use of rear- and front-projection techniques, the juxtaposition of colour and black-and-white images in the same frame, and techniques of superimposition. The film is glossy and highly cinematic, recalling the work of Alfred Hitchcock and Orson Welles, and drawing ostensibly on the German expressionist roots of *film noir*, as chapter two discussed. The influence of both Expressionism and *film noir* is seen throughout the trilogy in the paranoid and pessimistic sensibility it evokes. Hegemonic forces are seen as inescapable, but also as profoundly problematic. The films are overwritten with a dark and oppressive style designed to heighten the gloom of the ideological inscription underpinning the narratives. In *Europa*, key themes work with the film's technical prowess to highlight the expressionistic concerns at the heart of the narrative. What is to be understood as 'good' or 'evil'? What is the psychological importance of these values for an understanding of the politics of identity? How can cinema make space for idealism in the face of the apparently inescapable lure of hegemonic formations of power? Where might the individual find space for himself and his sense of subjectivity?[5]

Discourses of failed idealism and its function in prompting greater evils permeate the plots of all three films, although they are, perhaps, seen most clearly in *Europa*. The use of front- and rear-projection construes a vision of Europe that is articulated through cultural fantasies underpinning its recent history, as the previous chapter explored. In addition, the film is shot through with the complexities of identity and questions of gender. The dream-like qualities of *Europa* complement the nightmarish atmosphere of *The Element of Crime* and the folk-fable story of *Epidemic*. The psychological unravelling of the certainties of identity and history sits alongside the enigmas of time and power for von Trier, and he employs a key device to flesh out his stylistic debts to Expressionism and *film noir* which takes the form of the trope of hypnosis – a device that fittingly draws together the different thematic issues and concerns at the heart of this trilogy of films.

Hypnosis and Fatalistic Idealism

As discussed in chapter two, hypnosis is intricately connected to unconscious processes and provides an important means by which the origins of certain psychological symptoms and dispositions might be understood. It is also fundamentally about the relationship between the subject and the hypnotist and its function turns on the question of suggestibility. The hypnotist wields an immense amount of power and is able to manipulate the subject in terms of her/his sensibilities, emotions and memories.[6] The power of suggestion is all important in this context, and there is much at stake in the ethical formulation of any hypnotic relationship. For von Trier, hypnosis might be seen to extend to the materiality of the cinematic experience; film and the cinematic experience hypnotise spectators, lulling them into a softened sense of security in which the suggestibility of cinema might better operate.[7] To describe the 'Europa' trilogy as bound up with hypnosis, then, is to suggest that its films explore the structures of the mind in relation to pleasure, identity and meaning. It is important to consider this not just in relation to narrative, but also to film form and to the consumption of films by spectators.

In *The Element of Crime*, Fisher is transported through hypnosis from Cairo to a murky dystopian and watery apocalyptic vision of a ruinous Germany. The purpose of Fisher's hypnotic experience is clearly related to a case which he has been investigating for the past two months in Cairo, yet the film never returns us to Egypt in the end, as it leaves us hanging on Fisher's plea for the hypnotist to bring him back ('I want to wake up now – are you there? You can wake me up now. Are you there?'). It becomes apparent that the film is intended to navigate us through the mist of time in order to place Fisher in a very clearly defined ethical context in relation to his pursuit of an ideal. Despite the fact that Fisher is seen to be working for Commissioner Kramer, he immediately turns to his old tutor, Osborne. He takes up Osborne's notion of 'the element of crime' essential to any successful crime detection and places this at the heart of his investigation of the case of Harry Grey. In the end, Fisher becomes so drawn into the case that he takes on the identity of Harry Grey himself, literally re-living his movements and actions to the extent that he inevitably comes to commit the next in the series of murders. He thereby comes to grips with 'the element of crime' through direct experience of it as a perpetrator. Fisher/Harry Grey's actions cast suspicion on Osborne who is framed for the crime because of his apparent mental illness. Fisher goes free and Osborne commits suicide. The film ends with Fisher alone in a rain-sodden apocalyptic wilderness and he stares aimlessly into the eyes of a rat at the bottom of a storm drain, feebly attempting to persuade the hypnotist to awaken him.

The trope of hypnosis, here, removes the protagonist into a setting in which he is able to pursue an ideal. His very discernible idealistic motivations are seen throughout the film as he tries to follow Osborne's notions to the letter, unwittingly setting himself up to fall. Von Trier has commented that in his films, 'whenever there is a man in the lead role, at a certain point, this man finds out that the ideal doesn't hold' (Smith 2000: 25) and this is a trope that runs through the 'Europa' trilogy. In *Epidemic*'s film-within-a-film, Dr Mesmer unwittingly spreads the plague through the land in his attempt to bring medical attention and care to those who need it most. Interestingly, this fatal idealism is mirrored in the framing film, when the filmmakers try to persuade Claes Kastholm Hansen, the film consultant, of the potential of their film by using a hypnotist to evoke its content. The effect of the hypnosis is to bring the fictional plague into the reality of the writers' world as the female medium used by the hypnotist contracts the plague herself and infects everyone in the room. The fatalistic idealism of the male protagonist is also seen in *Europa* as we watch Leopold Kessler succumb to the activities of the Nazi terrorist group, the Werewolves, despite his resolve to resist their hold over him. His love for the *femme fatale* of the film, Katharina, leaves him open to emotional blackmail and he becomes an archetypal dupe for her betrayal. He agrees to plant a bomb on a train on behalf of the terrorists, and, despite the fact that he changes his mind and attempts to undo the plot, the bomb explodes and he is killed. In a very languorous closing sequence reminiscent of Charles Laughton's *The Night of the Hunter*, the film depicts Leo's death by drowning, a comment on the futility of his idealist agenda.

Throughout the film, the role of hypnosis is foregrounded through the use of a voice-over narrator (Max von Sydow). The voice-over is important in understanding the function of hypnosis on a number of levels. Firstly, it simulates the hypnotic setting; the voice-over addresses the subject in the second person, addressing itself to 'you'. This has the effect of structuring the spectator's identification with Leopold Kessler as it simultaneously narrates Leo's actions on the screen and addresses itself to the viewers

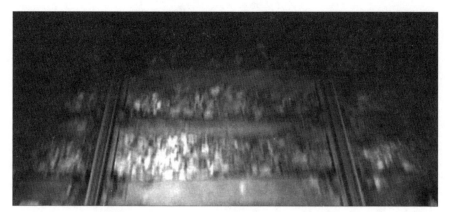

Fig. 11 Images of train tracks in *Europa* underscore the hypnotic voice-over

in the auditorium. The second-person mode of address in the voice-over thus conflates the spectator with the protagonist. It also configures key aspects of the *mise-en-scène*, as the train tracks are filmed at decreasing speed in order to lull the spectator into this structure of identification and in order to draw a parallel between the train track and film as a material object because of the similarity of their appearance.[8] The hypnotic voice-over, then, is multi-functional. It inscribes the key principles of the film's narrative structure; it configures the spectator's identification with the protagonist; it acts as an emblem of cinema and points to the ways in which film offers both a space of security and an opportunity to get to the origin of its concerns. Its alliance to psychological processes is also inscribed in this process of unravelling. Hypnosis decentres the subject and allows for the subversion of a bourgeois sensibility through its deployment of techniques that evoke the unconscious and the psychic mechanisms at play in the experience of trauma. As chapter two suggested, the difficult material underpinning the narrative in *Europa* relates to the ideological and historical context of war and the experience of guilt and shame it evokes. The trope of hypnosis thus opens up space in which to consider the implications of the unravelled subject in relation to the workings of power and ideology in society.

Hypnosis, Trauma and Spectatorship

This emphasis on hypnosis can be understood with reference to discourses of trauma. As we have seen, the themes of the 'Europa' trilogy as a whole are marked in terms of cultural trauma and notions of history encompassing crime, plague and war. Hypnosis figures largely in the history of trauma and its psychological treatment. In particular, the roots of psychoanalysis are to be found in the context of work on trauma and the hypnotic method. Influenced by Jean-Martin Charcot's work on hysteria, in which he stresses the displacement of the traumatic symptom from the injury sustaining it and the fact that the symptom emerges only belatedly, Freud and Breuer (1991) forged their foundational work on the unconscious through their investigation of the potential curative dimensions of the hypnotic method. That the trauma in this trilogy is cultural trauma suggests that the protagonists of these films are somehow working through a kind of cultural unconscious. What is more, it is arguable that trauma structures the identification of the spectator with the protagonists. This is, perhaps, seen most clearly in *Europa* in the film's conflated address to both protagonist and spectator, but it is also played out in the structures of identification in *The Element of Crime* and *Epidemic*. Von Trier uses hypnosis to alert the spectator to the importance of cultural trauma and, as a result, his films raise interesting issues of cinematic address.

As we move through the trilogy, the hypnotic elements of the films shift. In *The Element of Crime*, the hypnosis clearly works only at the narrative level; in *Epidemic*, the hypnosis is central to the collision of narrative worlds and this arguably prompts a measure of self-reflexivity in the spectator watching the narratives unfold – has s/he also become contaminated as a result of watching the films? The structure of the address has already begun to shift. In *Europa*, however, the shift is fully articulated as the voice-over narrator directly addresses the spectator as 'you', thereby mapping a spectatorial identification with Leopold Kessler and configuring the role of the spectator in terms of discomfort in the act of viewing.

This shift in the terms of the spectatorial address structures the spectator as active in that it demands reflection on the meaning of the films. In *Europa*, for example, the spectator is aligned with Kessler and is almost invited to suffer his feelings on his behalf, or at least to witness the slipperiness of his position through the act of identification with him. Throughout the trilogy, there is a striking absence of emotion. This absence in the protagonists of any emotional response to the situations in which they find themselves leaves no space for reflexivity in the narrative. In identifying with the protagonists who are eventually thwarted, the spectator struggles to make meaning for the films which thereby demand reflexive engagement. This is especially important in light of the way hypnosis draws our attention to socio-cultural trauma. Hypnosis, then, is important because it inflects the ethical concerns of the films. The ethical system of the films is anchored in their discourses of crime, medicine and war and can be understood in relation to masculinity and the mechanics of power at play in the trilogy.

Masculinity and the Mechanics of Power

The question of the mechanics of power runs through the 'Europa' trilogy. This is, perhaps, seen most clearly in *Europa*, where the setting in Germany in the period immediately following the end of World War II sets up the context of the experience of defeat as a key theme of the film. The arrival of Leopold Kessler, an American conscientious-objector of German descent, allegorises the presence of the United States Army in Germany and the conditions that this evokes in terms of the reconstruction of the country and the prevention of further recourse to war-mongering. At a socio-historical level, *Europa* raises ethical questions about the motivation of the American military and its intervention in the commercial interests of the country it has now occupied in the name of reconstruction. This is encapsulated in many scenes, perhaps the most memorable of which is the one in which von Trier plays a young Jew. His role is to bear false testimony in order to enable Max Hartmann (Jørgen Reenberg), the owner of the rail company, Zentropa, to be exonerated of any connection to Nazi activities in order that he might collaborate with American interests and help to ensure that the railways are kept 'safe'.

In constructing his narrative around power in this way, von Trier foregrounds the ethical problem of a relation to power and the inability of the individual to transcend the politics of the state. Interpellated by socio-economic and militarily-invested structures of ideology, Kessler is unable to desist from taking up an association with the Werewolves, despite his best efforts. His idealism is made explicit through the assumptions and projections made by other characters such as his uncle and members of the Hartmann family with regard to his reason for coming to Germany. It is, however, thwarted initially because of his love relationship with Katarina Hartmann. She seduces him into believing that 'fence-sitting' is ethically less justified than a firm commitment to an active political agenda. It is interesting here that von Trier uses the place of the subjugated other to elaborate such a position as ethically valid. Firstly, he uses the figure of the exploited young Jew to present a cynical perspective on the ethics of the American position in choosing to overlook earlier collaboration with the Nazis in order to further new collaboration with the project of reconstruction. Secondly, he uses the figure of the woman to throw into relief the question of the individual's relation to power and to ruling ideologies. In some ways, this turn to the place of the other is predictable in the context of von Trier's insistence on the masculinity of the trilogy. In this regard, it provides an opportunity to scrutinise the inter-relation of gender and ethics.

The question of gender and ethics has recently emerged in the field of feminist theory, and there has also been a turn to the question of ethics in relation to visual culture broadly defined.[9] In both fields, what seems to be at stake is the experience of difference which influences the cultural formation of otherness in all its guises. In von Trier's work, the distinction between the 'Europa' and 'Gold Heart' trilogies is specified in terms of sexual difference, with von Trier seeing the former as 'masculine' and the latter as 'feminine'.[10] The ethical concerns of the trilogy are arguably inflected through this deployment of gender. It is fascinating that the concern with ethics, alterity and difference at play in von Trier's work mirror similar thematic concerns of a key theorist of sexual difference, Luce Irigaray. In her recent work, Irigaray has sought to address the complexity of this inter-relation of sexual difference, gender and ethics and the next section explores how these ideas can be used to understand the relationship between ethics and masculinity in the 'Europa' trilogy.

Masculinity and Ethics in the 'Europa' Trilogy

The broad basis of Irigaray's philosophy is that, in the context of dominant ideology, discourses of gender eclipse the question of difference. This constructs a hegemonic *a priori* of sameness in which the masculine prevails; in other words, masculinity is aligned with positions of hegemonic power and otherness is marginalised and silenced in order to ensure that masculinity continues to dominate (see Irigaray 1985a; 1985b;

1993a; 1993b; 1996). As a theorist who is heavily invested in the importance of language to the development of speaking subjectivity, Irigaray often frames her discussion and critique of the symbolic order in terms of the inherent masculinism of the discourses that constitute and traverse it. Discourse, for Irigaray, is that which silences the other. For Irigaray, discourse usually silences the feminine, rendering it unspeakable. Drawing on (and responding to) philosophers such as Emmanuel Levinas, Maurice Merleau-Ponty and others, she places the question of sexual difference at the very heart of an interrogation of ethics because, she argues, the ethical relation is integral to development of subjectivity in- and for-itself. In order to become, speaking subjects need to recognise the other and to develop a means of engaging with it. For Irigaray, the feminine is usually cast in terms of the other, as that which is repressed and forced to function as the unconscious bedrock of masculinity. A politics of gender aiming to circumvent this structure would, in her view, necessitate recognition of the centrality of the other for any notion of the subject. She further emphasises that the basis of any ethical relation is a sense of wonderment and awe at the radical 'irreducibility of the other' (1996: 13). This acknowledgement that the other is both integral to and yet separate from the subject is fundamental to the possibility of any becoming and therefore to any ethical relation premised on difference.

That the 'Europa' trilogy is shaped through the masculine by von Trier is important in this context. On the one hand, the masculinism of the filmic concerns is overarchingly apparent at both the narrative and formal levels. The recourse to technique, a particular concern with history and the perceived inevitability of the protagonists' fall from grace conspire to produce a distinctively masculine relation to the theme of power. Discourse is inscribed through notions of technical expertise, the dominion of history and the unshakeability of a particular hegemonic version of masculine subjectivity in which prowess is measured in terms of sameness. However, this is complicated by von Trier's insistence on the fall of each protagonist and by the fact that each fall comes as a result of the protagonists' attempts to resist dominant power structures in order to attain an ideal. In *Epidemic*, for instance, Dr Mesmer's foray beyond the city walls is structured as a direct flouting of the demand of the newly-instated government made up of medics, which is set up to imply that there is a real danger inherent in Mesmer's plan. Of course, by the end of the film, we realise that this is actually little more than a narrative conceit, in that the medics withhold the vital information that the disease affecting the country is presently confined to the city itself and has not yet reached the countryside. In the framing film of *Epidemic*, too, we see that the filmmakers set out to bamboozle the film consultant into funding their film when faced with the loss of their long-term script project which he is expecting to receive. They humorously send up the conventions of filmmaking with their focus on dramaturgy, and yet remain blissfully unaware of the impending plague infection that will strike them by the end of the film when the fictional world they have mockingly constructed becomes their lived reality.

It is, then, as though von Trier is colonising a position of resistance against hegemonic power structures at one level and yet undercutting this position at another by cynically manipulating the outcome of any attempt at resistance. The idealistic protagonists in each of these films neither attain their ideal nor fall into the trap of sameness that the loss of an ideal arguably entails. Instead, each protagonist is thrust helplessly into the domain of the unspeakable (that is, the domain of the other), where prospects look grim and there is no hope. The state of the protagonists at the end of each film might be described in terms of abandonment or dereliction. In *The Element of Crime*, for example, Fisher is saddled with his own unspeakable knowledge that he is the true murderer and that Osborne has committed suicide as the ultimate gift to him. Along with this gift, however, comes the singular misery of not being able to speak one's guilt. As we see at the beginning of the film, Osborne's life is hardly productive at any level once he has gained an understanding of his life's project. He can merely await the arrival of Fisher as the heir to the melancholia that his experience has induced. There is a kind of endless return implicit here that is redolent of Friedrich Nietzsche (a favourite philosopher for von Trier). This ending also reminds us how the material recalled in the hypnotic trance is said by Breuer to be somehow split off from the rest of the psyche and therefore at the root of hysteria (see Laplanche & Pontalis 1988: 192). In some ways, then, Fisher himself becomes the cultural embodiment of this split-off material and the hysteria that ensues from it. At a discursive level, he himself becomes that which is unspeakable, unthinkable and therefore ripe for repression. The discursive implications are clear: the scrutiny of the workings of discourse results only in further subjugation. Fisher finds himself at the bottom of a dank and dark pit at the end of the film, pleading for release.

However, crucial to the unfolding of this narrative and the making of meaning in each of the films, is the role of the spectator. Von Trier does not withhold knowledge from the spectator, and, as a result, his films position the spectator as a source of ethical action. The films in this trilogy demand identification with the protagonist in order to foreground the complexity of his ethical journey. The question of ideals is rendered starkly in each film, leaving little room for the spectator to miss the commentary on the ethical problematic constructed in the films' endings. Von Trier's approach highlights the inevitability of the recuperative strategy at play in the hegemonic structure of power and this is important in understanding why the trilogy is a 'masculine' one. The masculinity lies not just in the narrative and formal content of the films, but also in relation to what the films suggest about ethics. In this context, the critique of a set of symbolic discourses premised on sameness put forth by Irigaray again seems to be of interest.

In her scrutiny of ethics, Irigaray examines the figure of Antigone at some length.[11] Drawing on Hegel, for whom Antigone stands for ethics, Irigaray comments that 'Antigone is silenced in her action … because she is neither master nor slave' (1993a: 119). In some ways, this perspective on Antigone resonates with the protagonists of von Trier's 'Europa' trilogy. Fisher, Mesmer and Kessler all stand in, to a degree, for Antigone, and in so doing they signify the trouble with ethics in a masculinist discursive setting. As Irigaray suggests, 'discourse is a tight fabric that turns back upon the subject and wraps around and imprisons him in return' (1993a: 120). Furthermore, the web of discourse entails that 'man is forced to search far and wide, within his memory' for the source of meaning. But by moving back into the past one risks losing the future' (ibid.). Moving back into the past in order to pursue a future, is, of course, facilitated in these films through the mechanism of hypnosis. Following Irigaray, the trope of hypnosis in the films thus underscores the impossibility of escaping discourse without recourse to an ethics which is shaped, not in relation to the dominant modality of sameness, but rather in terms of the space of the other. In the dominant discursive field, such a space is unspeakable and this accounts for the gloominess of the endings in the trilogy.

Von Trier's endeavour in the 'Europa' trilogy is evocative of this very enigma. The refusal of his protagonists to capitulate to the dominant locus of power in each of the films' endings suggests that the ethical struggles they have undertaken are fruitless because the mechanics of power is hegemonic and unshifting. Von Trier evokes the impossibility of pursuing an ideal in the discursive terrain of ideology: the pursuit of an ideal that runs counter to dominant ideological positions entails taking up an ethical position defined in relation to the other. Whereas Fisher in *The Element of Crime* becomes trapped in a realm of silence at the end of the film, in *Epidemic*, Mesmer literally seeks out a cave in which to hide himself in order to avoid contact with the plague (though, of course, it is only here that he comes to realise that he himself is the carrier of the disease),[12] while the filmmakers in the framing film become infected with a plague they themselves have constructed. At the end of *Europa*, Kessler succumbs to a watery grave and is seen floating along the river toward the sea while the voice-over reminds us that there are survivors who still live on and that 'you want to wake up, to free yourself from the image of Europa, but it is not possible'. What is more, the scenes of death and dereliction at the end of each film are accompanied by strangulated noises. For example, in *The Element of Crime*, the pained animalistic squeaks of the rat trapped in the storm drain mirror the discursive position of Fisher; in *Europa*, as Kessler drowns he tries to scream but the waters turn his shouts into senselessly muted sounds; in *Epidemic*, the blood-curdling scream of the medium is unbearable to us, just as the events she is witnessing under hypnosis are unbearable to her. The effects of these aspects of the filmic endings on the cinematic address coincide with the metaphorical and allegorical spaces carved out for the protagonists at the end of each film. As spectators, our identification with the protagonists is undercut in the endings which tend toward the collapsing of boundaries. The structures of spectatorship seem to unravel in this context. In this sense, the endings are readable in relation to the discursive disavowal of the other that helps to perpetuate hegemonic forces.

Each of the films' endings also turns on trauma and on an overwhelming sense of what Irigaray describes as 'dereliction'. The sense here is meant to connote a state of abandonment with no hope or place of refuge (Whitford 1991: 77–8).[13] Each of the films in von Trier's 'Europa' trilogy ends on a note of either dereliction in this sense or of actual death. The dereliction and/or death of the films' protagonists connects importantly to the ethical possibilities of the films. As already seen, the ethical position set out in these films seems to suggest that a masculinist discursive order restrains any effort to seek out ideals and that ethical principles are defined in relation to this hegemonic logic. Seen from this perspective, it is the recuperative strategy of the discursive order that inscribes the masculinity of the trilogy. The protagonists themselves set out to subvert the ontological demands of such hegemonic structures and, as a result, they are punished with death and/or the abyss of silence. Hegemonic masculine ontology cannot subvert the structures inside which it is inscribed. To do this entails occupying the domain of the other and hegemony operates to ensure that masculinity is not able to do this. This seems to be one way of making sense of the trilogy's ethical concerns.

Furthermore, for von Trier ethics seems to be bound up with the complex relationship between truth and authenticity. Rather than seeking truth, the protagonists in these films appear to be in search of a means of establishing an authentic sense of self in relation to a world rocked by apocalyptic catastrophe. As the previous chapter suggested, von Trier is pondering the ways in which it is possible to imagine what it means to be European (or even American) in light of the experiences of history. The threads of identity become unravelled by catastrophic world events such as war and plague, and von Trier's work sets out to scrutinise the impact of this on what it means to live in a world where such events are inescapable.

In this context, it is interesting that this trilogy of films signals von Trier's interest in religion and religiosity. In each of the films, we see parodic representations of faith and faithlessness. In *The Element of Crime* and *Europa*, von Trier himself plays the only characters marked out by their religious identification (in each case, the character is Jewish). (Ironically, of course, von Trier was later to discover that his father was not the Jewish Ulf Trier but rather an irreligious man named Hartmann,[14] with whom his mother had an affair in order to conceive a child with more artistic sensibilities (see Stevenson 2002: 63). Von Trier went on to abandon any personal association with Judaism and converted to the Catholic faith, a move that seems to signal a shift in his sensibility around the function of religion and systems of belief.) In *Epidemic*, faith fails the protagonists and is depicted as empty and hollow.

In the 'Europa' trilogy, then, faith fails its task in that it does not help to reveal spaces of authenticity in relation to history and experience. Instead, the image that von Trier constructs is rather pessimistic, pointing to the futility of the pursuit of authenticity. That all of this is achieved with meticulous attention to the schema of cinema, to its techniques and foibles, is testimony to von Trier's resolute belief in cinema as art and the importance of tragedy in formulating the credibility of the artistic endeavour. The debts to Richard Wagner, Nietzsche and Tarkovsky signal this clearly, as do the cinematic references to *film noir* and German Expressionism. Von Trier, as the *enfant terrible* of late twentieth-century cinema presents a rather bleak and gloomy perspective on humanity in these films, seeking to provoke both admiration for his talents and a radical questioning of his motifs and sensibilities in terms of what cinema can achieve. In subsequent work, this role as *provocateur* comes to be exaggerated and taken to extremes. Furthermore, while the themes and central questions of von Trier's work are to remain rooted in religion and the enigmas of human nature, his cinematic sensibility shifts immeasurably, shaking up the European scene and placing him firmly centre-stage with regard to the future of European film.

PART TWO

Transformations: TV/Film

CHAPTER FOUR

Reading The Kingdom: Authenticity, Artifice and the Postmodern Struggle

In 1994, von Trier's career took an important turn in direction as he accepted an invitation to make a television series for Danmarks Radio. *The Kingdom* (*Riget*, 1994) would set the scene for a new mode of filmmaking in which the director seemed to abandon his prior concerns with technical mastery in favour of hand-held freedom and the illusion of spontaneity which would herald the development of the Dogme 95 project shortly afterwards. *The Kingdom* and its sequel, *The Kingdom II* (*Riget II*, 1997), mark a crucial stage in the evolution of von Trier's international status and visibility. Initially made for Danish television, *The Kingdom* was released as a film at the Venice Film Festival in 1994 before being screened in Denmark. It subsequently went on to be screened at international film festivals, including Berlin and London, to almost universal critical acclaim.

Von Trier had created a remarkable hybrid form – a made-for-television cinematic epic which had both televisual and cinematic qualities but which also worked against the received key principles of both media, blending elements of the banal and everyday of popular television with the concerns of European 'art' cinema. Once again, formal constraints are disregarded in this work to startling effect. However, the textuality of both *The Kingdom* and *The Kingdom II* is also bold and innovative, as this chapter will explore. I shall discuss both instalments of the series as a homogeneous text in order to signal that the themes and issues under consideration cross the boundaries of these works to run through the text as a whole.

Critical commentary on *The Kingdom* signals a broad range of televisual references for this work. Von Trier himself has pointed to the influence of three key television texts in his formulation of both narrative and formal approach, citing Claude Barma's *Belphegor* (ORTF, 1965), David Lynch's *Twin Peaks* (ABC, 1990–91) and Barry Levinson's *Homicide: Life on the Street* (NBC, 1993–99).

Belphegor, a TV mini-series set in the Louvre in Paris, provides both narrative and formal substance for von Trier who picks up on the series' setting in a historical museum and ideas about the haunting of buildings emanating from the land on which they are built, as well as themes of spiritualism and the workings of secret societies. The episodic structure of this series is also evident in von Trier's structuring of *The Kingdom* in its television broadcast format in four distinct parts.[1] From *Homicide: Life on the Street*, von Trier explicitly develops the sense of style that characterises both parts of *The Kingdom* with shaky hand-held camera-work, disorienting camera movement and flagrant disregard for 'rules' of film language such as the 180-degree rule. The 'pseudo-documentary' effect of this approach helped to create the sense of 'rare authenticity and authority' that von Trier attributes to these films (Björkman 2003: 146). From *Twin Peaks*, von Trier takes his stylistic sensibility and a certain narrative disposition. Describing Lynch's series as 'a piece of left-handed work' (Andersen 2003: 94), von Trier frequently discusses the inspiration he took from it which can be seen in the soap opera structure of the series as well as in its quirky yet rather paranoid humour and its surreal staging of unlikely events linked to horror and the supernatural realm.

The Kingdom also draws explicitly on generic sensibilities associated with television drama formats such as soap opera, hospital drama and the detective series. The episodic plot structure and serial format can be understood as a 'flexi-narrative' as Glen Creeber has suggested (2002: 389). However, it is also indicative of the way television drama transcends the application of strict generic boundaries because of issues around broadcast scheduling and 'flow' and because of the tendency of television drama to participate in and draw upon several generic categorisations simultaneously (Feuer 1992; Neale 2001; Turner 2001). The dominant characteristic of *The Kingdom*, in terms of differentiating its textual substance, sits, perhaps, most easily in the category of 'telefantasy'. Following Catherine Johnson's definition, telefantasy needs to be understood in terms of its non-verisimilitudinous features, but also in terms of a concern with 'the stability of the fictional world, with the role of seeing, and with the image' (2005: 6).

Both *The Kingdom* and *The Kingdom II*, with their elaborate use of special effects to conjure up images of spirits, ghosts and monsters, clearly operate in a mode of telefantasy. However, the visual style and form of these texts complicates matters, as both texts also draw on a distinctively hand-held sensibility more familiar to viewers from documentary, a format which concerns itself with realism and notions of 'truth'.[2] These apparently contradictory generic attributes are foregrounded at several levels in the textuality of this work and they also reflect its hybrid status as neither a specifically televisual nor distinctively cinematic piece of work. In order to grapple further with these questions, it is necessary to set out the cinematic roots of *The Kingdom* and to chart its status as a *film*, which can be understood in relation to a number of literary concerns, as the next section discusses.

Literary and Cinematic Forebears

As a project, *The Kingdom* must be understood in relation to a number of literary and cinematic traditions. Aspects of the series which centre on the ghostly and the monstrous are influenced by a number of literary and theatrical movements which have broadly influenced the production of culture in northern Europe. These encompass ideas of the Gothic, the theatrical tradition of *Grand Guignol* and the broad-based cultural turn of Romanticism. Romanticism was a movement that dominated western Europe during the later eighteenth and early nineteenth centuries, in which concerns about emotion, aesthetics and the sublime were explored in response to the creeping rationalisation of post-Enlightenment Europe. With its interest in nation, mythology, imagination, feeling and questions of nature (as opposed to science), Romantic art and literature sought to overturn the cultural and social assertion of dispassionate discourses of secularity and science. In the British and German contexts, this gave rise to the Gothic tradition with its specific themes of mystery and the supernatural.[3]

Gothic art is often associated with the extremes of emotional experience, which results in a sense of gloom overlaid with excitement and dark, unspeakable thrills. It is often aligned with superstition and ritual and with the pursuit of the sublime. *The Kingdom* draws on these traditions and makes them manifest at both the level of narrative and form, with its hand-held, pacy camera-work exacerbating the excitement of the narrative themes throughout. It also draws on the *Grand Guignol* theatrical tradition and its tendency toward gruesome and macabre body horror that exploits the human propensity to be simultaneously fascinated and repelled by the interiority of the human body. The hospital setting of *The Kingdom* allows plenty of scope for von Trier to draw on this style in his staging of scenes such as those involving a post-mortem examination, 'live' brain surgery performed under hypnosis, the transplantation of a malignant hepatosarcoma into the healthy body of Dr Bondo (Baard Owe), the liver surgeon, and the numerous scenes with the decapitated head of a corpse which is sawn off by a medical student intent on using practical jokes as a way of seducing Camilla (Solbjørg Højfeldt), the nurse in the sleep laboratory.

The literary tradition underpinning this work is also at the heart of a great deal of German cinema which, as already seen, was highly influential for von Trier. Films such as *The Cabinet of Dr Caligari*, *Nosferatu* and *Vampyr* (Carl Theodor Dreyer, 1931) draw on similar traditions, foregrounding as they do themes which dominate in von Trier's work in *The Kingdom*: folklore, horror, monstrosity and the grotesque. As numerous commentators have remarked, these staples of German cinema can be read allegorically with reference to the social and cultural history of the era in which they were made (Eisner 1973; Kracauer 2004). However, as Thomas Elsaesser (1989) has aptly demonstrated, these films also need to be read in relation to the increasing competition between the German and French film industries and that of Hollywood, and the trope of the fantastic is intrinsic to the workings of this. The trope of fantasy, Elsaesser argues, is important in understanding the way that cinema allegorises social and cultural politics and constructs them discursively. *The Kingdom* and *The Kingdom II* are frequently read in terms of social commentary and a certain postmodern engagement with the capacity of cinema to mobilise discourse to comment on the formation of major discursive categories such as history and identity. The following section explores this in greater detail.

'Something is Rotten in the State of Denmark'[4]

Despite the global reach of *The Kingdom* and its sequel and the appeal of the series to audiences with no direct experience of everyday life in Denmark, there is something very culturally specific inherent in the text. This is signalled throughout in a number of ways. Firstly, the name of the hospital on which the series is based is 'Rigshospitalet', a real hospital in Copenhagen. Von Trier bastardises this name by changing it to 'Rigets hospital', a satirical reference to the nickname of the real hospital. ('Rigets' means 'of the kingdom' or 'of the realm' and has associations to both the historical denomination of the nation of Denmark and to the popular cultural belief in the land of the dead.) The title sequence of the film (repeated at the beginning of each episode in the televised version) draws attention to this dual meaning by creating a mythological back story about the land on which the hospital is built which is grounded in the folk history of Copenhagen.

The opening sequence consists of sepia-toned close-up shots of a bleak wasteland populated by shadowy figures bleaching cloth interspersed with submerged camera underwater shots that show tangled waterweeds and the murky depths of the waters of the swampland. It is accompanied by a voice-over which sets out the back story as follows:

> The Kingdom Hospital rests on ancient marshland, where the bleaching ponds once lay. Here the bleachers moistened their great spans of cloth. The steam from the cloth shrouded the place in permanent fog. Then the hospital was built here. The bleachers gave way to doctors, researchers – the best brains in the nation and the most perfect technology. To crown their work, they called the hospital 'The Kingdom'. Now life was to be charted and ignorance and superstition never to shake science again. Perhaps their arrogance became too pronounced like their persistent denial of the spiritual. For it is as if the cold and damp have returned. Tiny signs of fatigue are appearing in the solid, modern edifice. No living person knows it yet, but the portal to the Kingdom is opening once again.[5]

At the end of the voice-over, fingers and hands begin to push up through the earth and the opening sequence cuts to a title frame bearing the word 'Riget' hewn from stone which begins to crack as blood seeps through its cavities. In turn, the title frame cuts

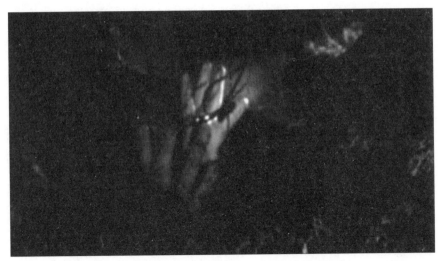

Fig. 12 Fingers push up through the earth in the opening sequence of *The Kingdom*

to a highly televisual fast-paced title sequence in which shots of the show's stars are inter-cut with glimpses of key scenes and cutaways to the ghostly ambulance captured by CCTV footage and views of the towering concrete building of the hospital itself.

The shots of the stars of the series in this opening sequence also indicate the cultural specificity of the text. Many of the actors involved are famous Danish television and theatre actors (Björkman 2003: 149) and many of them had been involved in *Matador* (Danmarks Radio, 1978–82; regular re-broadcasts), a popular and long-running television series which focuses on life in Denmark during the occupation of the country by Nazi forces. The domestic appeal of such stars is clear-cut, and the fact that they are well known from a TV drama focused on the historical specificity of the Danish national experience is also relevant for this discussion.

Several critics have commented on the concern with Danish national identity and its centrality to the plot of *The Kingdom*. Von Trier deploys the character of the Swedish doctor, Stig Helmer (Ernst-Hugo Järegård), as a comic foil throughout the series, making great play of his spurning of all things Danish and his caricatured attitude to the superiority of Sweden. The Danish national sensibility is an overt theme of the series, then, and this has provided material for the analysis of the social and discursive formations of identity depicted in the texts. For example, Glen Creeber (2002) has written effectively on the formation of nation in *The Kingdom* with reference to the way that mythology and history combine with discourses of power and science to produce a particularly televisual conception of nationhood. Drawing on the work of Michel Foucault, Creeber argues that

> *The Kingdom* appears to explore (via the metaphor of the hospital) different and varied aspects of Danish national life, particularly the complex and possibly fractured relationship between its dark and hidden past and its sanitised and ordered present. While Mrs Drusse's ghostly exploration of the

paranormal seems to uncover the dark and hidden history of 'the kingdom', the clinical and overtly rational world of the doctors and nurses appears to reveal a contemporary world governed by rationalism, bureaucracy and scientific intolerance. Indeed, although the logical world of the hospital appears to carry on as normal, Mrs Drusse seems to tap into a 'spiritual' substratum that lies deep somewhere within the hospital's vaults. (2002: 390)

Creeber goes further, drawing on psychoanalysis to sketch a topographical model of the hospital's spatial organisation as a metaphor of a sort of national unconscious which is rooted in the memory of spiritual and mythological cultural practices which stand in opposition to the highly rationalised discourses of contemporary European identity (2002: 391–4). Suggesting that '*The Kingdom* appears to represent and dissect a national "unconscious", exploring the role of cultural memory in the construction of both personal and national identity' (2002: 398), Creeber constructs a convincing reading of the sense of crisis that exists at both the level of national and personal identity in the context of postmodernism.

It is interesting to make links from this reading to the historical framework of film history, given its significance for von Trier, and to reflect on the ways in which *The Kingdom* and *The Kingdom II* draw attention to debates around cultural hegemony associated with television in Europe and with cinema in the global industrial context. 'Quality television' is often aligned with paradigms of taste and cultural value associated with socially elite groups and is arguably a measure of culturally hegemonic value formations. It is striking, in this regard, that critical acclaim around *The Kingdom* might be read as aligning it with the category of quality television despite its overt play with grotesque and sensationalist elements of 'lower' popular cultural forms such as the soap opera. Its complex status as both/neither film and/(n)or television is important in this context. Von Trier is able to draw on the cultural capital associated with European art cinema and his background as a particular exponent of that mode of filmmaking to lend 'authority' to this 'low' television format and to underscore the philosophical elements of the textual meaning. In the context of global cinema, however, by tapping into a more populist style, von Trier finds a way to exploit the demand for entertainment that ensures a wider global appeal for mainstream American cinema.[6] The hybrid form of *The Kingdom* seemingly begins to articulate some of the concerns around US cultural imperialism that will become more self-consciously expressed in von Trier's later work, as chapters eight and nine will explore.

In his discussion of German cinema, Thomas Elsaesser has suggested that

Any reasoning about the social or political meaning of films of the fantastic has to respect both the autonomy of the historical dimension and the autonomy of the textual level, and seek structures – not where they overlap or mirror each other, but at the points of contact, where there is evidence that the text has seized, worked over, displaced or objectified elements of the historical or social sphere, in order to bring them to representation within the text's own formal and generic constraints. (1989: 29)

The Kingdom is an excellent example of a text that holds these tensions in place to great effect. It simultaneously comments on social and historical assumptions about the relative cultural value of cinema and television while throwing assumptions about what constitutes each of those media formats into disarray and drawing attention to the economic principles at play. At the same time, the textuality of *The Kingdom* signals the complex effects of such paradoxes on the formation of subjectivity in the postmodern setting. This chapter will return to these ideas below.

Glen Creeber's reading of *The Kingdom* makes reference to a Foucauldian framework of analysis and draws attention to the importance of discourse in this work. Similarly, Timothy Tangherlini suggests that

> Foregrounded in his ideological critique of the modern Danish welfare state are the competing claims for legitimacy, authority and ultimately control made by an ultra-rationalist positivism represented by the hospital's senior physicians and a metaphysical spiritualism represented by the character Drusse. As such, one finds two competing discourses in von Trier's television kingdom. On the one hand there is the powerful and authoritative discourse of modern medical expertise endorsed and institutionalised by the state ... On the other hand, there is the marginalised discourse of folk belief – long derided in the positivist, critical and rational Western scientific discourse. (2001: 3–4)

For both Creeber and Tangherlini, *The Kingdom* exposes the domestic discontent around the Danish social welfare state and political unrest arising from debates around membership of the European Union that predominated in the country during the early 1990s (Tangherlini 2001: 4–5; Creeber 2002: 397–8). The supernatural ghostliness of von Trier's story is linked to this, acting as a metaphor for the need to get to grips with the historical antecedents of the contemporary context and signalling the ways in which the inscription of Danish national identity is discursively sustained and policed.

This is augmented in the more overtly satirical sequences of the text in which the overly bureaucratised medical establishment and its scenes of governance are repeatedly lampooned. A visit to the hospital by a government minister prompts Dr Moesgaard (Holger Juul Hansen) to abdicate responsibility for escorting the official on a tour of the institution to Swedish rival, Stig Helmer, on the grounds that Moesgaard is so proud of 'Operation Morning Air' that he cannot bear to take on the responsibility himself. Likening the visit to his experience as a child of having a painting he longed to show to his mother but only being capable of running away and hiding behind a door, Moesgaard hatches a plan not to be in his office when the minister arrives, suggesting that Helmer should tell him that he had been called away to operate 'in Odense or Hamburg ... or somewhere'. In the actual event, when the minister does arrive, he discovers Moesgaard hiding under his office desk and so he is forced to show him around the hospital, which naturally results in his unwitting discovery that regulations are being flouted at every turn. Firstly, the official party comes across the scene of Mrs Drusse (Kirsten Rolffes), Bulder (Jens Okking) and Dr Krogshøj

Fig. 13 The ghost of Mary (Annevig Schelde Ebbe) is exorcised by Mrs Drusse (Kirsten Rolffes), Bulder (Jens Okking) and Dr Krogshøj (Søren Pilmark) in *The Kingdom*

(Søren Pilmark) exorcising the ghost of Mary (Annevig Schelde Ebbe) in the basement corridor; secondly, the group encounters Dr Bondo's illicitly-organised liver transplant operation taking place in the Neurosurgery department as his fellow surgeons attempt to undo the previously unethical transplantation of a hepatosarcoma into his body by replacing it with a new healthy organ. Bondo protests that he does not want the operation, causing the minister great consternation. Thirdly, the group walks in on the attempt to abort Judith's (Birgitte Raaberg) monstrous foetus in the neurology examination room; lastly, the entourage visits the sleep laboratory only to find Camilla and Moesgaard's son, Mogge (Peter Mygind), having sex together. The minister declares that he has 'seen enough' and hastens the end of his visit. Thus, von Trier sends up issues of governance, respectability, the institutionalisation of medicine and perceived social authority in one fell swoop, drawing attention to the absurdities of the rational discursive authority attributed to the medical profession and drawing into focus issues around malpractice and the inappropriate use of resources.[7]

The social satire of *The Kingdom* operates at the level of what Tangherlini calls 'the front story' of the plot, the aspects of the narrative which centre on the daily reality of life in a hospital. This can be understood as defining the soap operatic quality of the text. Interpersonal relationships intersect with individual neuroses and the banality of the everyday to produce a flexi-narrative structured around familiarity and structures of recognition and identification. However, as a text, *The Kingdom* operates in other generic modes such as those of the detective story and the supernatural mystery and this has important consequences for the ways it comes to be interpreted. It is not enough to signal the discursive formation of the text and its allegorical and satirical functions. This is not a text that simply lampoons social practices around cultural memory and national identity. Instead, it also mobilises rather more fundamental questions around the structure of individual identity and subjectivity and it does this through its articulation of the idea of mystery at the heart of its narrative concerns. In this way, the text inscribes itself with reference to the philosophical concerns more familiar to viewers from European art cinema than from everyday television.

Creeber's reading of *The Kingdom* indicates this with reference to a psychoanalytic framework of analysis that foregrounds the way in which the topographical organisation of the hospital replicates a Freudian model of the unconscious. For Creeber, this is associated with issues around cultural memory and the importance of a national collective unconscious in the formation of individual identities. Yet there is also a marked concern with the uncanny running through von Trier's text, and this is repeatedly highlighted through the deployment of fantasy as the key generic sensibility within the text. Indeed, markers of the Gothic within *The Kingdom* signal the extent to which this aspect of the unconscious is significant within the development of the story.

At the heart of von Trier's engagement with the 'folk belief' underpinning his story is an on-going fascination with the relationship between past and present and with the ways in which this is expressed culturally in terms of history, fantasy and mythology. The theme of the uncanny resonates clearly through each of these aspects of the text at both the formal and narrative levels. The uncanny is inextricably linked to unconscious processes and to folklore but it also has important ramifications for understanding the complex layering of horror and comedy that runs through this ghostly detective story/soap opera. The next section explores the importance of the uncanny in relation to these ideas in order to raise questions about the status of this work as a mode of fantasy.

In the Kingdom of Abjection and the Uncanny

The uncanny is a complex notion. It relates in the first instance to the apparent familiarity of that which is deeply unfamiliar and alien to our sense of self. It is intricately bound up with unconscious processes and with a fear of death and the abyss. Nicholas Royle suggests that

> The uncanny is ghostly. It is concerned with the strange, weird and mysterious, with a flickering sense (but not conviction) of something supernatural. The uncanny involves feelings of uncertainty, in particular regarding the reality of who one is and what is being experienced ... But the uncanny is not simply an experience of strangeness or alienation. More specifically, it is a commingling of familiar and unfamiliar ... The uncanny has to do with the sense of a secret encounter: it is perhaps inseparable from an apprehension, however fleeting, of something that should have remained secret and hidden but has come to light ... At the same time, the uncanny is never far from something comic. (2003: 1–2)

The uncanny, then, is a remarkably apposite unconscious structure for any analysis of *The Kingdom*, a text which concerns itself with a series of collisions between past and present, life and death, rationality and spiritualism and which meditates on the strangely contingent sense of selfhood which permeates these structures and is easily thrown into question. Throughout *The Kingdom* and *The Kingdom II*, the uncanny makes itself manifest through the various encounters between the spirit world and the everyday life of the hospital. From the opening sequence of the first instalment with its internally-lit, driverless ambulance to the numerous instances in which transparent ghostly spirits occupy the frame alongside 'live' human characters, *The Kingdom* foregrounds such encounters as unquestionable within the logic of its story. Von Trier does not adopt an eerie *mise-en-scène* for such scenes; instead, the domain of the spiritual is depicted as part of the ordinary, everyday concerns of those inside the hospital. Mrs Drusse's regular staging of séances in her ward is not seen as remarkable in any way. Similarly, nurses and doctors alike seem oblivious to the monstrosity of Judith's baby (conceived with Mary's dead step-father, Aage Krüger (Udo Kier)) and to the appearance of ghosts, such as Mary, in the midst of operating theatres, archives and corridors. In fact, von Trier's depiction of such ghostly figures is presented as normative – the only point at which there is any debate about the importance of the ghostly is when Judith becomes transparent during her pregnancy and Dr Krogshøj seeks the advice of Mrs Drusse about what it might mean.

This rendition of the ghostly as normative is important for its perception as uncanny. The fact that neither hospital staff nor patients are unduly alarmed by the

Fig. 14 Judith's baby, Lillebror (Udo Kier), is monstrous and grotesque

Fig. 15 Image showing Judith (Birgitte Raaberg) becoming transparent during her pregnancy

visibility of the spirit world presents the unfamiliar in terms which re-cast it as *familiar*. This is precisely the structure of the uncanny. However, the place in which the uncanny is *felt* is outside the text (with one exception which is discussed below). The uncanny qualities of the text are thus felt by the spectator and this is mediated through the enunciation of the uncanny through structures of fantasy. As Tzvetan Todorov (1973) suggests, the fantastic depends on a structure of hesitation and uncertainty and underscores the delusory nature of perception. The fantastic troubles our most hallowed boundaries: boundaries between self and other, life and death and senses of time and space. Limits are transgressed and made uncertain. For the spectator of *The Kingdom*, uncertainty dominates. The normative presentation of ghosts as part of the material reality of the hospital setting troubles a notion of rational truth. Yet the text itself sets out to lampoon the very notion of rational discourse and seemingly places its faith in the discursive substratum of culture which is expressed through folk culture and the belief in the supernatural.

For the spectator, this presents a puzzling logic. As Creeber and Tangherlini have suggested, one response to this is to read the textual representation of the supernatural as a metaphor or allegory for what is socially and culturally repressed and to draw on the psychoanalytic tenet that the repressed always finds a way to return in order to articulate a reading of the text as a socio-cultural critique of rational discourse. However, as Freud (1991b) suggests, the mere representation of the uncanny is not sufficient to evoke the *experience* of the uncanny and it seems necessary to question the way *The Kingdom* works to produce a sense of the uncanny and its aims in doing so. In other words, what is it about *The Kingdom* that is uncanny and how does this bear meaning?

James Donald suggests that human beings have 'a *need* for an Other to define the terms and limits of identity' (1989: 237). Throughout *The Kingdom*, the idea of the other is everywhere in the text. For example, Stig Helmer stands for the 'foreign other'; the 'Man from Haiti' (Michael Simpson) stands for the 'racial other'; 'Little Brother' (Udo Kier) stands for the 'monstrous other'; Mary and the other ghosts stand for the 'irrational other' and Judith and Mrs Drusse stand for the 'feminine (m)other'. Identity in *The Kingdom* is thus thrown into question in its entirety and made to be ultimately rather unknowable – otherness seems to pervade the sense of self at almost every turn. What becomes uncanny in this regard is the unknowability of human subjectivity in the contemporary context of postmodernism. Following Donald, it is possible to read *The Kingdom* as a text that throws into relief the fundamental problem of postmodernism for the contemporary fragmented subject and this can be understood through the way in which *The Kingdom* brings together discourses of the popular, the uncanny and the fantastic to produce a mode of the sublime.

Donald suggests that

This ambiguity between normativity and heterogeneity can be seen in the deployment of 'the popular' not only in political rhetoric but also in aesthetic or cultural arguments ... the popular demands the familiar and the delimited – even when, as in melodramas and horror films, it is dealing with anxiety, irrationality and death. But the popular always denotes a centrifugal force as well as, and in tension with, its centripetal pull towards consensus; that is why some popular forms – especially the more offensive ones – *share* with the sublime a transgression of aesthetic boundaries and decorum. (1989: 246–7)

For Donald, the uncanny is closely bound up with notions of the sublime but also with the idea of abjection. Drawing on the work of Julia Kristeva, Donald foregrounds the way that the abject exists in the interstices of representational practices, occupying liminal territories associated with the transgression of borders and thereby exposing 'the fragility of the law' and disrupting the sustainability of meaning (1989: 242). One can see how such a description of the abject can be seen to be at play in *The Kingdom*. The case of Judith and the way she comes to occupy a rather uncertain status as existing somewhere in between the realm of the living and the realm of the dead is a clear example of this. In becoming transparent, it is not really the ghostliness of her transformation that becomes uncanny for both the spectator and Dr Krogshøj, but rather the fact that she seems to be both alive *and* dead, occupying the liminal zone described elsewhere in the text as the 'Swedenborg Room' whilst simultaneously carrying out her everyday life in the hospital as if she is anchored irreparably in the material reality of her existence. Her body becomes abject and this produces the uncanny for the spectator and for Dr Krogshøj, but it also elevates the textuality of *The Kingdom* to the arena of the sublime.

As Kristeva suggests, 'the abject is edged with the sublime' (1982: 11). *The Kingdom* becomes a point of constellation for an undoing of identity, a disturbance of its familiarity in a form that circumvents traditional modes of horror by masquerading as melodrama/soap opera and by presenting itself as a manifestation of the popular whilst maintaining links to the fantastic and to rather ethereal philosophical questions about what it means to exist. The effect of this is heightened by von Trier's use of the hand-held camera, signalling a formal pursuit of truth but in the context of a fiction in which reality is entirely undone at both the discursive and unconscious levels.

The Kingdom, then, holds in tandem the play of discourse, knowledge and identity on the one hand and the pull of the uncanny and the fantastic on the other. It presents the fantastic as a tangible source of truth as it simultaneously exposes the fragility of reality conceived through discursive structures and formations. This is crystallised in a number of key examples running through the text. Firstly, when Judith becomes transparent, she comes to embody the effects of the uncanny and she acts as a cipher through which the plot is able to unfold. It is striking that Judith becomes ghostly once she begins to realise that her pregnancy is far from normal – in fact, she ends up giving birth to the monstrous progeny of the ghost father of Mary, the spirit being tracked by Mrs Drusse. It is also interesting that it is to Mrs Drusse (the medium) that she and Dr Krogshøj turn for guidance and advice on what to do with this half-spirit child. Later, in *The Kingdom II*, Krogshøj becomes a zombie, inhabiting the space in between life and death while Mrs Drusse is almost killed in a road accident and is seen to enter the 'Swedenborg Room' in order to understand that her time on earth is not

Fig. 16 Mrs Drusse in the liminal zone of the 'Swedenborg Room' between the realm of the living and that of the dead in *The Kingdom II*

yet done and that she is being entrusted with a mission aimed at helping the spirits to reconcile their world with the official history of the hospital.

Each of these examples provides important plot motivation, linking *The Kingdom* to *The Kingdom II*. These elements of the plot also signal the ways in which the text as a whole manages to conjure something of the ineffable in its formal representations of the hinterland of the spirit world and the realm of abjection. It comments through the popular discursive medium of television on the stuff of high art cinema, bringing questions of the sublime into focus in relation to the lived experience of the ordinary and the everyday. This is perhaps what is most uncanny about this text. It cannot neatly be pigeonholed and resists boundaries of all sorts – von Trier produces for us an archly transgressive and highly postmodern text in which the confusions of contemporary individual identity are read in relation to perspectives on mythology, discourse and cultural memory but in which the mystery of what it means to be a human being are somehow explored and sustained throughout. The uncanny unfolds alongside the comic to formulate a text in which unconscious processes become almost palpable, though they remain highly unspeakable at the same time. This works not only at the level of narrative, but also in terms of the spatio-temporal construction of the text, as the next section will consider.

The Kingdom as Threshold

As we saw in chapter two, Bakhtin's ideas about the narrative deployment of space and time are useful in constructing an overview of the origins of meaning and the representability of events. In *The Kingdom*, as Creeber has shown, the spaces of the hospital are important in considering the way in which meaning is made within the narrative. The ghost of Mary is discovered by Mrs Drusse in the lift shaft and much of the plot unfolds at the basement level of the building, which is the setting for the exorcism of spirits, the illicit exploration of the archives, the meetings of the male medics who are members of the Lodge and for the exchange of goods ranging from specialist microscopes and cocaine to patient gowns and voodoo poison. At the ground-floor level, the action unfolds around the ghostly ambulance in the first instalment of the text and around its 'death-racing' in *The Kingdom II*. The upper floors provide the setting for clinical examinations, management meetings and the (mis)management of patients and hospital bureaucracy. In between lie the sleep and pathology laboratories. Creeber suggests that this layout reflects a crude structure of the mind according to the psychoanalytic topographical model of the mind, and this is interesting in making connections between the ideas explored in his reading of this work which are grounded in the idea of a national cultural unconscious.

However, it is also very striking that the division of these spatial arenas can be understood with reference to the separate and mutually resistant domains of 'official' and 'unoffical' discourse. The 'official' discourse of the rational, scientific and institutional circuits of exchange are aligned with the upper levels of the hospital while the 'unofficial' discourses of the spiritual, the supernatural and folklore unfold in its lower spaces. These 'official' and 'unofficial' spaces of *The Kingdom* also coincide with the discursive spaces of experience and identity made available inside them. When she is seen on the upper levels of the hospital, Mrs Drusse (the medium/detective of the piece) is often bewildered by the mystery of Mary and her haunting of the hospital. By contrast, it is in the basement corridors that she uncovers solutions to the problems she faces and begins to solve the mystery of how and why the ghosts are returning to do their haunting. Similarly, the basement houses a space aligned with 'truth' – the archive, which acts as a metaphor for the myriad histories competing for dominance in the world of the official spaces of the hospital wards and offices. It is in the archive that truth is seen to circulate as an object which is both repressed and insistent and in which the Foucauldian schema of power and knowledge is scrutinised and exposed. Moreover, it is in the basement that the Lodge meetings of the consultants convene to enact their rituals and explore ways of 'unofficially' undoing the 'official' standards of practice while seeking to protect the authority that apparent adherence to such practice confers. Here, too, the shamanistic therapist practices his new-age psychologies that entail making contact with the inner child and inner warrior in order to grapple with aspects of the personality. The basement, then, is a space of abasement, a space that troubles the rigour of official discourse and allows boundaries to be transgressed. This is a multi-layered space too, a palimpsest of hidden strata which become ever more sinister as they move further into the depths of the earth. It is in this space that the truths of history are able to be explored, allowing new stories to unfold in the chronotopic structure of this buried space with all its connotations of repression. The importance of the hospital as a threshold between material society and the spirit world is linked to the formation of this chronotopic structure and also to the expression of grotesque realism which runs throughout the text.

For Bakhtin, grotesque realism is an important feature of carnival. It is a form of parody that is opposed to 'high culture' and which undercuts discourses of authority and truth, thereby bringing it 'down to earth' (1984: 21). In addition, grotesque realism is associated with 'unofficial' carnival linked to folk culture. The emergence of the grotesque in the context of folk carnival would allow 'official' discourses to become sullied by 'unofficial' ones – hence the link between the grotesque and the comic, which can be seen as two sides of the same coin. Bakhtin argues that the dual-sidedness of the grotesque 'can only be expressed in unofficial culture. There is no space for it in the culture of the ruling classes ... official culture is founded on the principle of an immoveable and unchanging hierarchy in which the higher and lower never merge' (1984: 166). Images of grotesque realism abound in *The Kingdom*. The birth of Judith's monstrous baby, Little Brother, is the most striking example, but one might suggest that Mona, the brain-damaged victim of Stig Helmer's gross professional misconduct, also embodies a notion of the grotesque. In *The Kingdom II*, Krogshøj becomes a zombie, yet another manifestation of the grotesque.

In each of these cases, the grotesque encapsulates distortions of the healthy, living bodies of the material world. The grotesque bodies of the text hover at the limits of life, intruding into the domain of death. The liminality of the grotesque is bound up not just with the threshold between life and death but also with that between the official and unofficial ideologies circulating within the building. In order to become grotesque formations, bodies and identities need to occupy the liminal space between life and death which is associated with the supernatural and which is perceived as other in itself. The grotesque is centred on the notion of the threshold, a chronotopic formation which is about encounters and crisis.

In *The Kingdom*, then, the hospital enshrines the threshold between life and death, the material world and the supernatural realm. It opens up a space in which encounters between official and unofficial worlds can begin to take place. In this way, it becomes a metaphor for the way in which abjection undoes the sense of self, signalling the ways in which the collapse of ideological certainties leads to the collapse of faith in the structures of hegemony and the increased questioning of what it means to be a subject. The blending of humour and horror that is ever-present in *The Kingdom* can be seen as a postmodern response to the failures of subjectivity. The text arguably documents the turn away from faith in official discourses and a cultural turn toward the domain of the unknown, the supernatural. This can be seen as a return to medieval structures of 'knowledge' premised in folk belief which, in turn, can be read as a refusal of the logic of science and the notion of rationality. The effect of this on subjectivity is important – the subject begins to disintegrate and multiply. The way in which this text allows so many characters to occupy the liminal spaces between life and death simultaneously foregrounds this. It also raises important questions about the death of the subject and the possibilities of closure, as the next section will suggest.

Death and Desire in The Kingdom

The question of desire is one that has haunted psychoanalytic writings on subjectivity and the unconscious. For Freud (1991a), human desire is often to be framed in terms of the desire to look and the desire to know. Freud formulates the desire for knowledge in relation to the pleasure of voyeurism (which involves active looking) – in other words, epistemophilia parallels voyeurism in terms of the formation of desire and subjectivity. In *The Kingdom*, the desire to know is closely bound up with the mythologies surrounding the death of the subject. As Mrs Drusse, the spiritual detective of the text, seeks out the truth that has been buried in the hospital's history, she exposes the ways in which history is silenced by ideology and thwarts the possibilities of subjectivity as a result.

As we have seen, Mrs Drusse's adventures unfold in the hidden spaces of the hospital, in basement corridors and the lift shaft. In *The Kingdom*, she helps her dying friend to survive in 'Swedenborg Room' for long enough to assist her with some crucial information about the ghost of Mary – this is essential to Mrs Drusse's investigations. Later, in *The Kingdom II*, Mrs Drusse herself visits the 'Swedenborg Room' and comes face to face with this friend and Mary herself. At another key stage of her investigation, she is able to detect the voice of Mary in the recoded silence of the hearing-test booth – the laboratory worker, of course, is unable to hear this.[8] As with any fictional detective, Mrs Drusse has insight and knowledge that anticipates the narrative and moves it on. She becomes the means through which our knowledge of the unofficial histories of the hospital comes into being. Furthermore, it is through Mrs Drusse's investigations that we begin to decipher the mystery of the text; we are encouraged to identify with her insights and to entrust the narrative to her despite the overtly expressed view that she is a malingerer and a charlatan (Dr Helmer reiterates this view at numerous points throughout the text). Our identification with Mrs Drusse permits a new space of truth to emerge for the spectator: the space of death.

As a text, *The Kingdom* constitutes an elaborate analysis of what might be understood as death. In the context of the narrative, death is reduced to the expiration of bodily functions. Subjectivity seems to transcend the limits of the body, with various characters surviving as spirits, zombies or somehow held in the interim space between life and death. This is interesting with regard to the structure of identity that the text explores. It is as though von Trier's text suggests that identity is premised on the transcendence of bodily limits and the encounter with death. At one level, this echoes the director's religious sensibility and allows for the exploration of ontological concerns bound up with the Nietzschean 'eternal return' amongst other ideas, as discussed in chapter one. However, this also links back to ideas explored above in relation to abjection and to the postmodern context of the piece.

As discussed above, abjection figures importantly throughout *The Kingdom*, drawing attention to the fragility of human subjectivity and separating out the mind/body relation so that notions of where humanity lies become separate from corporeal specificity. This evokes a sense that the transcendence of bodily limits enables an encounter with death that is important for the realisation of a sense of subjectivity. Authentic subjectivity is not to be understood as anchored within the body but, rather, as something that resists the limits of the body and illustrates the importance of the spiritual realm, a realm which is often refused and refuted by ideological processes and discourse. There are interesting parallels here with the work of psychoanalyst Nicholas Abraham. In his paper on phantoms, Abraham suggests that death pervades religious belief and signals the importance of the pursuit of a sense of 'authenticity' for the human subject:

> The theme of the dead – who, having suffered repression by their family or society, cannot enjoy, even in death, a state of authenticity – appears to be omnipresent (whether overtly expressed or disguised) on the fringes of religions and, failing that, in rational systems. (1987: 171)

For Abraham, the 'phantom' is 'nothing but an invention of the living' – it is a construct, a signifier of 'the gaps left within us by the secrets of others' (ibid.). The phantom thus points to the failures or silences of rational systems in articulating the struggle for authenticity. In *The Kingdom*, then, the prevalence of spirits haunting the hospital can be read in relation to the ways in which dominant discourses of rationality, science and capital close down opportunities for authenticity. In this sense, *The Kingdom* appears to use the metaphor of the 'phantom' as a symptom of the postmodern condition. The pursuit of authenticity is ever more complex and fragmentary in the context of postmodern sensibilities around image and surface and the 'truth' of human experience is always in question.

This is illustrated at both the formal and narrative levels of *The Kingdom*. The pseudo-documentary style signals notions of 'truth' and its perception/creation through the media lens; the blending and blurring of genre boundaries complicates the sense of where the fiction of the text actually lies; the representation of spirits is of structural importance to the unfolding narrative – spirits abound in the plot and are of structural significance; in the broader context of the specificity of the text and its perceived media format, *The Kingdom*'s collapsing of the boundary between television, technology and cinema points to the ever closer imbrication of popular cultural entertainment and structures of ontological enquiry – to a certain extent, the broader cultural turn toward images of the supernatural can be understood in precisely these terms.[9]

It is interesting to note how this concern with the struggle for authenticity and the increasing sense of alienation in relation to dominant paradigms of discourse and rationality begin to emerge as key themes in von Trier's *oeuvre*. *The Kingdom* encapsulates the kernel of his ideas in relation to this theme, and points to future development of his output. Formal experimentation and a tendency to disregard the notion that there is a formal 'language' of cinema are key determinants of the ethos of Dogme 95 as the next chapter will explore. Postmodern provocation and an augmented sensibility of what the implications of the increasingly common sense of alienation and fragmentation that emerges in the pursuit of authenticity provide the impetus for narrative concerns and a re-visioning of the political effectivity of cinema, a trait that will run through von Trier's future work in increasingly visible measure. The importance of artifice as a mechanism though which human subjectivity can be scrutinised comes to occupy an increasingly important place in the organisation of von Trier's key concerns – this play with artifice and authenticity must be read as indicative of the postmodern context of the work that follows on from this text and as a sign of the complexity of any project that aims to continue to foreground the value of cinema as art, as an art form that has something valuable to express in the context of the contemporary cultural context of late capitalism and global flow. Arguably, the transnational appeal of cinema has a crucial role to play in preserving the importance of the art work as a mean of exploring the silences and forgetting of dominant ideologies as *The Kingdom* aptly demonstrates.

PART THREE

Dogme 95 and the 'Gold Heart' Trilogy

CHAPTER FIVE

A New Vision?: Dogme 95 and the Digital Revolution

In 1995, von Trier's career took an important change of direction with the launch of the Dogme 95 manifesto, an initiative in which von Trier, collaborating with a number of other Danish directors, launched a provocative series of statements which aimed to shake up the film industry and awaken it to its own complacency around the drive to make money. The manifesto was accompanied by a 'Vow of Chastity' containing ten rules to guide the production of films under the umbrella of the initiative.[1] With its focus on the technical possibilities of cinema at the end of the twentieth century, the Dogme 95 project helped von Trier to position himself at the forefront of the shifts in approaches to cinema heralded by developments in digital technology. In some respects, however, this was the outcome of chance rather than design, as the original manifesto and stipulations in the 'Vow of Chastity' did not directly speculate on the future of cinema being tied to digital progress. Instead, while, on the one hand, the manifesto suggests that 'a technological storm is raging, the result of which will be the ultimate democratisation of the cinema', it also adds that this is a technological storm 'of which the result is the elevation of cosmetics to God. By using new technology anyone at any time can wash the last grains of truth away in the deadly embrace of sensation' (von Trier 1995a).

The manifesto's references to technology are never specifically couched in terms of the digital age producing opportunities for anything other than the liberation of directors from the pressure to produce 'illusion films', defined as films that are 'cosmeticised to death' and full of 'superficial action'. In fact, with its stipulation that 'the film format must be Academy 35mm' (von Trier 1995b), the 'Vow of Chastity' appeared, at the outset at any rate, explicitly to reject the possibilities of the developments in digital camera technologies including video.[2] Despite this, however, many Dogme films have actually been shot on video. This is partly in response to the difficulties associated with using 35mm film cameras to record hand-held shots. As von Trier comments,

> the rule simply says that the film must be shot on 35mm film and in Academy which is a clearly defined format. But when you enter into a collective you have to submit to the collective ... Søren [Kragh-Jacobsen] made the smart move of interpreting the rule as referring to the *distribution* format. That the films, as he put it, could also be shot on 16mm – the crucial factor was only that they were distributed on 35mm ... I shall refrain from telling who was against, but the opponent then said afterwards: If it is only a distribution format, then of course you can also shoot your film on video – that must be fairly logical. We agreed on that which, to be frank, has been hilarious and has given some radically different possibilities. Mainly it has made the process much cheaper which of course also pleases me. And it has led to a trend where people around the world have started making these cheap, cheap Dogme films. They might not be completely according to the rules, but if it means that people who used to be limited by a notion of how a proper film should be, if those people now feel that they can make film – then I find that has a certain quality to it. (Rundle 1999)

It is important to acknowledge from the outset, then, that for the founders of the Dogme 95 movement, digital revolution was not a specific objective. Nevertheless, the work produced as a result of the manifesto is frequently linked to the digitalisation of cinema and there is a widespread perception that it has played a significant role in the apparent 'democratisation' of cinema that has accompanied these technological developments.

The focus of the movement in its original form is ostensibly motivated by the desire for change on the one hand and for rules on the other. The format of Dogme 95 as a media event closely follows the by now very familiar tendency of von Trier toward self-promotion. What is interesting is that von Trier's influence on the formation of Dogme 95 boldly sets up a framework for the future of cinema that is centred on his own approach to film as an art form. By deploying a manifesto, the 'Vow of Chastity' and a series of 'confessions' of failure to adhere to the self-imposed rules of the project, von Trier effectively places his cinematic reputation at the heart of the Dogme 95 project. In doing so, he shapes the launch of the movement as a media spectacle of international significance – the von Trier publicity machine is in full throttle throughout the making of the movement and its integration into the heart of debates around the future of cinema and the status of film as art. This chapter examines the key elements of von Trier's shaping of Dogme 95 and sets out the ways in which his influence has successfully begun to alter the impact of film in the digital age, despite the apparent refusal of the possibilities for democratisation made available by digital technologies seen in the original formulation of the project.

Manifestations

That Dogme 95 was launched via a manifesto should come as no surprise. Throughout his early work, von Trier had made repeated use of manifestos to preface and accompany his work, releasing these in press packs and through the channel of première screenings of his work.[3] The manifesto as a cultural form has always intrigued von Trier. He often comments on his interest in the Surrealist and Communist manifestos, as well as in the manifesto published by Dziga Vertov in 1926[4] which provided much of the inspiration for the work of Jean-Luc Godard's Dziga-Vertov group in the context of *la nouvelle vague* (Schepelern 2003: 59).[5]

The significance of the film manifesto throughout the history of cinema has been usefully discussed by Scott MacKenzie (2000 and 2003). Suggesting that most film manifestos seek to state aesthetic and political goals, MacKenzie draws on Janet Lyon to signal the key ways in which Dogme 95 makes an important move away from the assumption that

> the syntax of the manifesto is so narrowly controlled by exhortation, its style so insistently unmediated, that it appears to say only what it means, and to mean only what it says. The manifesto declares a position; the manifesto refuses dialogue or discussion; the manifesto fosters antagonism and scorns conciliation. It conveys resolute oppositionality and indulges no tolerance for the faint hearted. (Lyon cited in MacKenzie 2003: 49)

For MacKenzie, the focus in the Dogme 95 manifesto is on irony and provocation rather than on critique and politicised exhortation to action. He argues that Dogme's focus on issues of filmmaking practice and production rather than on the ideological positioning that can be read off such practice, marks it out as rather unique in its manifesto style. For the Dogme 95 brethren, the exhortations are stylistic and designed to prompt reflection on the substance of cinema and its artefacts. Whereas, as MacKenzie makes clear, manifestos are 'intrinsically tied not only to the cinema, but the immediate world surrounding the authors' and 'have had, in most cases, quite short lifespans', the Dogme 95 manifesto invokes a specific shift in emphasis, 'one which shifts from a properly ideological critique of cinematic production and its relation to the non-diegetical world, to a rhetoric which only addresses modes of production, and does so without offering an ideological critique' (2003: 50–1).

Dogme 95, then, pays homage to the modernist manifesto as a mode of interrogating the possibilities of cinema. In this sense, it is a typical by-product of von Trier's attempts to engage wittily with the history of cinema and, in so doing, to promote his own significance in its broader context. As is well-documented, the Dogme 95 manifesto stems from an idea of von Trier's and was very quickly formulated together with Thomas Vinterberg in advance of them sharing any specific ideas for films (Schepelern n.d.). It was initially formulated in response to an invitation to speak at an event to mark the centenary of cinema in Paris in 1995. For von Trier, this provided an opportunity to provoke and to create a new space for publicity. The manifesto was launched in a highly theatrical style, with von Trier simply declaring himself a representative of the newly-constituted movement, reading the manifesto and the accompanying 'Vow of Chastity' aloud and scattering red leaflets containing the same information into the audience at the Odéon in Paris before leaving with a flourish. At this point, neither von Trier nor Vinterberg had any funding in place. Nor did they have any Dogme films in production. What was being 'launched', then, appeared to be little more than a stunt designed to stimulate interest in von Trier's playful manipulations of cinema and its cultural appeal. In practice, however, this rather arch provocation would go on to provide substantial international visibility and a corresponding shift in the power of influence that von Trier would be able to wield.

An Ascetic Sensibility

The chief concerns of both the Dogme 95 manifesto and the 'Vow of Chastity' focus explicitly on matters of aesthetic consideration in relation to contemporary tendencies in the production of cinema. Making reference to the extensive individualism that pervades most commercial cinema and to the tendency toward 'illusion', 'predictability' (which is aligned with 'dramaturgy'), 'superficiality' and 'trickery', the manifesto sets itself out on a terrain of opposition to the domination of increasingly high-budget, action-centred and apparently 'meaningless' films. Its basic principles assert that cinema should be central to the endeavour of anyone who is serious about its importance and its future. While the manifesto expresses a yearning for *la nouvelle vague* in particular and for the key movements of art cinema since 1960, it explicitly articulates its motivations at the level of aesthetic concerns – the question of cinema as art is integral to its founding principles.

Similarly, the 'Vow of Chastity' sets out its rules with the explicit intention of shaping and restricting the practicalities of shooting a film in order better to guarantee forms of cinema which deal with what it wishes to describe as 'truth'. Despite the exhortation to disregard questions of good taste and aesthetic considerations, the central thrust of the documents underpinning this movement centre on the need to get back to basics with regard to filmmaking as a practice, to celebrate the ethos of cinema in order to get to grips with the stuff of life, its emotions, dilemmas and enigmas.

The truth of what it is to be a human being underlies all the assumptions and exhortations made in these two documents, and this signals the core sensibility of the movement which concerns itself with the status of film as art. By imposing upon its members exhortations to resist everyday practices of filmmaking such as the use of props, locations, non-diegetic sound, fixed cameras, lighting effects, and the use of optical filters, Dogme 95 creates a pared-down cinematic sensibility premised on technological restrictions. In addition, the requirements that Dogme 95 films should neither be generic, nor historical nor futuristic, together with the rule prohibiting the use of superfluous action to motivate the plot and another forbidding the accreditation of the director signal the ways in which von Trier and the other brethren wished to avoid the pitfalls of overly-commercial cinema. The rules concocted within the manifesto and the 'Vow of Chastity' amount to an exercise in austerity for the filmmakers who sign up to them, explicitly requiring filmmakers to consider reflectively their critical engagement with film as a medium and to produce innovative and inventive responses to the constraints imposed upon them by the rules. The sensibility here is clearly an ascetic one, and one that is simultaneously meant to engender both critique of current cinematic practice and innovations in response to the possibilities of cinematic technologies. The nomenclature of the Dogme 'brethren' seems highly appropriate in this rather monastic context and the religiosity of the language deployed by its key players self-consciously underscores the intention of being seen to 'save' cinema as a culturally and artistically valid form. It is interesting, too, that there is a certain romanticism at play in the selection of terms such as 'chastity' and this taps into a rather exhibitionistic desire by von Trier to be seen to 'hold back' and be seen as somehow 'pure' enough to advance cinema as an art form.

In its blatant disregard for the aesthetic conventions of popular cinema, Dogme 95 attempts to seize upon the specificity of cinema as an art form. It musters an almost puritanical discursive attitude in order to mobilise a drive toward authenticity, as discussed below.[6] Yet, it does all of this in a heavily ironised way, setting out its rather ascetic stall in such a playful and provocative style that it becomes impossible not to view the political self-observation and highly parodic tones associated with these documents as archly postmodern.

Postmodern Puritanism

The playful and highly ironic discursive style of the Dogme 95 manifesto and the 'Vow of Chastity' makes great play of inter-textuality on the one hand and pastiche on the other, and both these things combine to produce a distinctive postmodern edge for the movement. With its self-conscious rhetoric of asceticism and *faux*-religious discourse, the founding documentation of the movement recalls a great deal of von Trier's personal investment in religious belief. Its very terms of reference make this apparent: 'dogme' translates as 'dogma'; the pledge directors are expected to make is marked out as a set of 'vows'; chastity is a time-honoured component of both religious observance and ascetic self-discipline; the vows number ten in total and are resonant of a series of commandments. Members of the movement are referred to as 'brethren' and they are expected to provide 'confessions' or a list of 'sins' for which they receive reprimands from fellow brethren upon completion of the films. MacKenzie comments on the 'unholy marriage of the spirit of the Protestant work ethic and Catholic flagellation' at stake in the vow of chastity (2003: 53), and this is indicative of the personal tussle with religion that seems to lie at the heart of much of von Trier's life and work.

Von Trier's pursuit of a cinematic sensibility that is overlaid with religious overtones is not limited to the terms of the Dogme manifesto alone.[7] Rather, for von Trier, religiosity marks his discursive structuring of film from the outset. In his first manifesto, published to coincide with the release of *The Element of Crime*, von Trier stipulates that 'We want to see religion on the screen'. The third manifesto, published along-side *Europa*, is entitled 'I confess!' and von Trier deploys religious rhetoric to evoke the ways in which film should become 'miraculous', a way of divining 'the right path'; he concludes this manifesto by saying 'May God alone judge me for my alchemical attempts to create life from celluloid. But one thing is certain: life outside the cinema can never find its equal, because it is His creation, and therefore divine.' This repeated recourse to the domain of religion would suggest that the heavily ironised references to it in the Dogme 95 agenda are a consequence of von Trier's own avowed on-going interest in and commitment to religion as a mode of existence.

Having been brought up with a strictly atheist home-life, von Trier turned to organised religion when he married for the first time and became a Catholic. The need for religion in his life is described by von Trier as 'difficult' despite the fact that he has always 'had a longing to submit to external authority'. Suggesting that he 'felt a need for a sense of belonging to a community of faith', von Trier is often quick to signal the fact that it is not so much religious practice in which he is interested but rather the idea of God. As we saw in chapter one, von Trier's fascination with the work of Carl Theodor Dreyer is partially grounded in Dreyer's humanist approach to notions of God and, for von Trier, the pursuit of religion seems tied to an urge toward the discipline that was lacking in his childhood.

However, for von Trier, religion also seems to provide a framework through which the 'basic elements' of life can be scrutinised. In fact, he explicitly signals that, in his opinion, 'all the classic forms of religion also contain the basic elements that I would like to see in films ... in that they are emotionally moving' (Michelsen 2003: 12). This link between religion, film and emotion is fundamental to understanding the evolu-tion of von Trier's *oeuvre*. It is possible to chart these concerns across a range of his films, but those that emerged in the context of the Dogme 95 manifesto offer the most clear cut examples, with *Breaking the Waves* foregrounding religiosity most overtly.[8] What is interesting is how, in von Trier's work, religion becomes a means by which the importance of the irrational domain of affect and its role in the formation of our experience of the world is highlighted.

Drawing on the work of Stanley Cavell (1979) on the way the photographic medium allows us to see something that is not present while at the same time allowing us to remain unseen, Greg Watkins has suggested that

> film has a unique power in easing the peculiarly modern sense of displace-ment from reality, our condition of distance from it ... Popular film functions culturally as an opiate (and precisely in Marx's sense of that term). By natu-ralising almost mechanically the particularly modern forms of alienations, i.e., by making the distance between the viewer (self) and the world viewed (film) an apparently questionable 'matter-of-fact', the viewer is relieved of the burden of that distance. On the other hand ... many of the great 'auteurs' of filmmaking are precisely interested in unsettling that relationship once again, and, in the space of renewed dis-ease in the viewer, find other ways of addressing the modern human condition. (1999)

For Watkins, this new rendering of film is a religious one, and, in *Breaking the Waves*, von Trier is as masterful at deploying it as Tarkovsky. In Watkins' view, this film provides a model for the way film can embody something of the unspoken appeal of religion, by drawing in the viewer to contemplate the deeper ontological truths of human existence. There are clear parallels to be drawn here with the motivations made explicit in the framing of the Dogme 95 manifesto as ultimately geared toward the pursuit of 'truth'. While Peter Schepelern suggests that von Trier's drive in the early films is to be understood as the pursuit of the 'absolute control of the *auteur* artist who functioned as God or a puppeteer' (2003: 64), by the time of the production of the Dogme project, it is as though von Trier is seeking to draw attention to the way film can serve a higher spiritual function. Indeed, as Schepelern has also noted, Dogme can be read as 'a kind of aesthetic masochism … an artistic flagellation intended to cleanse the artist of all commercial vices, leaving him purer and better' (ibid.). One might go further to suggest that the 'spiritual cleansing process' enshrined in the Dogme 95 manifesto and the Vow of Chastity also affects the spectator, and that this is where the pursuit of 'truth' is tested for its veracity and integrity. In this context, it is important to consider the emphasis accorded to 'authenticity' in the Dogme project and to relate this to the stylistic shifts in fictional film language that are created by means of hand-held camera technologies and techniques and by the incorporation of 'the real' into the domain of fiction.

Fictions of the Real

Questions of 'the real' have been central to many debates in film and media studies over many years, with particular recent attention arising from a proliferation of documentary films and reality television spectacles. The pursuit of 'reality' is often framed in terms of 'authenticity', and implicit in the project of representing 'truth' is an assumption about the 'ordinariness' or 'familiarity' of events in question. Critics have pointed to the clear roots of the Dogme movement in the development of documentary modes such as Direct Cinema, *cinéma vérité* and Free Cinema (MacKenzie 2003; Stevenson 2003). In particular, MacKenzie's work on the ways in which Dogme 95 extends the remit of Free Cinema is interesting.

Free Cinema, a movement created in Britain during the 1950s, was established by filmmakers such as Karel Reisz, Tony Richardson and Lorenza Mazzetti with the aim of bringing together films made outside the structures of the film industry in a single screening.[9] For these directors, their films embodied an 'attitude' that had at its heart 'a belief in freedom, in the importance of people and in the significance of the everyday. As filmmakers, we believe that no film can be too personal' (Anderson *et al.* 1956). As John Ellis has suggested, the filmmakers sought to be

'free' rather than 'experimental' in order to emphasise that they understood their work as neither introverted nor esoteric, nor was their concern primarily with technique. 'Free' also as an expression of opposition to the way British filmmaking was organised at that time: it involved a hostility to the industry's

conventions of style and technique – the insistence on studio rather than location shooting, the preference for investing huge sums in a prestige production
rather than finance several more modest – and therefore, in their view, probably better films. It was also an opposition to the monopoly operating in film
distribution, and the refusal of producers and distributors to consider films
which were different, controversial. Here was involved not only the radical
demand for an 'independent cinema', using 16mm rather than 35mm (still
considered an 'amateurs' gauge') but also a concern to show that good films
were just as (if not more) likely to be made on small budgets as large. (1977)

Ellis also sets out the key stylistic elements of Free Cinema, signalling the reportage-
style, the frequent use of direct sound, photographic composition and angles, disjunc-
tions of editing and the ways in which these strategies were designed to produce films
that showed not what 'things really look like but how they really are'. It is also worth
noting that the impetus behind Free Cinema was motivated by technological developments in portable filmmaking equipment and the production of faster film stock.[10]

There are clear parallels here with aspects of the Dogme movement. A crucial
difference between Free Cinema and Dogme 95, however, is that the films of Free
Cinema were in fact documentaries and were profoundly bound up with issues of class
and social justice.[11] Nevertheless, for MacKenzie, in terms of its basis in a manifesto,
Free Cinema is the greatest forebear of Dogme 95. He emphasises the fact that 'like
Dogme, Free Cinema functioned both as a new way to make films and as a publicity
stunt in order to garner recognition within the public sphere' (2003: 51). There is
also a definitively instrumental attitude at the heart of each movement in terms of the
attempts of Lindsay Anderson and von Trier to mobilise people into action. MacKenzie
suggests that a crucial difference between the Free Cinema manifesto and the Dogme
95 manifesto is that the Dogme manifesto shifts the emphasis

from a properly ideological critique of cinematic production and its relation to the non-diegetical world, to a rhetoric which only addresses modes of
production, and does so without offering an ideological critique as a necessary
corollary to the goals of the aesthetic renunciations at the heart of the Dogma
project. (Ibid.)

While this claim seems a logical one in relation to the materiality of the approach
to filmmaking, it nevertheless seems to skirt around the ways in which Dogme films
often work as an allegory for a refusal of bourgeois values in everyday life as well as in
relation to the production of cinema. Several critics have signalled the way in which
von Trier's Dogme film, *The Idiots*, in particular, seems to illustrate the potential of
Dogme as a movement to produce a commentary on cinema as an institution (Gaut
2003; Rockwell 2003). In addition, MacKenzie's claim fails to take into account the
importance of the documentary aesthetic in relation to the *fictionality* of the films
produced through the Dogme movement. Whereas MacKenzie wishes to signal that
the experimentation at the level of filmic form is divorced from the content of the

films, it seems important to acknowledge that Dogme 95 is not merely concerned with aesthetics. The blurring of formal style and narrative content is readable as a highly politicised one and one that has implications for an understanding of filmic pleasure and debates around active spectatorship. In order to illustrate this, it is necessary to turn to the notion of affect in cinema. The emotionality at the core of the Dogme films is of central importance in understanding their political impact and this is seen to particular effect in von Trier's Dogme #2, *The Idiots*.

Affect, the Drive to Authenticity and the Pursuit of 'Truth'

The substance of the manifesto and set of vows underpinning Dogme 95 stipulate very clearly that the design of the project is to move away from the cinema of illusion toward a cinema of authenticity and truth. Several critics have commented on how this drive to authenticity has resulted in realist tendencies in the key Dogme films (Hampton 1995; Conrich & Tincknell 2000; Vestergaard Kau 2000; Christensen 2000a and 2000b). The relationship between film and realism is an established terrain of debate in film theory, and these critics draw on work by theorists such as Siegfried Kracauer (1960) and André Bazin (1967) to examine what is at stake in Dogme's pursuit of authenticity.

For Kracauer, filmic realism is related to the natural world and to the potential of photographic composition to relay something of that world. Suggesting that the use of staged sets and/or elaborate *mise-en-scène* detracts from the realist tendencies of cinema, Kracauer asserts that it is important to distinguish film from art:

> The concept of art does not, and cannot, cover truly "cinematic" films – films, that is, which incorporate aspects of physical reality with a view to making us experience them. And yet it is they, not the films reminiscent of traditional art works, which are valid aesthetically. If film is an art at all, it certainly should not be confused with the established arts … even the most creative filmmaker is much less independent of nature in the raw than the painter or poet. (1960: 40)

For Kracauer, then, the aesthetic achievement of a properly 'cinematic' film requires an evocation of experience in the spectator. In this respect, most Dogme films appear to meet the criteria. In *Festen* (Thomas Vinterberg, 1998), for example, the raw substance of the film's narrative takes up an immensely taboo subject, the revelation of paternal sexual abuse in the midst of a family gathering. The narrative manipulates the sensibilities of the spectator in its scrutiny of cultural attitudes and values, evoking a self-conscious monitoring of emotional response in its audience. In *The Idiots*, we are invited initially to empathise with Stoffer (Jens Albinus) and his friends as if their masquerade of mental retardation is real, and are thus invited to mirror Karen's (Bodil Jørgensen) immediate response to the group in the opening restaurant scene. We are as shocked as Karen is when the 'spassers' reveal the joke once they have climbed inside the taxi outside – we identify with Karen and share with her the puzzlement at what

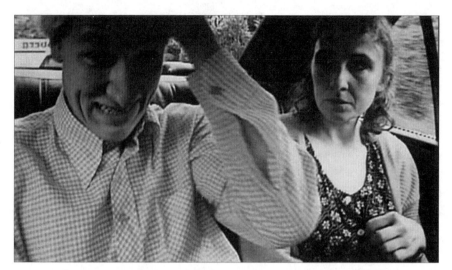

Fig. 17 In *The Idiots*, Karen's (Bodil Jørgensen) shock as the 'spassers' reveal their joke is apparent to the spectator

is going on. This has an important effect of the formulation of our emotional response to the film, which can be understood in terms of affect.

Affect can be generally understood as the observable expression of emotion, which may involve facial expressions, laughter, tears or blushing, amongst other things. The psychological dimension of emotion is what is at stake here; at times, human subjects may find themselves expressing emotional responses which they are not directly conscious of feeling but nevertheless the emotional state is an observable one. In other contexts, it is possible to observe an emotional response being felt within oneself without it being directly expressed – in other words, it is possible to constrain or repress specific emotional responses and the affective quality is sustained.

Accounts of how affect is to be understood often draw on the discourses of psychoanalysis in order to show the ways in which emotional states can function at the unconscious level as well as at the level of the conscious mind. For Freud, affect is related to the instincts or drives and to the changes in libidinal energies associated with the drives. Explicating Freud's position, Jean Laplanche and Jean-Bertrand Pontalis suggest that

> at times [affect] has a purely descriptive value, designating the emotional
> repercussions of an experience – usually a powerful one. Most often, however,
> its use presupposes a quantitative theory of cathexis ... The affect is defined as
> the subjective transposition of the quantity of instinctual energy ... It is hard
> to see how the term affect could remain intelligible without some reference to
> self-consciousness. (1988: 14)

Affect is thus to be understood as the emotional impact of an experience and as a quota of energy associated with events and experiences which may not be directly discharged but rather repressed. This makes it possible for affect to become buried within the psychic structures of the mind and to re-surface as a result of other experiences. In the context of film, it is possible that images might trigger such affective responses, enabling us to bring to the fore emotional energies and responses that may otherwise remain unaddressed. This is important for an understanding of how it becomes possible to bear unpleasurable images and even to experience pleasure in their viewing. It is interesting that much of von Trier's work appears to tap into such structures of affect and emotion, and *The Idiots* is a good example for analysis.

The question of affect is an important one in relation to all the films associated with the Dogme 95 brethren. These films strive toward authenticity, on the one hand, but also attempt to represent our emotional and psychological experiences of the world. In this respect, Dogme can be aligned with André Bazin's humanist view of cinematic realism. For Bazin, the value of cinema is to be found in what films reveal of reality – it is about the notion of truth or beauty in the world. As Ian Conrich and Estella Tincknell have suggested, 'Bazin regards a film to be truthful if unaltered by human intervention or manipulation. The film spectator's relationship to the image should be faithful to the experience of the image observed by the spectator in reality' (2000).

What is interesting in these discussions of the realism of the Dogme 95 project is the way its realism is tangled up with the aesthetics of the movement, which bear clear resemblance to documentary strategies. Yet, as Ove Christensen, has observed, 'the subjects of Dogma films are presumed to be fictitious and there is no intention to lure the audience to believe otherwise' (2000a). The use of documentary style raises more questions than it answers about the relationship of reality to fiction in the Dogme films, highlighting the way documentary style can be deployed in the context of fiction to throw the language of filmmaking and film-viewing into disarray. This uncertainty about the inter-relationship of truth, reality and fiction is encapsulated most clearly in *The Idiots* because of its very visible play with the signifiers of documentary. What is at stake in this rather meta-discursive play with the stuff of cinema? How does von Trier manipulate filmic conventions in order to re-visit the assumptions underpinning what makes a film 'cinematic'? What does this mean for the pleasures of watching such a film? And how does this play with documentary elevate the visibility of the psychological through affect?

Where the Truth Lies

Recent debates in documentary theory foreground the ever closer relation of documentary to fiction, of documentary actuality and its creative treatment to discourses of authorship and interpretation (Winston 1995; Corner 1996; Bruzzi 2000; Nichols 2001). In one sense, all images are fictions of the real. This is interesting in relation to a film such as *The Idiots* in which style and content are elaborated with specific reference to a discourse of 'realism' and 'authenticity'. The narrative follows the antics of a group of young people who masquerade as mentally ill, 'spassing' seemingly in order to explore social and cultural taboos around disability and identity. The film is shot with a hand-held camera, imitating a style of camera-work more usually associated with documentary. It also includes a number of to-camera 'talking head' interview segments, which help to lend the film and air of 'truthfulness' despite the fact that it is a work of pure fiction. This chapter will return to debates around 'authenticity' below.

The Idiots makes use of a range of documentary techniques that might be aligned with John Corner's 'evidential mode 1' (1996: 28) or with Bill Nichols' 'observational mode' (2001: 33) in which there is an emphasis on the everyday life of the protagonists witnessed by an unobtrusive camera. It also draws on documentary strategy in its use of sound. Here, then, we have a wealth of documentary strategies deployed for the purposes of a fiction. Yet this film is not an example of 'mockumentary' in the style of *This Is Spinal Tap* (Rob Reiner, 1984), for example. It is definitively *not* a fabricated documentary. Instead, this is fiction in the guise of what Nichols has defined as a performative mode of documentary (1996: 34), which is seen as creating affect and disrupting patterns of looking and pleasure in cinema in order to construct an active spectator.

In choosing to incorporate a hand-held camera, fly-on-the-wall aesthetic and to-camera interview segments into the narrative of *The Idiots*, von Trier calls upon our familiarity with the documentary format in order to heighten the claim to the real in this fiction. The interview segments of the narrative serve a dual function in this film. Shot three weeks after the six-week shoot (Knudsen 2003), they serve firstly to offer moments of reflexivity on the narrative. Secondly, however, they serve a narrative function in that they help to direct our patterns of identification with the fictional characters by anticipating the unfolding of narrative events and foregrounding events that we, as spectators, have not yet witnessed, flagging them as central to how the narrative should be read and understood.

The interview clips thus tailor our response to the story but they do so by masquerading as a form of truth-telling. The interview segments work in tandem with the camera throughout the film, echoing the intrusive quality of the camera's engagement with the actors. The camera is implicated in the action. Its role is intrusive, but inflected as testimonial. It is not overtly marked as authorial, as it creates a sense that the action is unfolding before it as if it were 'live'. The cinematic 'mistakes' of catching crew on film add to this feeling.

It is the camera that mediates the action. It directly addresses us as spectators, inviting us to participate in the unfolding of the narrative and thus to participate in the making of its meaning. This mode of cinematic address heightens the intensity of our relation to the film and its protagonists. Paradoxically, however, we are nevertheless unconsciously encouraged to maintain a relation to the narrative as fiction through the context of the interview clips. The formal attributes of the film are thus important in facilitating and establishing the framework of the spectator's response to the narrative. This has important consequences for the construction of affect in the closing sequence of the film, when Karen returns to her family home to 'spass' in front of them.

The interview segments position us as witnesses to the effects of Stoffer's experiment. In effect, our relationship to structures of identification in the film depends on an elaborate masquerade of truth-telling that is designed to evoke an emotional

Fig. 18 The documentary style of *The Idiots* is heightened in shots such as this one, in which a cameraman is 'mistakenly' caught on film

response, one that is premised in affect. The role of the camera as mediator to the spectator as witness is crucial here; it preserves our relationship to the fiction while dissimulating a mode of truth-telling that upsets our familiarity with the language of film.

However, in the closing sequence of the film, the direct address to the spectator is compromised, and it is wilfully disrupted in order to produce affect. In the film's closing sequence, the camera, which has until now functioned as a mediator of the action utilising a documentary aesthetic, suddenly abandons this aesthetic in favour of a much more familiar fictive mode, in which the camera anticipates the action. The apparent independence of the camera from the action we have witnessed until now is exposed as a fiction at this point, as the camera takes on the guise of Anders (Hans Henrik Clemensen), Karen's husband, as he strikes her. Here, the camera reveals itself as a channel for a pre-scripted fiction, anticipating and moving with Anders as he strikes Karen. For the spectator, the psychological violence of this moment is not rooted merely in the violence of the narrative at this point. The effect of this sudden shift from documentary masquerade into a fictive mode wrenches us from the perceived security of the address to us as it has so far been constituted. The affect of the moment is profound. We are rudely awoken to the fact of the fiction because the mode of cinematic address has altered. The affect of the moment comes, then, not just in response to the diegetic violence but also in response to the psychological violence imposed on us via the filmic form.

The shift in address is important because it reminds us that we are watching when we seemingly should not be. Psychoanalytic models are useful here in helping to explain the pleasures at stake in this kind of spectatorship. There is a great deal of commentary on the usefulness or otherwise of psychoanalysis for screen studies, documented by theorists such as Laura Mulvey (1975) and Steve Neale (1983) and numerous other

Fig. 19 The camera anticipates the action as Anders (Hans Henrik Clemensen) strikes Karen at the end of *The Idiots*

theorists who have engaged with debates around the cinematic apparatus, structures of the gaze and questions of gender and spectatorship. Building on the work of apparatus theorists such as Christian Metz (1981) and Jean-Louis Baudry (1985), we can read the shift in address at the end of *The Idiots* through a psychoanalytic lens to suggest that, as the camera anticipates Anders' striking of Karen, we are encouraged in our unconscious processes to recall the fantasies of the primal scene.[12] As spectators, we resist the urgent desire to announce our presence as we watch this scene and we are forced into the uncomfortable position of voyeur. The scene becomes simultaneously unpleasurable but strangely compelling and we continue to gaze upon it, despite the discomfort that it produces in us affectively.

Ethically, *The Idiots* appears to elude the morality of looking, encouraging us unconsciously to adopt the position of onlooker onto fantasy in order to maintain a relation to the fictional status of the film. At the same time, however, the film constructs itself as 'truth' through its exploitation of documentary style and strategy. It is only at the end when this slippage is made apparent to us that we find ourselves in the unbearable position of being offered no respite in the narrative closure from the fact of our voyeurism and the affect of the narrative trauma.

The Idiots does not allow us to get away with passive, voyeuristic looking. Instead, we are required actively to respond in order to salvage meaning. We are required to engage with the fictional material masquerading as truth in order to act as knowing spectators. The use of a documentary aesthetic sustains the sense of a direct address to the spectator throughout the body of the film. What is more, the narrative substance of the film centres on the ethically questionable antics of a group of middle-class young people who seek their 'inner idiot' by 'spassing' in a variety of public and private settings. The use of the documentary aesthetic, then, encourages us to pass judgement on the narrative as if it were real, and yet, as spectators, we know that the film is *not* a real documentary, and so our judgement does not have to be real either. The play of form and content here is crucial to our relation to the film as a whole.

This has an important set of effects on our experience of pleasure in this film. Traditionally, pleasure in cinema is deemed to come from the identifications we are able to make with protagonists and narrative events, from the certainty of dramaturgical development and from the tying up of loose ends in the moment of closure. In *The Idiots*, such expectations are disrupted. There is no space for 'illusion' in this film, no anchor point in which we might suddenly discern something of the familiarity of film language as we have come to know it. The complexity of the interweaving of notions of truth and fiction is cleverly nuanced in the strategies employed by von Trier and in his unwillingness to let us off the hook without paying for our psychological urge to look. The affect produced in the spectator is the payoff, and our own capacity to tolerate the emotional effect of this is called into action in order to provide us with a means of finding pleasure in the film. Effectively, the film forces us to consider our relation to the image, to speak an ethical or political perspective on our cinematic experience. This opens up a new space in which to consider spectatorial subjectivity, allowing us to (re-)view with a critical eye and a sense of subjectivity that is effectively addressed and deconstructed, ruptured and reconstituted through the practice of viewing.[13]

For von Trier, then, as for Bazin, the truth of a film unfolds in the experience of the spectator. His play with sadistic and masochistic tendencies here is important. It is as though he is seeking to elevate the realm of emotion in order to put the passion back into cinema. This is where the politics of Dogme lies. It re-reveals the extent of our psychological investment in cinematic pleasure. The function of film as art thus seems to be reconstituted and brought centre-stage in ways that resist any tendency toward illusion and which are therefore properly 'cinematic' in Kracauer's sense.[14] It is also important to note that *The Idiots* does not merely function in this specific 'cinematic' sense at the level of narrative. Its formal properties are an important element of the performative politics at the heart of the movement, as we shall see.

Dogme's Politicised Aesthetic and Its Critics

As Beryl Gaut, Ove Christensen and others have noted, *The Idiots* is a film about film-making as a pursuit. For Christensen,

> *The Idiots* is a film about acting and role-playing. One of the themes is the relation between playing a role and being a person ... The film is also about filmmaking. The editing in the film is discontinuous and the images are often blurred and shaky because of the lack of proper lighting and the hand-held camera. The editing draws attention to the film as a film. But it is also part of the documentary style. The stylistic oscillation between documentary (mini- mised or spontaneous aesthetics) and marked artificiality furthermore makes the film an investigation into the status of film and the grammar of film. In this sense, *The Idiots* is a film about its own making. (2000b)

For Gaut, *The Idiots* and *Festen* are films about *auteur* projects as well as the pursuit of truth (2003: 100). It is at the level of form, and particularly at the level of editing, that these Dogme films render themselves as self-reflexive pieces concerned with the dynamics of filmmaking as a practice. This is in keeping with the obvious levels of irony and knowingness that are deployed in the manifesto itself, of course, and it is important to note here that it is the combination of attention to self-reflexivity, the blurring of stylistic boundaries at both narrative and formal levels and the self-conscious and playful refusal of *auteurist* principles (despite the overt authoring of cinematic technique implicit in these films) that mark them out as politicised.

John Roberts suggests that Dogme 95 lacks political punch and is characterised by 'ideological reticence' (1999: 142). This seems to miss the point of the play with notions of realism, documentary strategy and fictionality, however, especially when one considers the status of the films as art. The politics of Dogme 95 appear to lie in the re-deployment of debates about the status of film as art and this is a direct response to the creeping commercialisation of the film world on a global scale. With its turn to an aesthetics premised in what Christensen has characterised as 'ugly cinema' (seen in films such as *Clerks* (Kevin Smith, 1994) and *The Blair Witch Project* (Daniel Myrick & Eduardo Sánchez, 1999) and in numerous contemporary reality television shows), Dogme 95 can be contextualised historically and discursively. Nevertheless, in its self-conscious referencing of debates around authorship and the idea of the new wave, the movement also deploys an ironised return to the dominant debates of film history and film theory, thereby revealing the ideological values underpinning the scholarship around cinema and positioning itself as a commentator upon it.

The manipulation of editing and film form characterises the key films emerging from the movement. This shows how the refusals embedded in the manifesto and its rules highlight the dilemmas facing filmmakers who wish to resist the increasing commercialisation of their art. The politics of Dogme 95 are implicit in the manifesto rather than overtly articulated but the signifiers are writ large in the editing techniques used in the films and in the deliberate construction of 'mistakes' such as catching a boom on camera or allowing a lens surface to retain droplets of water. The materiality of the act of making a film is highlighted in moments such as these, and this is important in helping to re-shape the ways in which what counts as cinema is understood. This is fundamentally about contradictions as the project seems to seek out means of alienating the viewers of its films whilst simultaneously encouraging them to pursue greater authenticity. Where Roberts holds that the voice of the filmmaker here is 'strangely formless' and 'subjectless', refusing 'to speak on *behalf* of anyone or anything' (ibid,.), I would suggest that in fact the opposite is the case. The voice of the filmmaker is made explicit in the duality of the manifesto and its rules and the films as texts. The politics of the filmmaker are articulated through the deployment of style, narrative and form and are designed to upset ideological assumptions about the nature of film as art and the authenticity of cinema as a space for the pursuit of the real.

Dogme 95 is fundamentally a 'cinematic' project, making room for itself to re-work the possibilities of its technologies for the sake of art. It also returns film theorists to a set of debates that are essential in the context of innovations in technologies and domains of filmic consumption. Just as the films of *la nouvelle vague* sought to re-establish what constituted the artistic value of cinema, the films produced through the Dogme 95 project can be seen as re-positioning the possibilities of cinema as an art form at the start of its second century. The authenticity of the Dogme 95 project, then, is bound up with time-hallowed questions about the nature of art and its substance. In its play with the expectations of the audience reading the films and with the habits of the filmmakers creating them, Dogme quietly draws attention to this, disrupting ideological assumptions about 'truth', 'reality', 'art' and 'cinema' as it goes. The ostensible disregard for the defects of 'good' filmmaking practice that is flaunted by Dogme films recalls the work of Rudolph Arnheim (1957) for whom, in order to become a work of art, a film needs to go beyond the aesthetic restrictions inherent in merely trying to replicate reality. The manipulation of reality through techniques such as editing is central to the artistic endeavour of cinema in his view. While Dogme explicitly resists the potential for inflecting reality through strategies of illusion, its formal play with editing and camera technique helps to render reality in a particularly cinematic way. It thus becomes an exemplar of the autonomy of film as an art in its own right in a way that resonates with Arnheim's assertions.

Art and Artistic Value

The question of the artistic value of Dogme 95 as a project by definition needs to take into account the extraordinary spread of the movement beyond the bounds of cinema. The back-to-basics ideals inherent in the Dogme manifesto and the Vow of Chastity have inspired a number of 'spin-off' reformulations of the project in fields ranging from documentary to dance and computer game design. In addition, there have been a number of parodies of the Dogme manifesto which make flippant play with its structure and rules. Mette Hjort offers an interesting overview of the details of these parodies, signalling key examples including the 'Lazy-98 manifesto' written by a group of Danish scriptwriters and further re-workings of the ten key rules written in relation to set design and film viewing as a practice (2003b: 140–1). For Hjort, both the parodies and the 'inter-artistic extensions' of the ideals of the movement to other spheres of cultural production are indicative of its capacity to create audiences. Highlighting the fact that the manifesto is central to and inseparable from the success of the films, Hjort suggests that

> inscribed … within these cinematic works is an invitation to audiences to adopt a meta-cinematic stance that makes a seemingly straightforward phenomenon of rule-following the basis for more momentous and substantive reflections on the history of cinema, including some if its false starts and current problems. Audiences are, of course, meant to engage in the kind of first-order process of meaning-making that allows them to make sense of the unfolding plot and to be moved by the characters with whom they are encouraged to align themselves. But by virtue of the Dogma frame, they are also expected to entertain second-order considerations having to do for

example, with the pervasiveness, origin and legitimacy of certain cinematic norms. (2003: 134)

It is this skilful interweaving of the manifesto with the material film objects that, for Hjort, accounts for the rapid globalisation of Dogme 95, with films being made, distributed and exhibited all around the world. There is a certain historical specificity implicit here, however, that is related to the role of the internet in structuring the accessibility of the Dogme project to filmmakers as well as critics and spectators, and it is this which seems important in any attempt to understand the political edge of this artistic 'meta-cinematic' endeavour.

The Dogme 95 website is in many ways as central to the visibility of the 'meta-cinematic' qualities of the movement as the manifesto, the rules and the films themselves. With its infamous logo of a flickering eye lodged in the backside of a dog, it immediately draws attention to the seemingly blasphemous discourse in which the project appears to be shrouded. Containing links to articles and interviews about the four founding brethren and the films they produced under the auspices of the movement, the website was originally managed by Nimbus and Zentropa, production companies co-owned by the directors themselves. In 2002, the Dogme 95 collective decided to close down the '*Dogmesecretariat*' with the result that the Dogme films that could be made by anyone at all based anywhere in the world could now be self-certificated (www.dogme95.dk/news/interview/pressemeddelelse.htm). For a number of critics, this heralded the end of Dogme as a movement (Gilbey 2002; Bell 2005). Nevertheless, the Dogme 95 website continues to be a central resource on which filmmakers can lodge a record of their Dogme films. It is now managed by an academic who keeps the website up to date with information about the number of films made and contact details for the production teams. Dogme is far from dead. It survives through the longevity of the internet, and the impetus of the movement continues to be productive around the world.

The role of the internet here, then, is rather crucial. It is what preserves Dogme as a political, meta-cinematic, artistic endeavour, and allows the democratising tendencies of the movement to survive beyond the personalities of those who conceived it. The Dogme 95 brethren may personally have withdrawn from the project, but the legacy of it survives and continues to develop through a kind of grass-roots, low-budget initiative that encourages individuals to make films and to make their films known by virtue of the accessibility of digital technologies. Discussing the work of Jürgen Habermas, Oskar Negt and Alexander Kluge, Hjort makes an important point about the development of counter-publics in forming spaces for the exploration of interests that diverge form the bourgeois public sphere (2003: 148). For Hjort, this is important in shaping the ways in which Dogme films such as *The Idiots* open up spaces in which 'difficult' or 'controversial' subject matters are placed into the public arena prompting discussion. It is also the case, however, that counter-publics are making increasing use of the internet as a means of articulating counter-hegemonic principles and politics (Brecher *et al.* 2000; Smith 2003).[15] The new social movements that have emerged in the early twenty-first century harness the potential of the internet to communicate modes of counter-hegemonic activity and politicking, creating a new space for the re-shaping of ideological assumptions. The inherent political intention in this democratisation of communications is echoed in the Dogme 95 project and its deployment of the internet as a means of maintaining its currency. The on-going longevity of the project inspires von Trier to make frequent reference to the scope of the movement in recent interviews, stating that he would

> find it amusing if Dogme could continue to exist like a little pill you could take when there was too much of the other kind of thing, too much refinement and distanciation. You'd then take a little Dogme pill and feel much better afterwards, because you'd be grounded again. I also think Dogme could provide an amusing form of discipline if it could exist as a kind of test that even the experienced directors would have to take every now and again. (Bondebjerg 2003: 222)

For von Trier, there is a certain pride at stake in the way in which Dogme 95 has succeeded in attaining a form of democratisation of the cinema. His own position as an 'experienced director' has profited from this endeavour, underscoring his reputation as an evolving *auteur* whose impact on twenty-first-century cinema is to be measured not only in terms of his cinematic output but also in terms of his influence on the new formations unfolding across the industry. Increasingly von Trier characterises his work with reference to his collaborative ventures in filmmaking, some of which are at the level of production rather than direction. Recent press coverage has made a great deal of his theatrical relationship with the co-owner of Zentropa, Peter Aalbeck Jensen (Bell 2005). Von Trier is now portrayed as a newly avuncular figure for aspiring directors seeking to establish themselves as producing newly creative cinema. Klaus Birch sees him 'poised above us like a wizard, waving his wand to see what happens' (Christensen 2003: 188). At the same time, however, there has been a marked shift in the style of von Trier's own filmmaking, with many of his most recent pieces being overtly politically inflected and motivated. The 'U-S-A – Land of Opportunities' trilogy extends the pared-down sensibility seen in the Dogme project to produce a neo-Brechtian aesthetic that relies heavily on theatrical strategy, as chapter eight will discuss. The meta-cinematic discourse of Dogme 95 with its refusal of illusion has shifted once again. The politics, however, have arguably become more explicit, as the next chapter sets out to demonstrate.

CHAPTER SIX

Narrative Structure, Narrative Codes and Questions of Genre and Spectatorship

As we have already seen, von Trier's Dogme 95 project had a huge impact on the stylistic sensibility of his work, marking an elaborate shift away from a highly technical approach to filmmaking toward a style that seems much freer and more liberal. The previous chapter characterised this shift as a return to the basic tenets of cinema, presenting a self-proclaimed pared-down aesthetic which echoes a tone associated with the new wave movements of twentieth-century cinema. This shift, however, was not merely an aesthetic one. In re-positioning himself as a camera-wielding director, von Trier also begins to fashion narrative in different ways.

Turning away from a very specific neo-expressionist approach to film form, which for von Trier had always been associated with masculinity and notions of precision, the work that follows on from the Dogme project occupies quite a different terrain. In an echo of his television pieces, von Trier's Dogme-inflected work in the 'Gold Heart' trilogy maintains a refusal of the traditional mainstream 'happy' ending, but seeks out a new form of narrative structure in which dominant themes encompass emotional trauma, transgression and, ultimately, transcendence. The trilogy is comprised of *Breaking the Waves*, *The Idiots* and *Dancer in the Dark*. The film narratives become modern day morality tales, but their effect depends very much on the formal elements of the narrative construction and on the impact of this on the spectator, as this chapter will explore. The films in this trilogy are sharply differentiated from those in the 'Europa' trilogy because of the concern with emotion that runs through them. The affective quality of these films is important in understanding their narrative devices, and this is seen most clearly in the way von Trier draws on generic sensibilities in each of these films.

Questions of genre in film are not unproblematic and film theory grapples extensively with the question of what we are to understand by this term.[1] Much of this debate centres on the distinction between film style and genre, signalling the ways in which 'genre' as category seems to be constructed on the basis of commercial appeal and industrial approaches to categorisation and also rendered in culturally-specific ways.[2] Considerations of genre also emerged in the context of the 'auteurist' approach to film theory, with particular attention being paid to the deployment of binary oppositional structures in the body of works by any given director (Wollen 1998). Other approaches to the idea of genre in film signalled the need to take account of the iconographic aspects of genre (Buscombe 1986) or to acknowledge the way genres help to do the work of cultural rituals around social integration (Schatz 1981). In an important contribution to the debate on genre, Steve Neale suggests that genres are 'systems of orientations, expectations and conventions that circulate between industry, text and subject' (1980: 19). For Neale, then, genre is shaped as much by the audience's expectations as it is through textual convention. Genres are not fixed and nor do they have fixed boundaries. Instead, generic conventions bleed across the perceived boundaries of film, producing hybrid generic forms. In many ways, von Trier's work can be seen as exemplary of this tendency, as the following section will explore. We might suggest that the 'Gold Heart' trilogy of films works to illustrate Robert Stam's observation that

> the most useful way of using genre, perhaps, is to see it as a set of discursive resources, a trampoline for creativity, by which a given director can gentrify a 'low' genre, vulgarise a 'noble' genre, inject new energy into an exhausted genre, pour new progressive content into a conservative genre, or parody a genre that deserves ridicule. Thus we move from static taxonomy to active, transformative operations. (2000: 129–30)

Melodramatic Tensions

The question of genre runs through the 'Gold Heart' trilogy, in which there is a particular focus on the genre of melodrama. Von Trier's turn to melodrama finds its origins in the television series, *The Kingdom* (as discussed in chapter four). Melodrama, of course, is often associated with soap opera and with 'the woman's film' and this is interesting in helping to signal how we might understand von Trier's claim that the 'Gold Heart' trilogy is a distinctively 'feminine' trilogy.[3] For von Trier, in this work, melodrama provides the raw ingredients for narrative structure and strategy; it becomes the touchstone of the trilogy, in a sense. However, as this section will make clear, none of the films is a straightforward rendition of melodrama in its traditional guise. Von Trier takes up the fundamentals of melodrama but he complicates them and compromises our responses to them by hybridising the style with reference to such seemingly incongruous forms as the documentary, comedy and the musical. In order to examine the effects of these 'transformative operations' it is necessary to set out the ways in which von Trier draws on the cinematic melodramatic tradition.

Cinematic melodrama has its origins in nineteenth-century theatre and is associated with class issues and an appeal to mass audiences.[4] It is often juxtaposed with 'classic realist' texts which are seen to reproduce bourgeois ideologies. By contrast, with all its associations with key cultural figures such as Bertolt Brecht and Douglas Sirk,[5] and with ideas of what is socially and culturally repressed (and often, therefore, signified in terms of femininity, a recurring signifier of what is ideologically ambivalent), melodrama is frequently understood to have radical political potential. As Martha Vicinus has stated, 'melodrama sides with the powerless' (cited in Gledhill 1987: 21). In its excessive stylisation, attention to the realm of emotion and (often explicit) depiction of ideological failure, melodrama offers a mode of cinema in which notions of lifestyle and the experience of everyday psychological and social pressures are represented in such a way as to capitalise on film-industrial practices whilst at the same time disrupting them. Melodrama is frequently identified in neo-Marxist criticism as the site of a kind of social critique that is rather at odds with the capitalist agenda of Hollywood as an industry (Elsaesser 1987). In terms of the focus in melodrama on conflict and questions of morality and ethics, it begins to become clear why this genre of cinema appeals to a director such as von Trier. As already seen, while his early films pay extraordinary attention to technique and intricately storyboarded detail, there is an over-arching concern with questions of right and wrong and with notions of idealism. By turning away from the masculine structures implicit in the early work, it seems natural that von Trier should take up a more melodramatic approach to his work.

That each of the films in the 'Gold Heart' trilogy is rooted in melodrama can be seen at first glance from the basic plot details. *Breaking the Waves* has been called 'a primordial melodrama' (Anon.: n.d.) with its focus on a young woman, Bess (Emily Watson), whose faith and desire are called into question by dint of her unquestioning love for her dying husband, Jan (Stellan Skarsgård). In *The Idiots*, the melodrama unfolds quietly against a backdrop of a pseudo-documentary comic style, reaching its crescendo in the film's closing sequence when Karen returns to her family home after going missing for several weeks after the death of her child in order to 'spass' in front of them. Lastly, *Dancer in the Dark* is a musical melodrama,[6] a clearly hybrid form, in which the musical components of the film are rendered operatic in quality by the insistence of the melodramatic character of the narrative (discussed in more detail below).

The melodramatic qualities of these films, however, are not merely marked at the level of story and plot. An important facet of melodrama is the way unspeakable aspects of the story are articulated through film form and stylistic devices. Frequently, the most emotionally challenging moments of melodrama are expressed through attention to iconographic elements of the *mise-en-scène* and to non-diegetic narrative devices such as music (Elsaesser 1987). In melodrama, as is well documented, such generic conventions are often inscribed in excess, a facet of narrative that is designed to echo the psychological, ideological and emotional complexity of the situations in which central characters find themselves. For von Trier, of course, excess holds broad appeal. Tracing back his approach to filmmaking, one can discern quite clearly the propensity for excessive indulgence that is writ large in his work. The genre of melo-drama, then, would seem an inevitable draw for him.

Von Trier's melodramatic sensibility in this trilogy is present and inscribed in different ways in each film. As mentioned above, *Breaking the Waves* has been described as a 'primordial melodrama' and many critics comment on how the film encompasses a broad sweep of melodramatic generic conventions. The plot centres around the maso-chistic tendencies of the central character, Bess, and her willing self-subjugation in response to her husband's deteriorating health. The focus of the film is on the emotional impact of these events, for both the characters in the narrative and the viewers in the auditorium. Much of the film is concerned with the structures of emotional experi-ence around Bess's decline, and these are related via a series of tableaux depicting her ever-weakening grip on everyday models of comportment and culturally-sanctioned moral standards. The community in which Bess lives is represented as a predominantly pious one, one that is defined with reference to a strictly cloistered religious sensibility which is closely allied to the power structures at play on the small island. In addition, the Church elders appear distinctly 'out of time', evoking a certain quality of inevita-bility with regard to this sensibility. As is often the case in melodrama, the repressive attributes of the community are symbolised through the *mise-en-scène*: the kirk is small and austere; Bess's family home is rather threadbare and basic; the oil-rig is isolated and filled with incipient dangers; Jan's sick-rooms are pokey and small; and the hospital rooms feels cramped and oppressive despite the fact that we see no other real patients in these scenes. In the interior shots of the film, von Trier makes great use of close-ups to further reinforce this cramped atmosphere and this stands in marked contrast to the liberating and expansive shots of the wild landscape outside and its openness. In the melodramatic tradition, such a contrast can be read as a reference to the question of femininity and the impossibility of female desire. The wilderness is often symbolic of that which cannot be vocalised, and this is interesting in connection with Bess's burgeoning sense of sexuality and desire in this film, as discussed below.

Such symbolism is iconic of the repressive attitudes of the Church on the island, but it also highlights the increasingly oppressive atmosphere surrounding Bess, who becomes ostracised by her community as a result of her attempts to satisfy Jan's requests by engaging with strangers in brutal sexual acts devoid of any sentiment. We see her literal and emotional isolation echoed in scenes in which she is seen travelling around the bleak and barren landscape of the island, in search of sexual activity to report back to Jan. This sense of burgeoning isolation and abandonment is symbolised earlier in the film, as Bess, awaiting a telephone call from Jan while he is away on the rig, waits inside the cramped telephone box, where she eventually falls asleep. The small space of the telephone box represents the only space available to Bess for the exploration of her desire for Jan. It provides her with a safe haven for a while, as she awaits Jan's call and she can fall asleep knowing it will come to wake her.

The stuff of melodrama is highly dependent upon the psychical reality of its characters' emotional lives. Narrative strategies tend to centre on the displacement

Fig. 20 In *Breaking the Waves*, Bess's (Emily Watson) growing sense of isolation is symbolised by the cramped space of the telephone box

of emotional energies and on the making of metaphor and narrative parallels. In *Breaking the Waves*, one such parallel is drawn between the conversations that Bess has on the telephone with Jan and the ones with God, which she vocalises for us, thereby expressing something of the interiority of her rather complex structure of belief. Is 'love' to be understood in religious terms or is it rather premised on carnal desire? As Bess herself will later observe, 'How can you love a word? You cannot love words. You cannot be in love with a word. You can love another human being. That's perfection.' Fragility is a key thematic throughout the film, with Bess's perceived mental instability providing the key narrative marker for this. However, in the end, it becomes clear that the real fragility lies around the religious doctrine upon which the Church elders' control of life on the island is built. Despite the powerful image of the glass being crushed in the hand of one of the elders seen during Bess and Jan's wedding scene, the power of the Church is exposed as a predominantly ideological construct through von Trier's deployment of the melodramatic style. At the end of the film, when Dodo (Katrin Cartlidge) rages against the Church's insistence that Bess must not be buried on hallowed ground, the patriarchal structure is also exposed.

Melodrama is frequently associated with social and ideological critique, as we have seen, and in the case of von Trier's work here, this is also clearly the case. Bess functions as a kind of rebus puzzle for the audience, as her character and her excessive behaviour are increasingly depicted through the *mise-en-scène* rather than through more traditional means of characterisation. Her increasingly cheap and crude dress sense and her insistence on travelling around on a bicycle (marking her out as the 'island bike') symbolise Bess's increasing sense of loneliness and isolation on the one hand, but also her rather manic commitment to living out excessive sexual fantasies (which seem as much a product of her imagination as of Jan's exhortations for her to 'go with another

Fig. 21 In *Breaking the Waves*, the psychological dimension of melodrama is neatly expressed in the scene where a beer can is crushed as a gesture of male strength

man') in the name of a pursuit of goodness. The narrative structure of the film, which is organised into chapters heralded by a series of digitally-enhanced inter-titles which are accompanied by pop music tracks from the 1970s, underscores this.

Breaking the Waves is structured into seven chapters and an epilogue.[7] Each chapter is prefaced by an inter-title of a moving image sequence that is held in a static shot, evoking memories of the 'tableaux' associated with traditional melodrama. These chapter headings signal the rather novelistic structure of the film, which harks

Fig. 22 Bess's excessive sexual behaviour is signified by both her costume and her use of a bicycle to travel around the barren landscape

back to the origins of melodrama in the Romantic period. In many ways, *Breaking the Waves* picks up on key themes of Romanticism, articulating the importance of emotional life in helping to shape the aesthetic concerns of art and culture. It also taps into the imagery of Romanticism, making links between the landscape and the psychological terrain of sexual confusion and femininity.[8] Romanticism focused on the heroic individual,[9] seeking to illustrate the ways in which the sublime can be aligned with individual experiences of heightened emotional experience, often linked to the supernatural, but usually treated in a naturalistic style, as if to underscore the importance of emotionality in the formation of the individual subject. It is interesting that, in *Breaking the Waves*, the romanticised chapter headings are accompanied by popular songs from the 1970s.[10] The use of music in melodrama is a fundamental aspect of the genre as, Thomas Elsaesser has suggested:

> Melodrama is a dramatic narrative in which musical accompaniment marks the emotional effects. … it allows melodramatic elements to be seen as constituents of a system of punctuation, giving expressive colour and chromatic contrast to the story-line by orchestrating the emotional ups and downs of the intrigue. (1987: 50)

It is worth noting here that *Breaking the Waves* has very little in the way of a substantial film score and that, in addition to the music used to illustrate the chapter headings, the film uses snippets of a few more tracks (also taken from the 'glam rock' era) and parts of Bach's 'Siciliana'. In terms of the melodramatic orchestration of the emotions of the film, then, the use of 'glam rock' classics points to the typical concerns of this musical genre which focused on rebellion, overt sexuality and the construction of a very artificial mask of femininity. The resonances with Bess's inner turmoil are clear here. Struggling to come to terms with her growing sexual maturity and its displacement of what she understands as love, Bess struggles to maintain the very strict standards required by the Presbyterian Church to which she belongs. Her simultaneous guilt and sense of liberation is not overtly spoken in the film. Instead, the musical interludes presented as chapter breaks in the unfolding story of her life signal the ways in which she *feels*. The exaggerated and excessive 'glamorous' style of the performers of these songs prefigures Bess's transformation from a quiet, mousy girl into a parody of prostitution.

There is a certain allegorical quality to such parallels, raising questions around the socio-historical perception of female desire and expectations of femininity in the context of the early 1970s. That the narrative turns on goodness is highly apposite here, and the social and ideological implications of the film as melodrama arguably centre on these concerns. This is echoed in the stylised camera work which draws on a specific documentary aesthetic, as this chapter will discuss later. The melodramatic tensions seen in *Breaking the Waves* persist in von Trier's subsequent work on *The Idiots* and *Dancer in the Dark*. The next section considers how this melodramatic mode evolves and contributes to the evolution of von Trier's hybridised style.

At first glance, it is difficult to pigeon-hole *The Idiots* in terms of generic sensibility. This film is definitively *not* a melodrama in terms of its aesthetics. There is no sustained use of music to convey unspoken emotion, nor is there an elaborately conceived *mise-en-scène* designed to reflect the emotional turmoil of the characters. As the film unfolds, however, its melodramatic tensions emerge, focusing on the depth of emotional turmoil underpinning the characters' actions. This is particularly seen in the case of Karen, who, at the outset of the film, appears to be something of an outsider. She occupies markedly liminal and marginal spaces in relation to Stoffer's group of 'idiots', only making the decision to 'spass' once she has begun to acknowledge her own overwhelming sense of loss. As viewers of this film, we are not privy to any background information on each of the characters, yet there is an overarching sense of sadness that permeates the film, and this renders the narrative as one inscribed in and through the experience of loss. As with *Breaking the Waves*, there is an implicit critique of social values running through the narrative of the film, and, although the tensions that this produces are sometimes darkly humorous, the film's extraordinarily painful closing sequence reinforces the melodramatic strain running through it. Arguably, the aesthetic style of the film displaces the sense of melodrama through its construction of affect in the spectator (see chapter five for further discussion of this). I will return to these issues below.

It is interesting to note that *The Idiots* makes use of a very short musical interlude in the film's opening sequence as we see Karen taking a ride in a horse and trap. This short piece of music is rather haunting, evoking something of the sadness of Karen's life, especially as it is reprised over the credit sequence at the end of the film. Despite the overt refusal of melodramatic convention in this film, it is, nevertheless, emotionally very intense. The emotionality of this film and its ability to evoke tears marks it out as bearing some of the melodramatic tensions of the trilogy. This chapter will go on to argue that these are further reinforced through the narrative excesses and style.

By contrast, *Dancer in the Dark* is von Trier's most overt example of the melodramatic style. As a musical, this film privileges Selma's (Björk) song and dance sequences, using them to foreground the psychological experiences and perspectives of the main character. It is of note, here, that these sequences are shot in enhanced highly-saturated colour in comparison to the rather flat hues of the 'reality' scenes,[11] and that, until the climax of the film, the musical sequences clearly reflect Selma's interior fantasy world rather than any real, 'lived' reality. Reviewers have commented that von Trier 'milks' the melodrama as much as possible in these scenes, using the hand-held camera aesthetic to enhance the rawness of the heroine's emotional vulnerability and to foster the spectator's identification with her.[12] By heightening the visual excesses of the fantasy song and dance sequences, von Trier foregrounds Selma's psychical state, deploying traditional melodramatic conventions such as vibrant colour schemes, music and heightened scenes of pathos around Selma's social and personal circumstances. As an immigrant factory worker struggling to make ends meet, the fact that Selma is also saving to pay for an operation to save her son's eyesight is also the stuff of classic melodrama. The emphasis on the potential for maternal sacrifice emphasises the film's articulation of goodness and places the film firmly within a strong tradition of the sub-genre of 'maternal melodrama' seen in 'women's pictures' such as *Stella Dallas* (King Vidor, 1937) and *Mildred Pierce* (Michael Curtiz, 1945). What distinguishes von Trier's melodrama, however, is his by now familiar use of a very particular hand-held video pseudo-documentary style and a very particular approach to the question of narrative excess. These tendencies cut to the heart of von Trier's very specific personal style and help to shed light on the ways in which the director resists the boundaries of generic convention in each of the films within this trilogy.

An Excess of Style

As noted above, the cinematic style of the 'Gold Heart' trilogy is inflected with the spirit of Dogme 95. In each of the films making up this trilogy, the aesthetic is one that is cast in terms of 'realism' and the pursuit of authenticity. This is largely articulated through the use of hand-held video cameras and through an approach to montage and editing that foregrounds the ease with which it is possible to seemingly disregard 'film language' in the construction of narrative meaning. The hand-held style of shooting films is more usually associated with the genre of documentary, representing as it does something of the attempt to capture the 'truth' of the moment on film and to relay the immediacy of events to the cinema spectator. In the context of fiction films, the style is thus unexpected and somewhat disconcerting.[13]

This blatant disregard for the conventional language of cinema can be understood in a number of ways. Firstly, it signals a concern with realism and the importance of realism in making films that grapple with the everyday reality of emotional difficulty. Secondly, the often exaggerated and entirely free-moving camera-work reflects the kind of excessive indulgence familiar to viewers of von Trier's earlier works and thereby maintains a certain mode of authorship running through his work. Thirdly, the rendition of an epic genre such as melodrama through recourse to techniques more traditionally associated with an often localised documentary style disrupts expectations with regard to the fictionality of the narrative material; it is as though the use of a realist or documentary style helps to authenticate the emotional and psychological states of being depicted on the screen, demonstrating the authenticity of these feelings and producing a quality of rawness that it is difficult to ignore. In this way, von Trier's use of this style helps to circumvent straightforward processes of identification such as those which might be fostered in mainstream Hollywood films. This has the effect of placing the spectator in almost unbearable positions of emotional engagement with characters and narrative events, producing a new position of affect as it does so. The excessive quality so often ascribed to von Trier's work makes its mark in this juxtaposition of style and substance, as the following discussion shows.

Von Trier's approach to the question of cinematography in this trilogy evolves with each of the films. Famously, von Trier made use of one hundred static cameras in each of the musical sequences on *Dancer in the Dark* in an attempt to capture a sense of 'live transmission' for the musical numbers. On a traditional film-shoot using 35mm film, such indulgence would be impossible because of the question of cost. On *Dancer in the Dark*, however, the use of digital cameras enabled von Trier to pursue this technique in an effort to show that 'the modern musical's greatest strength should be that it's trying to get away from everything artificial' (Björkman 2003: 229). On

Breaking the Waves, von Trier maintained his authorial distance from the camera-work, using cinematographer Robbie Müller to produce the desired 'look' for the film, and later complaining that 'the images were far too beautiful' (227). In the subsequent films, von Trier himself takes up the camera, arguing that doing so allows him much greater freedom to work with the actors and to capture unexpected elements of the performances, using the zoom when it seems appropriate to heighten the mood of any given scene.

This freer style of working enables von Trier to improvise on his scripts, working closely with actors to pinpoint the sensibility of characterisation and dramaturgy. It also allows for a much more excessive mode of film-making, one that is made memorable by the insistent use of large close-up shots of the protagonists' faces in scenes of heightened emotional fragility. For von Trier, this helps to create 'a rare authenticity and authority' (146), enabling greater expressivity of emotion and feeling. Examples of such shots abound in this trilogy, including such moments as Bess' visit to the cinema with Jan to watch *Lassie*, and, later, her first act of sexual intercourse with a stranger as Jan lies in mortal danger on the hospital operating table. In *The Idiots*, von Trier's use of the close-up on the faces of Karen and Susanne (Anne Louise Hassing) as they discuss the pain of Karen's separation from her family is almost unbearable in its scrutiny of the personal dilemma facing this woman. In *Dancer in the Dark*, Selma's song as she

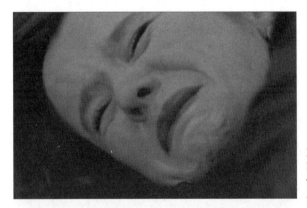

Fig. 23 A close-up on Bess's face as she has intercourse with a stranger in *Breaking the Waves*

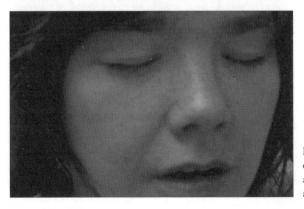

Fig. 24 A large close-up on the face of Selma (Björk) as she awaits her hanging at the end of *Dancer in the Dark*

awaits her execution is again accompanied by a painfully interrogative piece of close-up camera-work, exposing the rawness of her emotions, as, for the first time, she allows the psychological pain hitherto expressed in musical sequences carried out in her imagination to spill over into reality. The hand-held camera aesthetic works to enhance the melodrama of such moments, lending them a raw sensibility which produces affect in the spectator, in ways discussed above in chapter five. This is dependent on the use of a documentary aesthetic, as that discussion made clear, because it is important to ground the narratives in a modality of realism in order to produce a specific mode of identification for the spectator.

In Pursuit of the Real

The pursuit of the 'authentic' realist style associated with a documentary aesthetic is important in any attempt to understand von Trier's manipulation of cinematic genre. It should by now be familiar that von Trier often aims to exceed boundaries, by pushing the familiar strategies of cinema to their extreme. In many ways, *Europa* represented a pinnacle of artistic achievement in this regard, as it enabled von Trier to demonstrate his finely-honed technical appreciation of the possibilities of cinema. As he himself has noted, the move away from this highly-stylised approach constituted 'a liberation from aesthetics' for him (Björkman 2003: 215). However, as we have also seen, this apparent lack of aesthetic constraint is not without its own aesthetic demands. The hand-held camera style in itself becomes iconographic of a particular drive toward authenticity in the context of cultures of postmodernism (see chapter five for further discussion of this). In this respect, it is interesting to consider the ways in which von Trier is manipulating generic formats as a way of rejuvenating particular modes of cinema for the postmodern spectator of the late twentieth century who is inscribed in an endless pursuit of the meaning of identity and a search for a 'self' which might be considered 'authentic'.

Much has been written on the dilemmas facing the postmodern subject of late capitalism in terms of the increasing sense of fragmentation and loss that is felt in everyday life and the tendency to idealise elevated conceptions of what the 'self' should be (Lasch 1978; Frosh 1991; Giddens 1991 and 1992; Craib 1994; Richards 1994; Elliott 1996). Such work configures postmodern subjectivity in terms of reflexivity and a desire to witness oneself being seen to be a subject by (the) other(s). This is often depicted as the result of an emergent 'therapy' culture in which the subject appears to need to authenticate the experience of everyday emotion by recourse to models readily found in visual culture. It is not enough, in other words, to feel for oneself; the dilemmas of postmodernity require emotional sensibility to be authenticated through the act of being witnessed.[14] This cultural phenomenon has been linked to the emergence and popularity of reality television in the late twentieth and early twenty-first centuries (Biressi & Nunn 2005: 95–107) and is grounded in the ever more narcissistic formation of the individual psyche (Lasch 1978).

This focus on the question of the individual psyche is at the heart of von Trier's re-fashioning of the melodramatic style. This is seen most clearly in *Dancer in the Dark*,

Fig. 25 The fantasy sequences of *Dancer in the Dark* express Selma's interior world and foreground emotional sensibilities

his musical melodrama. Throughout the film, Selma uses her capacity to hear the beauty of music in the sounds of the banality of everyday life to sustain her through moments of intense emotional and personal difficulty. Her interior world provides the substance of the musical interludes in this film, depicting the ways in which she is able to find emotional stability in the face of the overwhelming threats to her subjective integration that come at various points throughout the narrative. Upon discovering that her landlord, Bill (David Morse), has stolen the money she has been saving for her son's eye operation, Selma bravely tackles him in order to ask for it back. In the ensuing confrontation, she inadvertently kills Bill, and immediately the film cuts to a musical sequence in which the dead Bill returns to life and dances with Selma, providing her with reassurance in the face of the inevitable adversity that will follow. Similarly, in the courtroom sequence, Selma plays out a fantasy in which the austere District Attorney is portrayed dancing and frolicking around the courtroom in a blatant reconfiguration of his hard-nosed legalistic agenda.

Von Trier has commented at length on his intentions in formulating the musical scenes in such a way. Firstly, the intention is to draw attention to Selma's inherent goodness and to the ways in which she is psychologically able to manage the disintegration of her life. Secondly, the musical sequences are designed to heighten the emotional vulnerability of the protagonist in order to lend the film a more operatic quality. As von Trier has commented,

> What I was trying to do was give the musical a more dangerous function. Not in a stylistic way though. I wanted to create a tighter atmosphere and arouse emotions that the musical genre usually holds at a distance. The classic musical is a sort of descendant of operetta. Opera, on the other hand, allows

itself an entirely different register and range as far as emotions are concerned, and it was that sort of intensity I was after ... I think it ought to be possible to develop the film musical considerably in this respect, and be more adventurous. But that would require the development of film, and greater sophistication in the audience: back to the situation where you could sit and let the tears gush. (Björkman 2003: 234)[15]

At the end of the film, of course, Selma's musical interludes cease to be purely psychological as she awaits a decision about whether or not she must wear a hood whilst being hanged. In a heart-wrenching sequence which involves a great deal of mobile camera-work and frequent close-ups on Selma's anguished facial expression, von Trier ties together the emotional and pseudo-realist traits of the film, allowing the intensity of the film to reach an extraordinary crescendo that culminates in Selma's hanging and a cut to a black screen devoid of respite for the by now rather harrowed spectator. This tying together of the emotional and realist qualities of the film reminds us that we are watching a film in which movement between registers is eventually collapsed (as we saw in the closing sequence of *The Idiots*). We are reminded of our own emotional investment in the film as a result of this process, and made aware of our heightened sense of emotional affect and its impact on our viewing pleasure. This neatly illustrates the ways in which von Trier's conflation of apparently incongruous cinematic sensibilities works to position us as spectators who must work to make sense of his films.[16]

That von Trier should turn toward a discourse of reflexivity by adopting a cinematic style grounded in realism should not be surprising given his interest in the spiritual dimension of identity and experience. His pursuit of humanist ideals of 'goodness' and spiritual significance can be read through the lens of the *faux* realism of the work in this trilogy. Anthony Giddens (1991; 1992) has shown how the decline of the significance of religion in everyday life can be linked to the 'democratisation' of emotions for the subject. Seeking solace in interpersonal relationships, the subject turns to discourses of emotionality in order to pursue a sense of being in the world. Everyday life becomes a question of performing identities according to the emotional agenda of any given situation, with the result that a sense of identity becomes contingent on the recognition of one's pain/joy/anger/trauma/jealousy by the other. In a discussion of the 'spastic aesthetics' of *The Idiots*, Ole Christensen suggests that

> basically the film is about role playing and being. What does it mean to be someone and what does it mean to pretend to be someone? Is being a consequence of acting or does acting make a disguise of an individual's character? Is the individual a persona, a mask? This concerns the status of fiction in relation to reality. In this respect *The Idiots* is about identity and character and thus also about film as medium and as art. (2000b)

The pursuit of authenticity in this trilogy through the filmic discourse of realism can thus be understood in two important ways. Firstly, it helps to shake the spectator out of her (complacent) familiarity with the language of cinematic genres in order to inflect the treatment of a generic 'body of techniques into a stylistic principle that carrie(s) the distinct overtones of spiritual crisis' (Elsaesser 1987: 49). Secondly, it heightens the emotional intensity of narrative themes by appealing to the sense of identity that is grounded in structures of looking within the contemporary postmodern context. In so doing, it conjures up important questions around the pleasures of identification and spectatorship in these films, as the next section will elaborate.

Affect and Femininity

The textual and formal excesses of the 'Gold Heart' trilogy are arguably transfigured into affect for the spectator. Many critics have commented on the 'unbearable' emotional intensity of these films, regardless of whether they choose critically to acclaim or deni-grate the film. The levels of excess at the formal, narrative and technical levels of these films is matched by the excessive response that is demanded of the spectator. The films in this trilogy famously elicit polarised responses running the whole gamut of emotions from declarations of his genius (for example, Mairs 1998; Matthews 2000) to explosive invective rejecting his work as monstrous and offensive (see US Confer-ence of Catholic Bishops 2004). It is interesting to observe the emotive language at play in these responses to von Trier's work and to consider the ways in which he has allegedly become 'the *enfant terrible*' of contemporary cinema. It is also interesting to consider the impact of these films in terms of film theory's understanding of the pleasures of spectatorship.

In an interesting article on the problem of femininity in *Breaking the Waves* and its constructions of spectatorial pleasure, Suzy Gordon suggests that

> *Breaking the Waves* appears to defy any appropriation by feminism. At the
> film's close, a woman's self-sacrifice in the name of love – her capitulation to
> sexual abuse and then death – is affirmed as an act of righteousness. And yet
> the film's treatise on 'goodness' gives way to a destructiveness that not only
> requires the woman's demise but also articulates her power. (2004: 206)

Gordon goes on to suggest that, by drawing on the psychoanalytic work of Melanie Klein on the importance of negativity in the formation of identity, it is possible to return to the rather stalled debate within feminist film theory on the question of the female spectator and to re-think it by casting the experience of negativity as central to the formation of female identity and desire. In some senses, then, Gordon appears to suggest that the film cannot really offer 'pleasure' in any meaningful sense of everyday emotional reward. Instead, the pleasures of the film seem to circulate around the spec-tator's identification with the psychical reality of the protagonist's experience, and this seems important in terms of the discussion above around the relation of von Trier's work to contemporary attempts to articulate the psychical dilemmas of postmodern subjectivity. Throughout the 'Gold Heart' trilogy, the emphasis is on the way that the traumatic appears to go hand-in-hand with the possibility of attaining transcendence, a theme which is peculiarly redolent of our times. Many argue that 'trauma culture' (Luckhurst 2003) places us in an increasingly voyeuristic, tabloid-esque and de-sensitised relation to the visual field. The pseudo-documentary style seen at play throughout the trilogy seems to provoke an overly-heightened (traumatic) affective response in the spectator, as I have discussed elsewhere (Bainbridge 2004a).

In this regard, it is interesting to consider the question of the attribution of the label 'feminine' to this trilogy of films. As several critics have suggested in extensive analysis of *Breaking the Waves*, the association of femininity to notions of 'goodness', 'martyrdom' and 'transcendence' is not unproblematic (Nelson 1997; Bekkenkamp 1998; Heath 1998; Makarushka 1998; Mercadente 2001; Restuccia 2001; Faber 2003; Penner & Stichele Vander 2003). While for Stephen Heath, Bess becomes a symbol of divine love incarnate, for Irena Makarushka, her 'transgressing goodness' accords her a level of sexual agency which offers some perspective on the film's pleasure for women. By contrast, for Alyda Faber, Bess is nothing short of an indicator of the insuperability of phallic law, suggesting that von Trier's fable is overarchingly patriarchal in its structure.

The emphasis on the femininity of the trilogy and its exploration with reference to *Breaking the Waves* by these critics is interesting. Each of the critical engagements with this film is articulated only with reference to the textuality of the film; the filmic form is not considered. The feminine has long been associated with the notion of excess (especially in a Lacanian psychoanalytic framework, where it is aligned with *jouissance*, an indescribable sensual ecstasy which might be understood in relation to the death drive); von Trier appears to be putting the excess to work in order to heighten the transcendental moments in his films, moments which he himself figures in terms of (and through) the feminine. In this respect, one might suggest that it is as much through the formal aspects of the films as through their textuality that von Trier arrives at his assertion that the films operate in some sense as feminine.

It is worth noting that he does not suggest that they are femin*ist* but rather femin-*ine*. This is a complex opposition but one that foregrounds von Trier's disavowal of a specifically feminist political sensibility in his depiction of women. Reading with von Trier, here, one could suggest that the films of the 'Gold Heart' trilogy evoke something of the apparent 'unspeakability' of certain aspects of feminine subjectivities. Much French feminist thought in the psychoanalytic tradition deploys this very premise, articulating a commentary on the particular difficulties associated with attempting to represent femininity within a patriarchal cultural context. Literary theory and criticism often applies these ideas to the work of women writers, attempting to construct a poetics of the feminine. I have argued elsewhere that it is possible to draw on the work of Luce Irigaray to understand the ways in which cinema (and particularly films made by women) opens up spaces in which to consider the silences of femininity as they are played out in the psychic mechanisms of fantasy, enunciation and identification (Bainbridge 2002). While it is difficult to suggest that von Trier is purposefully deploying a version of feminine subjectivity, his work nevertheless offers a useful textual reference point for the difficulty of expressing certain aspects of feminine desire and pleasure.

Irigaray, for instance, suggests that female desire is inscribed in the disavowed and repressed bedrock of symbolic patterns of discourse and representation that underpin dominant ideology. Sketching the ways in which woman is cast as 'other' in many social and cultural contexts, her work develops to suggest that theorising loving relations between the (heterosexual) couple is a crucial step in constructing a feminine position of enunciation. For Irigaray, phallogocentric discourse has always excluded the feminine from its parameters, with the result that female subjectivity cannot adequately be represented. In order to begin to formulate an understanding of the effects of this on female subjectivity, Irigaray argues for a certain set of discursive practices designed to mediate the experience of these unspeakable silences. Thus the film offers a useful context in which to begin to express this because of its important relationship to the psychic processes of fantasy and identification.

In the films of the 'Gold Heart' trilogy, the silences discussed by Irigaray make themselves felt in the tensions between narrative content and film form. The use of melodramatic, emotional strategies and the contrast between these and the documentary style of the films contribute to the specifically feminine concern of the narratives. For example, as already mentioned, each of the films in the trilogy makes important use of close-up shots on the faces of the protagonists at key moments of emotional sensitivity and spectatorial identification. The use of the close-up in these sequences ties the spectator into an emotionally-complex structure of identification with the female protagonists, offering insight into their unspoken emotional trauma around the ways in which the social forces of their worlds proscribe any means of being understood on their own terms.

This is the nature of affect in cinema, and as spectators we are almost compelled to respond in some way. Our emotional responses to the filmic narratives are relational; they depend not only on *what* we see but on *how* it is seen and on *how we feel* about what we see. The relationship between narrative and film form is crucial here, and this allows us to understand the pleasure of these films for the viewing spectator. The emotional intensity of the films depends on the sensitivity of the spectator. Cinematic affect, then, enables viewers to hold in place the psychical resonances of narrative content with the impression of authenticity that is created through the filmic style. It is arguable that this helps to make the sensibility of the films more 'feminine' because of their heightening of treatment of emotion. While this suggests that von Trier's formulation of 'femininity' is far from unproblematic, it also opens up an interesting space in which to consider the relationship between film form, content and affect in the formation of cinematic pleasure. Gordon's suggestion that this inevitably constructs a notion of spectatorship that is inscribed in negativity is accurate in as far as it references the ways in which dominant cultural modes of cinema disavow the spaces of the feminine and leave little room for its pleasurable articulation. Having said that, however, there is an important component of femininity which is aligned with emotional literacy and von Trier's films do seem to depend on this. The pleasures of seeing this on screen may be difficult to articulate, but, alongside the ambivalence expressed in Gordon's negativity-centred reading, there is a certain pleasure of recognition that comes from witnessing the psychical inscription of femininity that is seen in the films' clever articulations of the silences with which femininity is usually associated. The ethical implications of this are complex, however, as the next section will explore.

The End Justifies the Means

In each of the films comprising this trilogy, as we have seen, the female protagonist undergoes a life-threatening experience that is framed very clearly through notions of trauma and which seems to evoke issues of an ethical nature. At the end of *Breaking the Waves*, Bess is violently and fatally raped and is refused a religious burial by the Church elders because of the perception that she had become wanton (perhaps through madness) and had lost all of her religious piety in acting out her husband's sexual desires. Jan steals Bess's body and takes it out to the oil rig so that she can be buried at sea. The film closes with an extraordinary epilogue, showing large-scale fantasy bells pealing in the sky, high up above the rig, a shot that echoes the chapter headings and their evocation of the realm of fantasy. The explicit fantasy of this moment rescues the spectator from the almost unbearable moment of Bess's death, sparing the spectator the bleakest of endings.[17] At the end of this film, Bess appears to be vindicated – Jan *does* walk again following her sacrifice and it is as though this closing image underscores the mystical possibility that Bess was right after all. In the subsequent films in this trilogy, however, the spectator is increasingly left at risk in the film's endings.

In *The Idiots*, the mystery of Karen's return to her family is motivated by a desire to succeed where the other 'idiots' have failed, by 'spassing' in a personally significant context. In a painful sequence, she dribbles her food, allowing her cake to ooze from the corner of her mouth, until her husband, Anders, slaps her across the face. Karen stands and decides to leave with Susanne and the film ends suddenly in a moment of bleak despair. The emotional dereliction of the moment is unavoidable here.

In *Dancer in the Dark*, the public hanging of Selma culminates in our view of her dangling body being closed off from prying eyes by the drawing of curtains whilst the camera cranes up the scene, allowing us momentarily to glimpse the grief and bereavement experienced by those with whom Selma has engaged in the course of the narrative. The film ends with a lyric from Selma's dying song superimposed on the final scenes and crane shot to a densely black shot encompassed in silence. The meaning of closure is indisputable here. Plunged into darkness on screen as well as off (the cinematic auditorium is still in darkness as the film ends), the spectator is shattered by the unbearable weight of such an ending.[18]

At the point of narrative closure in each of these films, von Trier fosters in the spectator an extraordinary sense of identification with the protagonist. Yet it is also at this point that he sets about shattering that very illusion by ripping the life of the protagonist away in either a real or metaphorical way, just as he had done in the 'Europa' trilogy of films. However, in the 'Gold Heart' trilogy, the discursive framework has shifted and this has a number of ethical implications that centre on the themes of love and goodness. There is a new concern with the notion of 'love', a notion that hardly appears in the previous films. In her pursuit of love, each protagonist subjects herself to unspeakable trauma.[19] This is a marked difference from the films of

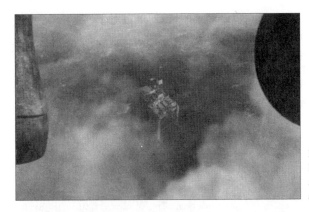

Fig. 26 The bells pealing for Bess's goodness at the end of *Breaking the Waves* offer some respite to the spectator

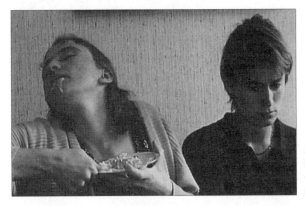

Fig. 27 Karen's act of 'spassing' in front of her family at the end of *The Idiots* makes for difficult viewing

Fig. 28 The spectator is not spared at the end of *Dancer in the Dark* when Selma is hanged and her dangling body is left on view

the earlier trilogy, in which the trauma that befalls the male protagonists is mediated through their attempt to navigate structures of power. In the 'Gold Heart' trilogy, the narrative trauma, which is constructed through personal and intimate relationships, is paralleled by a trauma that is evoked in the spectator. Just as there is a shift away from the terrain of power toward the terrain of love, there is also a corresponding shift in the way trauma is motivated in the films and in their ethical investment in structures of feeling and affect rather than in structures of discourse and power.

There is also a shift in the aesthetic concerns of the films which are grounded in a more unstructured documentary-style aesthetic discussed above. Where in the earlier trilogy, von Trier was concerned to disestablish the conventions of cinema through consummate technical skill and knowledge of film history, here he adopts a much greater sense of immediacy, albeit one that harks back to the aspirations of new wave cinema. As we have seen, such a shift in aesthetics foregrounds a turn to the domain of the emotions and affect and this, in turn, impacts on the ethical structure not merely of the films themselves, but also of the spectator's response to them. Questions of femininity are important here, as this chapter has begun to signal and there are clear implications for understanding the paradoxical pleasures associated with viewing such emotionally wrought films. The strategies identified here in relation to affect and ethics have important consequences for our understanding of how the films might be seen as feminine despite the fact that they cannot realistically be described as feminist. Following on the work of philosophers of the feminine, such as Luce Irigaray, it is possible to suggest that von Trier's films capture elements of the socio-cultural formation of femininity and its silences and enable them to be articulated, albeit it with all their contradictions and enigmatic structures on show. Arguably, this tendency in his work is structured around the experience of difference. The next chapter sets out a broader analysis of the politics of difference in von Trier's trilogy; it charts the way these films move toward a more geopolitical strain in von Trier's engagement with cinema as his work receives ever wider critical attention.

CHAPTER SEVEN

Screening Difference in the 'Gold Heart' Trilogy

Von Trier's second trilogy of films is known as the 'Gold Heart' trilogy because he frequently cites a children's fable with this name as his source of inspiration for this work.[1] Throughout the trilogy, as discussed in the previous chapter, there is a clear shift in aesthetic concerns and narrative construction that owes a great deal to the formulation of the Dogme 95 project. Dogme strategies permeate each of the films in this trilogy, marking a distinct shift from the highly contrived technical sensibilities that characterise von Trier's early work. As several critics have documented, this turn away from a very careful and composed style of working toward a more chaotic and creative mode of filmmaking came at a time of great personal change for von Trier. It was during filming that he left his first wife in order to begin a new relationship during the period between the completion of *Breaking the Waves* and the inception of work on *The Idiots* (Stevenson 2002: 87–9). In this context, it is fascinating that von Trier is often keen (in interviews but also in his own manifestos) to label this trilogy as distinctively 'feminine' (as discussed in chapter six). Running throughout the films in this trilogy is a sensibility that is centred on debates around identity and difference. Arguably, the femininity von Trier attributes to this trilogy of films inflects the treatment of difference more broadly defined in the films. This chapter considers the ways in which this trilogy grapples with cultural modes of difference and investigates the underlying femininity implicit here. It also raises the question of masculinity in relation to these concerns, drawing attention to the ways in which von Trier's approach to his work seems to remain rooted in a particular set of formations of masculinity.

The Question of Difference

As we have already seen, manifestos have formed an important part of von Trier's engagement with cinema.[2] In each of the manifestos, his aim has been to stimulate the potential of art cinema to produce 'the real thing, fascination, experience', to reveal 'creativity without making a secret of eternity' and to illustrate how art 'stems from a genuine inner need to play with life and to incorporate it into [our] own private world'. Interestingly, four of the five manifestos relating to the 'Europa' and 'Gold Heart' trilogies signal such concerns as the terrain of *men*, issuing a call for 'hetero-sexual films, made for, about and by men' while the fifth, entitled 'The Selma Mani-festo' (2000), uses the figure of Selma from *Dancer in the Dark* to conjure up a vision of '*someone who loves all of life!*' (italics in original) and therefore embodies the pinnacle of artistic endeavour.

This development from a concern with the potential of cinema to elaborate a particularly male perspective on the world toward a position allegedly more inflected by the feminine is one that has been signalled by von Trier and his critics in a variety of contexts. In an interview with Gavin Smith, for instance, von Trier has even gone so far as to suggest that he 'feel[s] kind of female [himself], to some degree' as a result of this shift from the masculine 'Europa' series of films to the feminine 'Gold Heart' trilogy (2000: 25). In making this shift, however, von Trier has maintained and devel-oped several key thematic concerns relating to cultural constructions of difference and its relation to questions of ethics and idealism. Arguably, the shift in the apparently gendered inflection of von Trier's work has turned on these concerns, as I will discuss toward the end of this chapter. In order to contextualise this discussion, it is first necessary to sketch out some of the modes of cultural difference that can be seen in this work.

Cultural differences take many forms and are usually defined with reference to a presumed hegemonic standard which, in the West, is frequently characterised as white, patriarchal, heterosexual, Western and male. Aspects of identity that escape inclusion within this dominant category of power and ideological influence are understood as marked by their difference from that hegemonic standard. Thus, cultural differences can be defined in terms of gender, ethnicity, age, religious creed, sexuality and social class, for example. The 'Gold Heart' trilogy deals with various modalities of difference and its cultural construction and representation. A number of critics have suggested that von Trier's treatment of difference in these films is highly politicised and culturally transgressive (Makarushka 1998; Darke 2001; Walters 2004). This suggests that the films foreground cultural inscriptions and refusals of categories of difference in ways that transcend images of difference as we are used to perceiving them in cinema. How, then, does von Trier mobilise discourses of difference in these films? This chapter will discuss von Trier's treatment of differences such as disability, class and national identity before going on to scrutinise the underlying attention focused on gender differences.

Disability

Questions of disability and embodied difference are most obviously central to the narrative structure in *The Idiots*, but this theme resonates through both *Breaking the Waves* and *Dancer in the Dark* too.[3] In *Breaking the Waves*, Bess struggles not only with the sudden paralysis of her husband, Jan, as a result of her prayer to have him returned to her from the oil rig on which he works; she also appears to be labelled as suffering from mental illness of some sort.[4] There are various allusions throughout the film to her mental instability and Jan is gradually persuaded to sign a form to permit her to be sectioned under the Mental Health Act. In *Dancer in the Dark*, Selma is incapacitated by her incipient blindness and the core of the narrative focuses on her struggle to earn enough money to ensure that her son, Gene (Vladica Kostic), is not subject to the same experience by raising enough money for a private operation on his eyes. In *The Idiots*, of course, the narrative turns on attitudes to learning disabilities, as the Søllerød group established by Stoffer indulges in 'spassing', or drawing out their 'inner idiot'.

In each of these representations, von Trier appears, on the one hand, to be courting critical controversy, which has certainly been forthcoming.[5] On the other, however, there is much at stake politically in the representations he affords us. As Paul Darke has suggested, *The Idiots* is 'one of the most politically and socially astute films to be made this century' (2001). Darke argues that *The Idiots* deploys a representation of disability that conforms to the Social Model of Disability, which suggests that 'normality' is a repressive social construct. His analysis neatly illustrates how von Trier's film draws attention to the hypocrisies and contradictions of social processes. The structures of cultural and hegemonic forces which privilege able-bodied subjectivities are characterised as repressive and monolithic in their unshifting attitudes to anything that appears to be intellectually, emotionally, morally or physically different from 'the norm'. *The Idiots* makes use of strategies of darkly comic humour to underscore this.

We see 'the idiots' at large in a number of social contexts, each of which seems to eke out the cultural attitudes of shame and ignorance that frequently accompany encounters with disability. In the restaurant scene at the beginning of the film, for example, we witness Karen's first encounter with Stoffer's group of 'idiots'. As Karen's food arrives, Susanne begins to spoon-feed Stoffer and he begins to throw back his head, resisting Susanne's assistance. We notice that Henrik (Troels Lyby) is also seemingly confused about how to deal with his food. As Karen looks on, Stoffer creates a scene by knocking crockery to the floor and then wandering around from table to table picking up people's napkins and greeting them all with an overly friendly 'hi'. The waiter and other diners grow visibly uncomfortable as he does this, with the waiter suggesting that he is 'concerned' for the other diners. Susanne begins to try to get her companions to leave the restaurant and Karen, having been taken by the hand by Stoffer, agrees to go outside with them. Shortly afterwards, as she joins them in their taxi, their deceit is revealed to both her and the audience, and we become aware of the fact that Stoffer and his friends have 'performed' this scenario in order to avoid paying their restaurant bill and that this 'spassing' (as they call it) is part of their everyday activity.

It is striking in this sequence of the film that the apparent disability of members of the group is something that leaves others feeling 'uncomfortable' but also that the discomfort cannot be appropriately articulated because of the predominant tendency toward political correctness. Similarly, when 'the idiots' visit the Rockwool factory for a tour, we see the ways in which disability is often patronised. In these early scenes in the film, it is not yet clear to the viewer what the intention of Stoffer's group of friends is, and we are forced into a number of encounters with bourgeois ideals and attitudes that are discomforting for the spectator and which seem to demand self-reflexive scrutiny on the part of the audience. This is seen most clearly when potential buyers for Stoffer's uncle's house have their intentions comically undermined as Stoffer tells them that there is a home for the 'handicapped' next door and that the residents like to come and visit the house. As the couple are shown around they encounter a number of the 'idiots' pretending to be visiting from the institution next door for a tea party in the garden. Struggling to retain their composure and to come across as liberal and tolerant in their outlook, the man and woman are increasingly lampooned, together with the bourgeois sensibility they represent. Similarly, when Uncle Svend (Erik Wedersøe) comes to visit the house, he sees a number of the 'idiots' engaged in ludicrous activities such as hoovering the wet flagstones on the path and sizing up the re-glazing job on the shed by throwing a stone through the window.

While von Trier deploys comedy and satire here to great effect, such scenes are very heavily politicised and there is a clear commentary on the hypocrisy of bourgeois, liberal ideals of 'normality'. Disability as a hidden arena replete with socio-cultural taboos of all sorts is repeatedly made visible throughout the film. Von Trier appears to be casting disability itself as social process, as a consequence of an over-investment in hegemonic structures of 'normality'. His perspective appears to suggest that society values structures of sameness over difference and that it will do anything to maintain the boundaries that this entails.

In many ways, von Trier's film demonstrates the extremes to which liberal bourgeois culture will go in order to preserve its notions of 'normality' and 'control'. While it never quite becomes clear what the purpose of Stoffer's group is, its very existence illustrates the extent to which von Trier takes issue with the blind willingness of contemporary liberal society to disavow difference. It takes some time for Karen to emerge as the protagonist of the film and the various perspectives on the purpose of the group we witness suggest a number of functions. In the end, the group has a different purpose for each of its members, a point made most clearly, perhaps, when Josephine's father (Anders Hove) turns up at the house to collect her and to enforce her medication on her. At this point in the film, it becomes clear that each of the characters has their own particular vulnerability and that their allegiance to Stoffer's group appears to offer some means of grappling with this.

The relationship of the individual to the group is marked out here as one inscribed through cultural processes that marginalise difference. There are clear resonances with the work of Freud (1991d) on group processes here. As Freud suggests, the individual loses his or her inhibitions when they become part of a group and this enables them to express emotions and ideas that have hitherto remained repressed.

Furthermore, this move toward allowing the return of the repressed cultivates a more primitive sensibility within the group, as much of what is repressed relates to dominant social taboos around sexuality and aggression. The identifications formulated within the group maintain levels of obedience to the designated leader and enable the expression of repressed sensibilities as a result. As the fellowship of the group works to provide spaces in which repressed material is sanctioned as that which needs to find expression, feelings of otherness and marginality are arguably brought to the fore. Difference, then, finds a safe haven within groups, a notion that sustains the contemporary fascination with support groups for people who wish to explore their (often embodied) difference from the 'norm' with others who have similar experiences. From this perspective, the group provides respite from the effects of being marginalised, but it carries with it demands of allegiance to charismatic leaders and a process of re-working one's own identity in order better to conform to the group.

In *The Idiots*, of course, allegiance is evinced through the act of 'spassing' in a public setting, and, more meaningfully, in one that has personal significance for the individual performing the 'spass'. As the leader of the group, Stoffer suggests that this is both a test of the commitment of individuals to the ideals of the group and the ultimate mode of resistant self-expression in the face of the everyday marginality experienced by individuals such as Karen. Karen becomes the only 'idiot' to carry 'spassing' over into her everyday life, showing both the extent of her marginalised sensibility but also the inherent weakness of group ideals – without the safety of the group in which to seek out more primitive modes of being, group members frequently lack the confidence to persist.

The spectrum of relationships in and around Stoffer's group of 'idiots' also highlights the difficulty of differentiating between 'normality' and 'otherness'. It is often not clear that there is a stable boundary between mental instability and the supposed performance by members of the group. When Stoffer rages at the local council official who appears at the house to suggest that he might wish to know that a grant might be available to assist him with moving his 'home for the retarded', it quickly becomes clear that he has lost control and, as he strips off his clothes whilst giving chase to the official, he becomes increasingly aggressive and rather maniacal to the point where his friends need to strap him down in order to allow him space and time to recover.

Other examples of the blurred edge between 'idiocy' or 'spassing' and the 'real' lived experience of mental illness or instability are seen in the scene between Josephine (Louise Mieritz) and Jeppe (Nikolaj Lie Kaas) as they maintain their 'spassing' personalities in a tender love scene, and in the closing scene when Karen 'spasses' in front of her family. The politics of 'normality' are thrown into disarray in such scenes, and, for the spectator, it further undermines any knowledge of what the purpose of the 'spassing' is. At times political invective and masquerade designed to expose socio-cultural hostility to those that do not conform to the 'norms' of behaviour, the 'spassing' also becomes a form of therapy for the individuals concerned, and, as the film unfolds, it becomes increasingly clear that the commitment to 'spassing' for each of the 'idiots' is personally motivated to some degree.

This blurring of the boundary between mental stability and mental illness is also central to *Breaking the Waves* where we see the tensions play out through Bess's relationship to the village community and the attitudes to her experiences expressed by the Church in which she places so much faith. While Bess is portrayed at various points throughout the film as somewhat 'simple-minded', it is only once she has begun to act on Jan's instructions to immerse herself in sexual activity the better to please him that she really seems to descend into madness. Bess's madness and her consequent banishment from the religious community are intricately tied up with von Trier's explorations of faith and goodness, as this chapter will go on to discuss below. The 'Gold Heart' trilogy of films also explores issues of class identity and difference, as the next section suggests.

Social Class

The question of social class is not an overarching theme in von Trier's work. Nevertheless, it does pervade his films at both the narrative and formal levels. It is arguable that in the 'Gold Heart' trilogy, the political edge of issues around class is brought to the fore because of the documentary-style, 'realist' aesthetic von Trier adopts in each of the three films. As we saw in chapters five and six, the turn to a documentary-style aesthetic was central to the development of the Dogme 95 project, a project that underpins the films in this trilogy. In fact, for von Trier, the 'realist' aesthetic of these films is fundamental to their impact on the audience. He has commented, for example, that it was very important to him to make *Breaking the Waves* with a distinctive realist aesthetic because

> if I had made *Breaking the Waves* with conventional techniques, I think it would have been unbearable … The film would have been far too sickly. … The raw, documentary style that I imposed on the film, which actually dissolves and contradicts it, means that we can accept the story as it is. (Björkman 2003: 166)

This hand-held aesthetic runs through *The Idiots* and *Dancer in the Dark* too. It is deeply resonant of a particular school of documentary filmmaking associated with the representation of everyday, ordinary social existence and the social politics surrounding it. There is particular resonance with the work of directors such as Ken Loach in this regard, a director whose work von Trier acknowledges is influential for him (Björkman 2003: 29). It is arguable that discourses of social class run through the gamut of von Trier's work, and can be seen very clearly in both the 'Europa' trilogy and *The Kingdom* series. This chapter, however, suggests that, as a thematic, the notion of social class is explored most overtly in the 'Gold Heart' trilogy, though the reading that follows will also include reference to other works made by the director.

The question of class is clearly articulated in each of the films in the 'Gold Heart' trilogy. In *Breaking the Waves*, the story unfolds in a small Presbyterian community in the Scottish Western Isles. The community is a simple one, and it is made clear that Bess is from a working-class family context through both the narrative and *mise-en-scène*. Similarly Jan, the Danish oil-rig worker, is presented as a manual, itinerant labourer, a man with no fixed abode who comes to Scotland through the desire to earn a living. The film deploys Dr Richardson (Adrian Rawlins) as a key figure of a bourgeois sensibility (albeit a sympathetic one), but it also presents him as an outsider in the midst of the community, thereby associating middle-class values as external to the community at the heart of the film. The emphasis here is on the simple life, one that is free of the shackles of materialist desire and consumption.

In *Dancer in the Dark*, the class divisions between characters are more pronounced. Centring on the factory workplace of Selma, this film again associates itself with a concern for the everyday working individual. It is interesting that many of the factory workers are foreign nationals, who have come to America in order to make money, in order to aspire to the promises of the American Dream. The American Dream is embodied in the film through the more socially aspirant characters of Bill and Linda (Cara Seymour), with Linda putting great pressure on Bill to provide for ever more impossible material possessions and markers of social mobility. Their lower-middle-class sensibilities and aspirations lie at the heart of the narrative, of course, in that it is Bill's need to provide for his wife that underpins his theft of Selma's savings which provides the motive for Selma's attach on him.

Once more, the *mise-en-scène* provides a great deal of context for the discursive representation of these matters, showing Selma living in an impoverished trailer setting, and contrasting this with the comparative luxury of Bill and Linda's house. In the scene with the bicycle, too, class sensibilities and differences are articulated clearly, with Selma becoming quite angry at the insistence of Bill, Kathy and Jeff (Peter Stormmare) that Gene should be allowed to have a bicycle like the other kids at school. The

Fig. 29 Class divisions in *Dancer in the Dark* are reflected in the domestic environments of the characters: Selma's trailer is much less luxurious than the home of Bill (David Morse) and Linda (Cara Seymour)

question of the American Dream and its association with patterns of consumption on the one hand and with the social struggle of immigrant workers on the other is carefully set up throughout the film, finding its neatest expression in the courtroom scene when the workings of social hierarchies come into play in determining Selma's fate.

In *The Idiots*, as already seen, the question of bourgeois values runs through the film as a whole and is a motivating element on Stoffer's formation of the group sensibility. In this film, however, it is interesting that von Trier's articulation of the question of class is in itself rather bourgeois, signalling the ways in which the concerns of a liberalist agenda are often closely bound up with bourgeois values and aspirations, and underscoring the difficulty of separating these things out. In many ways, Stoffer's project would never work without his bourgeois roots providing space in which to undertake it – he makes use of a house belonging to his uncle, does not seem to work for a living and seems to lurch from one position of liberalism to another with no coherent political agenda. Despite his railing against the system, Stoffer is as willing as other members of the group to make use of Axel's (Knud Romer Jørgensen) credit card when it is given to Katrine (Anne-Grethe Bjarup Riis) and she buys supplies for the birthday party which becomes a nude orgy. Commentators have remarked on how the class sensibility in this film seems to be linked to von Trier's own up-bringing in a communist-sympathising family, in which there was often a sense of communal living (Stevenson 2002).

Lars von Trier's depiction of social class and the political and cultural values associated with it is thus far from simple. Von Trier often presents perspectives on class in knowing ways. This can be seen in some of the early films too: in *The Element of Crime*, for example, the hotel receptionist, Schmuck of Ages (played by von Trier himself), suggests something of the hopelessness of working-class identity in contemporary Europe. In *The Kingdom*, too, the hierarchisation of doctors within the hospital setting is lampooned throughout, especially in the context of the male doctors' club. Meanwhile working-class characters such as Mrs Drusse are associated both with everyday ordinariness and the supernatural, irrational realms of the unknown encompassing spiritualism and mediumship. How, then, are such free-ranging depictions of class to be understood in von Trier's work? Unlike Ken Loach and others, von Trier does not seem set on a particular class-based political position. Instead he appears to be interested in the dynamics of the social processes around class and their effect on the notion of the individual. In this respect, the work of Pierre Bourdieu (1977, 1984 and 1986) is of interest in formulating a reading of this work.

Writing on the importance of the everyday in formulating a sense of how social structures function, Bourdieu suggests that the individual is constructed within a social space. In other words, any effort to understand the individual needs to take into account the social context in which the individual is to be found. The social context of the individual, which Bourdieu terms the 'habitus', is a combination of embodied and mental cultural constructs which both affect and are affected by the individual. The individual is thus influenced by her/his surroundings, but s/he also maintains subjectivity in relation to them, and thereby affects their surroundings. Within the habitus, power functions on the basis of various forms of capital. Capital is not merely to be understood in economic terms but can be social, cultural or symbolic in Bourdieu's account. Social capital is rooted in the relation to groups and the connections between individuals that are promoted within and between groups. Cultural capital, on the other hand, relates to forms of knowledge and levels of skill. Cultural capital evolves through education and systems of expectation and it helps to determine the social status held by individuals. Lastly, symbolic capital refers to the system of prestige and honour conferred upon individuals and to the power inherent within that prestige. It is possible for symbolic capital to be used against other, less-empowered or less dominant individuals in order to ensure obedience to preferred systems – Bourdieu suggests that this is to be understood as symbolic violence and that this is fundamental to efforts to perpetuate dominant ideological systems and practices.

In the 'Gold Heart' trilogy, issues of capital in Bourdieu's sense abound. In *The Idiots*, for example, the habitus of each of the 'idiots' is altered by the shift in social capital that accrues to them as they participate in Stoffer's project. However, the role of each of them is determined within the group by the particular cultural capital they have to contribute. In general terms, this means that Stoffer becomes the group's designated leader because he seems best able to articulate a sense of how the social capital of the group might best be mobilised. For example, it is he who determines that the group should attempt to sell poorly-made Christmas decorations by going from door-to-door in the Søllerød neighbourhood in mid-summer, and it is he who places demands on other members of the group in terms of 'spassing' in contexts of personal significance. At times, he seems most vested in symbolic capital too, as it is he who maintains a mask of 'normality' in order to show around the couple interested in buying his uncle's house and it is he who deals with his uncle's visit and the call by the local social worker. Nevertheless, as is often the case in von Trier's work, this superficial reading does not go far enough. By the end of the film, it becomes clear that the real symbolic capital in this film is held by Karen. By 'spassing' in front of her family, she comes to transcend the rather facile limitations of Stoffer's social outlook, presenting a much more 'authentic' rendition of his objectives that is made all the more powerful by the fact that Karen does indeed seem to be rather a dispossessed character whose life experiences have not provided her with the material or emotional means by which she might escape the confines of her lower-middle-class origins which appear to be so repressive.

In *Breaking the Waves*, of course, it is Dr Richardson who appears to wield the most cultural and symbolic capital. As a medical doctor and as an outsider, Dr Richardson is an incarnation of the dominant cultural norm of white, middle-class masculinity. As an outsider, he is not as incessantly interpellated by the very strict ethical sensibilities of the Presbyterian Church. Nor is he under any illusions as to the ways in which alternative worldviews are available to those who seek respite from the constraints of living in such a community. For example, he is very sympathetic to Bess's earlier experiences of grief after the death of her brother, which was regarded as an episode of madness by members of her family who committed her to hospital as a result. Dr Richardson, by dint of his profession and also of his status as an outsider with seemingly greater experience of the world, is imbued with a huge amount of cultural capital, to the extent that he is able to comment on the abuses of symbolic capital in the course of life on the small island and thereby able to offer paths around it. As a medical doctor, Dr Richardson is also imbued with a certain amount of personal and professional authority, seen in the scenes when he is called upon to try to convince Bess of her mistaken commitment to attempting to cure Jan through her sexually permissive behaviour and, later, when he declares that Bess is liable to be sectioned under the Mental Health Act and when, during the inquest into her death, he gives evidence as an expert witness. Dr Richardson acts as a symbol for the kind of rational, white middle-class masculinity that usually resists commitment to a spiritual approach to life as something that is ill-informed and insignificant. It is interesting, then, that by the end of the film, even Dr Richardson has become converted to the possibility that Bess did, indeed, represent the possibilities of transcendence. It is as though von Trier is attempting to demonstrate the rich potential of belief as a means of escaping hegemonic structures of ideological normativity in order to get to the essence of what is most at stake in human nature. Even for Dr Richardson, who can be seen as an embodiment of the dominant paradigm of cultural capital and its inscription through a certain mode of rational scientific endeavour aligned with masculinity, the appeal of the irrational and the structure of belief as an escape route holds appeal. Von Trier has suggested that he has 'always had a weakness for the irrational' (Björkman 2003: 205) and it therefore appears to be no accident that the groundedness of Dr Richardson's faith in science should be shaken in a film such as this. Von Trier has repeatedly suggested that the irrational female characters of this trilogy are facets of his own personality and his own sensibility around the importance of the irrational realm. By giving these ideas figuration through the construction of doubt in the context of the safest categories of (male) identity, anchored in hegemonic formations of what is to be understood as masculine, von Trier throws into question some of the fundamental assumptions underpinning contemporary perspectives on formations of subjectivity.

To an extent, this can be understood in relation to Bourdieu's notion of 'habitus', the system of commonalities that binds together players in any given social category. For Bourdieu, class inflects habitus in important ways, revealing the homology of experience shared between members of any given class grouping. As we have already seen, for Bourdieu, symbolic capital is of the essence, here, and it is closely bound up with political and economic structures of power. Much of the inscription of power within Western class systems is articulated through the dominance of a certain mode of dominant masculinity which is premised on an adherence to values sustained through apparently neutral social practices associated with professionalism and education. Dr Richardson, of course, embodies just such a mode of masculinity, and, as such, he wields a great deal of cultural and symbolic capital.

By contrast, the men who work on the oil rig are not quite so well-inscribed in relation to social structures of power emerging from the class habitus around masculinity. Jan and his fellow oil-rig workers make up an immigrant community of white men who are defined in terms of their working-class attributes. The cultural capital wielded by Jan and his fellow workers is defined in the film with reference to humour and music rather than with reference to economic or professional status. As such, these men are configured as 'strangers' or 'outsiders' in ways that contrast markedly with the 'outsider' status of Dr Richardson, which seems to accord him an increased authority because of his professionally empowered role. Jan and his fellow workers have very little symbolic capital in the film, which makes them figures of light relief at certain points throughout the narrative and which spells out the ways in which class habitus is more important than gender habitus in terms of providing access to symbolic capital. As itinerant workers, Jan and his friends demonstrate the ways in which, for those are of lower social status, practices around identity come to be formulated in relation to one's sense of community rather than through one's access to symbolic structures of social power. As such, they provide a counter-point to the rather dour community of Church elders and display a means of escaping the oppressively restrictive mode of being sanctioned by them. Whereas, for the Church elders, faith is the only guiding principle through which it is possible to conduct a 'good' life, for the oil rig workers, the 'good life' is defined with broader reference to sensuality and the appreciation of music, humour, dance and love.

It is as though von Trier's fracturing of the habitus of masculinity into three distinct terrains characterised in terms of Puritanism, rationality and freedom sets up the terms against which the scrutiny of femininity will be conducted throughout the film. For each of the modes of masculinity on offer in this film, Bess's femininity is transcendent of its chief concerns and appears to occupy a completely different terrain of ontological concerns. The habitus of masculinity is thus set up as something which is bound up with history and the deployment of power which is socially orchestrated and perpetu-ated. For von Trier, this all seems rather empty in the end, as the emphasis on the appeal of Bess and her articulation of goodness for each of the groups suggests.[6]

At first glimpse, Bess seems to lack cultural capital, and this is shored up in a number of key scenes. For example, we see Bess's bedroom adorned with kitsch pictures of kittens, suggesting a 'soft', infantile sensibility. Home life is conjured as basic and rather strict and Bess is frequently treated as a child, being labelled 'not right in the head' at various points throughout the narrative. The wedding of Bess and Jan is also laden with signifiers of a working-class sensibility, with people bringing along cans of beer in plastic carrier bags. It is fascinating to watch the circulation of cultural capital in this scene, and to note the hierarchisation of power in moments such as the arm-wrestling scene. There is an unspoken assertion of power that comes when, in response to Terry's 'manly' performance of drinking down a whole can of beer in one go before crushing the can in his hand, one of the church elders matches him, firstly by drinking down a whole glass of fruit juice and then by crushing the empty glass in his hand. The film is replete with symbolic violence of this kind, highlighting the struggle for power that seems to characterise life in this small community as well as highlighting the important dimension of class in the construction of sites of this power struggle. Throughout the film, this struggle is inscribed as a particularly masculine one, as this scene at the wedding suggests.

However, Bess, as a woman (and as an infantilised woman, at that), transcends the petty concerns of class-based patriarchal politics and their vested manifestations of power. For Bess, her binding contracts are the personally inscribed ones she makes with Jan and with God. As her story unfolds, we see that, despite being cast out by the Church elders and her family, and despite the best efforts of Dr Richardson and Dodo to preserve her by having her sectioned and treated under the Mental Health Act, Bess manages to create an ontological space of her own in which to establish her subjectivity. By literally staking her life on the power of faith and belief, Bess seems to operate without regard for the cultural capital that is so valued within her community. In so doing, remarkably, she seems to amass symbolic capital of her own, as we see once she has died. This seems to be constituted as a rather romantic, saintly aura and it inflects the responses of other characters in the film to what Bess's life stood for. In his testimony to the coroner's court, Dr Richardson attempts to change his medical report to suggest that Bess died because she 'suffered from being good', and this despite the fact that he had been willing to section Bess only hours before her death. The miraculous recovery made by Jan also confers symbolic capital upon Bess, and this is used to provide both comic relief and critical commentary in the scenes that deal with the attitudes of the Church elders toward burying Bess's body. Jan, of course, manages to steal her body from the coffin, taking it to the rig for a burial at sea. The final scenes of the film, in which we see bells pealing for Bess high up in the heavens, underscore the symbolic capital that this film attaches to 'goodness'. Despite the seemingly absurd abstraction of this ending, it ensures that the significance of the film's central themes is taken to heart: the importance of faith, love and transcendence is paramount.

Echoing the ending of Dreyer's *Ordet*, in which Inger (Birgitte Federspiel) miraculously returns from the dead as a result of the love and faith of her daughter, *Breaking the Waves* depicts the ways in which simple faith, goodness and love can facilitate the kind of humanist ideal of subjectivity that seems to bear meaning for von Trier. It also raises important questions about the ways in which power structures are used and abused, suggesting that love and faith provide alternative sources of power for the individual, and suggesting that power can be based on belief rather than on structure of class and hegemonically-defined exchanges of power.[7]

The question of cultural capital in *Dancer in the Dark* is intricately bound up with the economic capacity for consumption, on the one hand, and with cultural identity on the other. Many of the characters in this film are immigrant workers who labour in a factory and lead fairly impoverished lives, aiming to overcome their impoverishment through hard work and community. By contrast, Bill and Linda are depicted as aspiring middle-class consumers who pursue a lifestyle characterised by conspicuous consumption. It is interesting that the terrain of morality in this film again unfolds in the domain of those with the least cultural capital and that the possession of symbolic capital and the potential for symbolic violence that this carries is allied to power structures within the film. These concerns are not only bound up with issues of social class, however, but also concern questions of nation, as the next section will explore.

Questions of Nation and Cultural Difference

As a discursive construct, the question of nation runs through much of von Trier's *oeuvre*. From the earliest short films, including *Images of a Relief* with its concern to represent sympathy for a Nazi officer, and throughout the 'Europa' trilogy with its depiction of an apocalyptic vision of Germany as the heart of Europe, von Trier has signalled a concern with what Rosalind Galt has called 'national and supranational spaces' (2005: 4).[8] National identity was also at stake in the dark comic humour of *The Kingdom*, as we saw in chapter four. In *Dancer in the Dark*, however, von Trier turns his attention outward, moving beyond Europe to present an image of America and American identity. Given von Trier's phobias about travel, and his blatantly expressed disinterest in actually visiting the United States, it is not surprising that American commentators have been quick to criticise von Trier in relation to the version of America he presents in this film and the ones that follow on from it.

It seems that, at stake here, is the question of cultural inscription within paradigms of national identity and imagination. Arguably, *Dancer in the Dark* presents a distinctively European perspective on how America functions as a sign in the contemporary global context. Its protagonist, Selma, is of Czech origin and has come to the US specifically in order to be able to make enough money to ensure that Gene is able to have the sight-saving operation she herself has never been able to have. As a basic premise of the plot, this storyline taps into a number of contemporary issues around (economic) migration; processes of globalisation, the transnational perspective on the American dream and, importantly, to issues around cinema as an artistic form though which the 'imagined communities' of national and hybrid-national identities are formulated (Anderson 1983).

For Selma, it is clear that 'America' can be understood as the place that is constructed within the cinematic imaginary. As the fantasy scenes of *Dancer in the Dark* make clear, it is through Hollywood in general, and through Hollywood musicals in particular, that she constructs her ambition and her personal dreams. For Selma, the American Dream as embodied in Hollywood cinema comes to constitute the promise of her migratory home, despite the day-to-day reality of her fairly limited and grim existence as an exploited factory worker.[9] In constructing his protagonist in this way, von Trier draws attention to the way in which Hollywood cinema has come to provide an important point of reference for non-US consumers of film and shows how Hollywood representations of the US help to furnish such consumers with notions of what 'America' might be. The 'transnational reach' (Crofts 1998: 390) of US cinema arguably produces an imagined geopolitical construct for consumers in the global market, and, for von Trier, this is important.

Since the critical reception of this film prompted criticism of the director for attempting to depict a country he had never visited by constructing artificial locations meant to serve as iconic emblems of 'Americana' at the Zentropa studios, von Trier has vociferously defended his right to represent this country in any way he sees fit. Citing Franz Kafka's novel *Amerika* as a precedent, von Trier suggests that

> I daresay I know more about America from various media than the Americans did about Morocco when they made *Casablanca*. They never went there either. Humphrey Bogart never set foot in the town ... These days it's hard not to pick up information about America. I mean, ninety per cent of all

news and films comes from the USA. I reckon it ought to be interesting for Americans to see how a non-American who has never visited the USA regards their country. And Kafka wrote an extremely interesting novel called *Amerika*, and he'd never been there either. (Björkman 2003: 244–5)

Von Trier's position here is a provocative one, especially in the current geopolitical context. Nevertheless, it raises interesting points about the nature of cultural identity in an increasingly globalised world, drawing attention to the ways in which contemporary film spectators make what Paul Willemen has called 'a ventriloquist identification' with the ideological position of the cinematic subject presented in US films (1994: 213). The upshot of this is that the idea of nation begins to disintegrate into a kind of culturally-hybrid imaginary in which the rhetorical and ideological formations the mythologised 'America' seen on the silver screen come to provide a touchstone for the aspirations and endeavours of the citizen of the global village.

For von Trier, then, an important facet of the globalised work appears to be the freedom it brings to re-formulate dominant mythologies. This works not just at the level of the text, but also at the levels of production and distribution, as the Dogme 95 project makes clear. Mette Hjort has written on the globalising function of the Dogme movement, arguing that a key element of the movement is its creation of a 'metaculture' which makes 'discourses about, or reflections on the cinematic work for which an audience is sought, an integral part of the product's appeal' (2003b: 134). Arguing that the specificity of the Dogme ethos is fundamental to the global visibility of the project, Hjort suggests that the project is 'very much about the creation of publics, about the forging of a social space where a given cultural expression can simply become visible in the first instance, and perhaps ultimately resonate with genuine significance' (2003b: 135). Her discussion aptly demonstrates the ways in which this works to produce 'talk about, and reflection on filmmaking' (ibid.). In Hjort's account, Dogme works to do without images of national stereotypes in favour of depicting a more deeply shared culture for audiences in a global context. It is impossible to separate out the textual themes of the Dogme films from the rules under which they are made, as Hjort makes clear. Drawing on the work of Nancy Fraser on counter-publics as spaces which allow for practices of identity that resist the demands of dominant or official public sphere, she suggests that Dogme 95 works to situate itself as a metacultural opportunity to navigate the space between official and unofficial publics, and that, as a project, this is at the very heart of the Dogme rules and manifesto. For example, *The Idiots* is seen to bring 'into public focus the very realities for which the counter-public centred around disability is claiming greater attention' (2003b: 152), but it also opened up debates on the international scene of its reception around censorship and film classification:

> By ingeniously linking metaculture to public criticism, Dogma 95 effectively mobilises and forges links between a series of counter-publics that are committed in various ways to challenging dominant arrangements. Dogma 95, in short, is about stimulating creativity and finding a voice, but it is also

about building audiences – a network of audiences with a genuinely global reach. (2003: 155)

Hjort's conclusion, here, opens up interesting perspectives on how we might begin to read the representation of 'America' in *Dancer in the Dark* (and in more recent films such as *Dogville* and *Manderlay*) as a kind of metacultural move. In articulating a view of the US as it is perceived from outside, von Trier is setting his work up as a space for countering the apparent 'inevitability' of the creeping Americanisation of visual media through processes of globalisation. In his depiction of a version of 'America' that is constituted from a European perspective (and from the perspective of a globally visible art cinema director and producer), films such as *Dancer in the Dark*, *Dogville* and *Manderlay* contribute toward the undoing of the imagined community of the Hollywood audience, revealing it as a construct that is motivated by a mode of cultural imperialism that is designed to 'democratise' a very particular rhetoric of industry, capital and media entertainment. The complexity of this move needs to be read, as Hjort quite rightly suggests, at the level of film-industrial practice, but it also resonates with discourses of nation that have come to predominate in the context of late capitalism, globalisation and the geopolitical effects of neo-liberalism, as discussed in chapter eight.

The scope of cultural difference in von Trier's work is thus laden with possibility. Much of the 'Gold Heart' trilogy pays attention to forms of cultural difference through reference to dominant mythologies. In this respect, it is important to return to the question of the femininity of the work. The next section returns to this theme in an attempt to make a link back to the question of ethics in these films.

Femininity, Trauma and Divine Transcendence

Femininity is often aligned with the experience of otherness in dominant cultural contexts and can be seen as providing a 'model' of sorts for the understanding of other cultural manifestations of difference. Nevertheless, the assumption of parity between modalities of difference is not unproblematic because it tends to elide differences into one all-consuming category. That femininity is the marker von Trier attributes to the 'Gold Heart' trilogy indicates the specific importance of gender in terms of his understanding of difference.

Clearly, the films of this trilogy can be seen as 'feminine' firstly because of the gender of their protagonists. In addition, in each of the films, the female protagonist undergoes a profoundly challenging or life-threatening experience. In *Breaking the Waves*, we witness Bess's unbearable propensity for self-sacrifice as she forces herself into prostitution in a desperate attempt to persuade God to save and cure Jan after his accident. Bess's sacrifice culminates in her violent and fatal rape and her weary observation that she may have been mistaken in her attempts to sustain her husband through her acts of obedience to his desires. Bess's death is made more difficult to bear by the signifiers of madness attributed to her and by the fact that Jan does indeed recover and survive once she has died. In *The Idiots*, Karen's enigmatic commitment to Stoffer's group is not revealed until the end of the narrative when she returns to her family home in order to 'spass' in front of her family. Only at this point do we learn that she has run away from home because of the death of her child and her complex inability to attend his funeral. We hear that her family has presumed her dead and we watch as she dribbles her food and acts as an 'idiot' incurring a slap from her husband, Anders. Finally, with the help of Susanne, she decides to leave. Finally, in *Dancer in the Dark*, Selma discovers that her landlord, Bill, has stolen her savings. His subsequent refusal to return the money to her results in her killing him. We watch as she is subjected to a gruelling trial which is followed by imprisonment and her hanging at the end of the film.

For each of the female protagonists, then, there is a discourse of self-sacrifice that runs through the narrative, a trope which is well-wrought in the context of cultural stereotypes of femininity. Indeed, von Trier has been criticised in relation to this trilogy for his misogyny and manipulative attitudes to women (Dalton 2004; Matheou 2004; Thomas 2004). As I have argued elsewhere, however, it is possible to read against the grain of the films to produce a reading that positions the apparent misogyny of the films in relation to the discourses of ethics and religion that they also evoke and to read this alongside thinkers such as Luce Irigaray in order to draw conclusions about the ways in which the feminine is wrought in relation to trauma in contemporary cultural context (Bainbridge 2004b). Each of the films foregrounds themes of personal trauma but the question of ethics is re-cast so that it deals not with notions of ideals but rather with perceptions of goodness. Much of what has been written on this film has centred on the trope of goodness and Bess's status a martyr. What is most striking about this film, however, especially in terms of its relation to the other films in the trilogy, is the highly traumatic effect of Jan's demands on Bess. Whilst embodying goodness, she undergoes trauma of the most intense variety and it is interesting that this gets buried inside the analysis of goodness that predominates around this film. The femininity of the trilogy can be read through this lens of trauma and this chapter will go on to suggest that the inter-relation of trauma and femininity is of crucial importance in marking out von Trier's concern with processes of othering and differentiation. As we have seen, each film examines the martyrdom implicit in pursuing an ideal of goodness to its extreme, and, in so doing, depicts its female protagonist as a martyr to her very specific cause. In contrast to the films of the 'Europa' trilogy, then, those of the 'Gold Heart' trilogy pursue a moment of transcendence despite the accusations of misogyny that the texts provoke. How, then, is it possible to get to grips with the apparent 'femininity' of this trilogy?

In contrast to the films of the 'Europa' trilogy, where the trauma is evoked in terms of the socio-historical framework of the narratives, the trauma at the narrative level in the 'Gold Heart' trilogy is firmly couched within the realm of the personal. This suggests an interesting ethical shift. Where the earlier films configure a notion of the other through discursive and culturally-inflected perspectives that seem inscribed in a logic of sameness, the 'Gold Heart' trilogy of films inscribes the subject/other relationship in terms of the 'I/you' (or perhaps 'I/thou') relationship. Here, then, alterity, or otherness, is overtly linked to subjectivity and the ethical framework of the films shifts to inhabit a space marked by the experience of difference.

The 'I/you' structure of the trauma also invokes the notion of the divine in its focus on love, as we shall see below. This structure permits a shift in the cinematic address of the films in ways that place trauma at the heart of the spectator's relationship to the films (Bainbridge 2004a). In *Dancer in the Dark*, for example, the closing scene of Selma's hanging is deeply inscribed with affect for the spectator. The affective violence of this moment, constituting as it does the narrative closure, is formidable and the spectator must struggle with the affect evoked in her to wrestle meaning and value from the film.

As with trauma, the turn to the question of love is foregrounded at both formal and narrative levels of each film. In *Breaking the Waves*, we clearly see this at play in a number of contexts. Von Trier makes extensive use of intense close-ups on Bess, emphasising in this way the emotive investment of the character, and forging paths of intense identification for the spectator. While the narrative itself appears to present the view that love premised on intimacy and sexuality (in other words, a profoundly humanist form of love) offers scope for moments of transcendence in ways that the more dogmatic religious love does not, the film's epilogue presents an entirely contrary view. In the epilogue, when we see the oversized fantasy bells pealing in the heavens for Bess's goodness, the transcendent possibilities of love are seen to be achievable only through obedience to the divine. Von Trier is arguably drawing on an important distinction between religious practice grounded in dogma and the transcendent possibilities of a relation to the divine.

For von Trier, then, a notion of the divine is implicit in the transcendent ethical possibilities of love. In her extensive philosophical examination of the construction of femininity in terms of difference, Irigaray (1993b) suggests that love has its base in ethics and is determined in relation to the divine. The divine, for Irigaray, is an important facet of the discursive order, and yet it has largely been appropriated for the domain of the masculine. As such, religion is thus as inescapable as any other modality of discourse, and she is keen to assert the need for the feminine to find a way of inscribing itself within/upon notions of the divine in order to seek a relation to God in particular rather than to religion in general. This is a very important distinction in Irigaray's work, as it is designed to make apparent the importance of the acknowledgement and respect for the other in the formulation of an ethical relation. As Margaret Whitford comments, 'when Irigaray comes to talk about the ideal on woman's side, she employs the vocabulary of the divine' (1991: 140).

The parallels with von Trier here are remarkable. Just as Irigaray argues for notions such as the 'sensible transcendental' and 'the divine' as central to any attempt to access an 'ethics of sexual difference', von Trier dismisses a discursive notion of religious activity and belief in favour of a notion of 'God' that seems more connected to the possibility of transcending the human condition. It is fascinating that his scrutiny of this dynamic is couched in gendered terms. Arguably, von Trier's work can be seen as foregrounding the potential of the feminine as that which has been consistently proscribed from the discursive framework of a masculinist order to function as a channel for the transcendence of the humanistic view of the subject. Such a reading opens up a perspective on his work that frames it in terms of radical artistic potential.

Despite this, as we have seen, his work is frequently read as deeply misogynistic and remarks on the sadism implicit in his treatment of women abound (see, for example, Wise 2003). To some extent, this kind of response is arguably evoked through a traditional discursive framework which privileges sameness over difference. Such a discourse struggles to articulate the place of the other in terms which avoid essentialism. This results in a return to a binaristic subject/other relation in which power structures based on oppositions which diminish the other continue to dominate. At one level, it is possible to read von Trier's association of women with masochistic tendencies as a strategy typical of this patriarchal discursive system. Von Trier appears to elide femininity with masochism and therefore to perpetuate a patriarchal view of femininity as irrevocably 'other'. However, it is also arguable that he is responding to cultural assumptions and dominant perceptions of what is to be understood as femininity. Von Trier's work can thus be seen to draw attention to the way femininity often exceeds the boundaries imposed on it by patriarchal systems. As we have already seen, excess is a key trope of both narrative and form for von Trier, as each of the films in this trilogy shows.[10]

Following Irigaray, then, von Trier's 'Gold Heart' trilogy seems effectively to capture a notion of ethics that might be seen 'feminine'. In contrast to the 'Europa' trilogy, where von Trier seems to frame the ethical potential of his protagonists as hopeless and unspeakable, in the 'Gold Heart' trilogy, transcendence is achieved at the end of each film. Bess's salvation comes in the epilogue when the bells ring out for her, while Karen's transcendent moment is embodied in the scene of her 'spassing' in her family home. Selma, as we have seen, goes happily to her death once she has the knowledge that Gene's sight has been saved and that all her efforts have not been in vain. Of course, the literal or metaphorical/metaphysical loss of the protagonists (to death in the cases of *Breaking the Waves* and *Dancer in the Dark*) is a stark cost for such moments of transcendence, but it is important to acknowledge the substantial difference in the affective quality of these deaths when compared to the rather more anaesthetised response constructed in the deaths of the 'Europa' trilogy.

Perhaps what von Trier enables us to discern is the differential potential of gender to illustrate the ethical capacities of art. In this sense, while his work may not encompass an obviously *feminist* agenda, it might be said to present a radical space for thinking about the discursive and ethical components of politics, and therefore to constitute a radical artistic endeavour. This sense of radicalism moves beyond the 'Gold Heart' trilogy and becomes more overtly geopolitical in the 'U-S-A – Land of Opportunities' trilogy, in which von Trier adopts a very pared-down theatrical aesthetic for his films, as if to heighten the political impact of them, as the next chapter explores.

PART FOUR

Experimentation at the Boundaries

CHAPTER EIGHT

A Trilogy in the Making: Dogville and Manderlay

Questions of politics and the global pattern of power and influence dominate the recent turn in the cinema of Lars von Trier. As the last chapter made clear, debates around ethics and the formation of radical ideas have come to play an important part in his filmmaking over the course of the last ten years or so. This comes to a head in the work included in the 'U-S-A – Land of Opportunities' series of films, the first two of which have been made and released, with the final instalment (*Wasington*) in pre-production at the time of writing. The films of this trilogy concern themselves overtly with geopolitical assumptions rooted in the notion of 'America' von Trier first set out to explore in *Dancer in the Dark*, and this has been the target of a great deal of critical commentary, as the next section will explore. However, despite the apparently overt attack on a specifically American identity made in this work, many of the themes and issues explored also tap into a broader notion of cultural history that links to contemporary silences around events such as the Holocaust and issues linked to racism. In particular, von Trier has signalled the relevance of debates around immigration currently unfolding in Denmark as relevant to the structure of his thinking in relation to the narrative themes of these films (Hoberman 2004).

Von Trier adopts a pared-down theatrical aesthetic in this work that is reminiscent of the 'epic theatre' of Bertolt Brecht and, as a result, these films can be read allegorically as didactic pieces contrived to invoke self-reflection despite the apparent critical controversies surrounding them. There is much here that works as a form of meditation on what film might achieve, and the meta-cinematic analysis that seems to have run through a great deal of von Trier's work is seen again in this context. This chapter sets out these key themes and ideas and foregrounds the ways in which these films attempt to breach the frontiers of film in order to extend their reach into the domain of debates around political subjectivity and postmodern aesthetics.

Images of America: Critique, Fantasy and Symbolisation

With the release of *Dogville* in 2003, von Trier became the focus of a number of debates around 'anti-American' sensibilities in response to global events unfolding in the Middle East, Iraq and Afghanistan and in the 'war on terror'. For many critics, von Trier's own comments on what drove him to make the films helped to inscribe this attitude; for instance, von Trier's statements on the 'anti-American' position of the films include:

> I've never been to America, but there's an impression … Americans sometimes forget what they represent in the world. (Norman 2003: 23)

> I would love to start a Free America campaign because we have just had a Free Iraq campaign. You could say I'm a communist, but I'm not. I want to free America because, from over here, I see a lot of shit in America. Maybe (this idea) comes to me from journalists who are lying. America is not what it should be. (Gibbons 2003: 5)

> I learned when I was very small that if you are strong, you also have to be just and good, and that's not something you see in America at all. I like the individual Americans I know very much, but this is more of an image of a country I do not know but that I have a feeling about. I don't think that Americans are more evil than others but then again, I don't see them as less evil than the bandit states Mr Bush has been talking so much about. I think that people are more or less the same everywhere. What can I say about America? Power corrupts. And that's a fact. Then again, since they are so powerful, it's okay to tease because I can't harm America, right? (von Trier 2003)

There is much here to illustrate the intentionally provocative stance taken by von Trier. However, as Nigel Andrews also commented in the press,

> Dunderheads calling themselves critics have said that *Dogville* is 'anti-American'. But it isn't about America at all – it's about von Trier's fantasy USA: an extension of the one he created in *Dancer in the Dark*. Reality, free association and archetypes swirl together to form a playground of the unconscious. (2003b: 17)

This image of 'America' is one that is grounded in the transnational global context of media consumption. Von Trier is often keen to highlight the fact that America is responsible for a good deal of what circulates as 'popular culture', with national television broadcasting schedules incorporating US programming on a regular basis and with the international film market dominated by the output of Hollywood studios. In addition, other facets of 'American' life are globally significant as a direct consequence of structures of commerce and capital. In the context of global politics, of course, America has come to occupy a central position in the formation of the 'coalition of the willing' in the 'war against terror' and the neoconservative agenda to bring 'democratisation' to nation states such as Iraq through invasion and occupation if need be is of stark consequence and significance in the contemporary geopolitical climate. Andrews and others have suggested that von Trier's remarks about the meaning of 'America' in his images of this country need to be understood in this context. It *is* possible to see this work as 'a total indictment of American global culture' (Anderson 2003: 10) but it is also interesting to reflect on the fantasy of 'America' that dominates von Trier's imagination.

Von Trier's representation of 'America' is archetypal, drawing on a number of signs familiar to us from film history (as we saw in relation to *Europa* and *Dancer in the Dark*) and also from mythology and the circulation of global capital and commerce ('America' as 'the land of the free', home of the 'American dream' and the 'America' of popular cultural representations seen in many film and television texts, for example *American Beauty* (Sam Mendes, 1999) and *Six Feet Under* (HBO, 2001–05) evoke elements of American suburbia with series such as *Sex and the City* (HBO, 1998–2004) and various localised versions of *CSI* (CBS, 2000–) and films such as *Panic Room* (David Fincher, 2002) illustrating aspects of urban life). It is a fantasised vision of the 'America' that is consumed in the global context.

Psychoanalysis posits fantasy as a dualistic concept. On the one hand, it enables desire to be dramatised and makes available to the protagonist an array of subject positions and identifications. On the other hand, however, fantasy also has a defensive structure, allowing for the partial return of repressed material and offering mechanisms such as projection, splitting and negation as a means of making such material safe. For Jean Laplanche and Jean-Bertrand Pontalis, fantasy is also 'a purely illusory production which cannot be sustained when it is confronted with a correct apprehension of reality' (1988: 317). Heather Nunn suggests that fantasy 'can be seen as a stepping out of, and back into, the social world, and crucially, as an active creation, which shapes and is shaped by that world' (2002: 22).

This is interesting in attempting to understand how fantasy functions for von Trier in his 'realisation' of 'America'. The image of 'America' with which we are confronted in his work is one that is shaped through fantasies that circulate via the silver screen in cinema, in particular, and through the notion of 'reality' that is produced as a result. The 'America' that is consumed as an object of global consumption constructs the 'reality' of what 'America' *is* in the global cultural imagination. Von Trier articulates this as follows:

America is a good subject because such a big, big part of our lives has to do with America. ... America is kind of sitting on the world, there's no question about it. And therefore I'm making films that have to do with America, because America fills about 60% of my brain. All the words in there, all the things I've experienced in my life, about 60% of them – and I'm not very happy about that – is American. So in fact I am American, but I can't go there to vote, I can't change anything because I'm from a small country. And that is why I make films about America.[1]

This articulation of what 'America' symbolises in its global hegemonic formation is very important for any attempt to understand what von Trier is out to achieve in terms of the political effects of his films. In her account of the psychic formation of the individual, Melanie Klein (1988) argues that there are a number of mechanisms at play in the relationship between human subjects and the objects they encounter in the world. Suggesting that for every relationship with an object in the external world, there is a parallel psychical relationship with an inner object representing it, Klein argues that symbolisation is an important aspect of how we begin to make sense of the world around us. Symbols are made in order to provide a means through which to organise responses to fear and anxiety and in order to enable the individual to manage the emotional impact of inner objects and aspects of significant objects in the external world that come to be introjected to form part of the self. Symbolisation helps to externalise such elements and feeds into processes of creativity and the expression of emotion.

There are parallels here with the structures of recuperation at play in the workings of hegemony. In representing a version of 'America' premised on the apparently naturalised 'reality' of its signs and mythologies in the structure of global consumption, von Trier draws attention to the subtle processes implicit in cultural hegemony, highlighting its unspoken mechanisms and throwing into question the way in which the ideological and cultural values associated with it become unquestioningly introjected. The structures of introjection at stake in the hegemonic process nevertheless produce psychic anxiety and fears and these need to find an outlet through which to be expressed. Cinema, with all its connotations of fantasy and storytelling, provides an arena in which to explore such ideas, and it is possible to ascribe this meta-cinematic structure to von Trier's work as it draws so explicitly on received discourses of 'the cinematic'.

For von Trier, then, the political potential of cinema depends on its ability to undo the received hegemonic structure of its normative context of consumption. Both *Dogville* and *Manderlay* draw on several cinematic genres associated with popular Hollywood film production, referencing the gangster film, the melodrama and the western amongst others. However, the formal construction of these films appears to resist the familiar structures of film language, drawing instead on theatrical techniques of stylisation instead. This has an important bearing on the political significance of these films, as the next section explores.

Alienation, Artifice and Authenticity

As is well documented, *Dogville* and *Manderlay* adopt a stark, highly theatrical *mise-en-scène* influenced by Bertolt Brecht and Trevor Nunn's RSC production of *Nicholas*

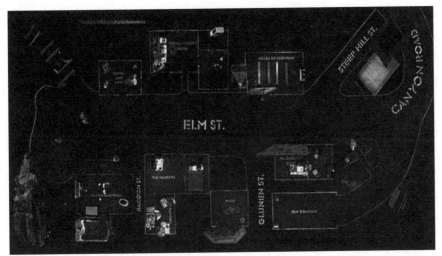

Fig. 30 The diagrammatic overhead shot at the opening of *Dogville* signals the theatricality of the film

Nickleby from 1980. Each film was made in a hangar in Sweden, with sets consisting of chalk marks/black paint lines drawn on the floor and a sparse selection of props and scenery designed to evoke associations to the landscapes of the stories.[2] The theatricality of the sets self-consciously references Brechtian political stage drama and the Marxist-inflected notion of 'epic theatre'.

For Brecht, writing between the 1920s and 1940s, theatre provided an arena in which to explore the capacity of culture to bring politics to the masses. Influenced by Marxism, Brecht worked to obviate the unquestioning consumption of drama through its strategies of identification and emotional catharsis. Instead, he posited a mode of theatre in which space for critical reflection is opened up for the spectator, a space that might induce political reaction and the desire to take action and effect change once the play was over. In developing this theory of 'epic theatre', Brecht formulated the *Verfremdungseffekt*, or the 'alienation technique', in which mechanisms of distancing were employed persistently to remind spectators that they were viewing a fictional work, a drama. By the use of placards, the reading aloud of stage directions, direct address to the spectator and the use of unconventional lighting arrangements and sparse set design, Brecht suggested that the spectator would be empowered to acknowledge that the drama was little more than a construction, and, by extension, that reality was also a construction and that they had it within their power to effect social change (Esslin 1974).

The influence of this Brechtian formulation of theatre on von Trier's work in *Dogville* and *Manderlay* is striking. As he himself has commented,

> I was also inspired to a degree by Bertolt Brecht and his kind of very simple, pared-down theatre. My theory is that you forget very quickly that there are no houses or whatever. This makes you invent the town for yourself but more importantly, it makes you zoom in on the people. The houses are not there

so you can't be distracted by them and the audience doesn't miss them after a time because of this agreement you have with them that they will never arrive.[3]

For von Trier, the pared-down aesthetic is thus first and foremost driven through an aesthetic designed to elicit greater attention to the characters and their actions. There is no distraction proffered by the films, no resort to the spectacle associated with cinema in the later twentieth and early twenty-first centuries. Instead, the narrative framework is stripped bare, the better to shape an understanding of the characters' motivations and the better to re-work cinematic assumptions and conventions. As a result of the stylisation of these narratives, the moral sensibilities and questions of ethical choice are foregrounded and made inescapable. In addition, the question of what is properly filmic is drawn into focus, as further discussed below. In many ways, this is not a surprising development of the aesthetic sensibility at play in the Dogme 95 movement. It becomes an almost logical extension of the back-to-basics philosophy at play in that context. However, it also taps into the fact that the Brechtian aesthetic has broadly been canonised within contemporary theatre practice and that its political sensibility is well documented.

In this regard, von Trier steps into the domain of the postmodern once again. By foregrounding the moral and ethical dilemmas underpinning his stories and by throwing into question the formation of the properly cinematic, von Trier's work crystallises issues around the political value and function of art.

Dogville sets this up very neatly in its ironic referencing of the pinnacles of modernist and classical culture. The presentation of the film in its opening intertitle references literature, music and theatre as well as cinema, suggesting that the text is premised at the boundaries and intersections of these cultural forms: the film is presented 'as told in nine chapters and a prologue' and the opening sequence deploys a voice-over by the narrator (John Hurt) intercut with strains of a classical music score which accompanies an overview of the *staging* of the drama and draws attention to the *cinematic* movement of the camera which swoops down from an overhead direct shot of the townscape laid out as a map into a close-up shot of the radio in Thomas Edison's house. From the outset, then, *Dogville* juxtaposes the apparently literary and theatrical roots of its conventions (the presence of the omniscient narrator; the splitting of the story into *chapters*; the austere set and sparse props, and so on) with its cinematic specificity (which is relayed through the means of highly visible camera-work, editing, and the extensive expression of a ubiquitous mobile viewpoint). The alienation effect thus unfolds in this slippage between the folds of high culture and the specificity of cinema – the spectator is made aware of the importance of the camera through the use of hand-held tracking shots, close-ups and crash zooms. That this is cinema is a fact foregrounded throughout the film and the distancing effect of this draws attention to the making of cinema and to its status with regard to storytelling and myth-making.

The narrative concerns of *Dogville* are premised on time-honoured archetypal themes centring on good and evil, moral rectitude and the question of 'grace'. At one

Fig. 31 When Grace (Nicole Kidman) arrives in Dogville, she is wearing a floor-length coat with a fur-lined collar, connoting the *femme fatale* familiar to us from *film noir*

level, von Trier is self-consciously referencing the themes of his previous work in the 'Gold Heart' trilogy of films and the theme of martyrdom is re-visited in this film, albeit with a less idealistic outcome. However, von Trier is also signalling the ways in which the basic themes of popular stories centre on biblical and mythological ideals. Moreover, the focus on the cinematic points to the ways in which classical Hollywood genres depend on such themes in the narratives they portray. Both *Dogville* and *Manderlay* are set in the 1930s, a decade which saw the inception of the heyday of American commercial cinema. When Grace (Nicole Kidman) appears for the first time in *Dogville* she is dressed in a glamorous floor-length coat with a fur-lined collar, connoting the figure of the *femme fatale* of *film noir*. Her trustworthiness is also immediately thrown into question because of the fact that she is a fugitive, and the appearance of the automobile in pursuit of her also structures associations between her and the gangster movies that dominated the output of classical Hollywood.

The inception of cinema as an industry is also referenced implicitly in the choice of 'Thomas Edison Jr' as the name of the film's male protagonist. Thomas Edison was the inventor of the phonograph and a pioneer of electric light production and also held the patent for the motion picture camera. In 1908, he started the Motion Picture Patents Company (MPPC), a conglomerate organisation consisting of nine cinema studios which held the patents for many of the components required for filmmaking. The inception of Hollywood as the location for the burgeoning American film industry is purportedly linked to the draconian measures adopted by the MPPC in pursuit of appropriate fees for the use of patented inventions (Parkinson 1995). Edison, then, can be seen to have played a formative role in the shaping of the commercialisation of cinema and von Trier's choice of this name for his protagonist neatly draws attention to the importance of film history underpinning his work in this film. *Manderlay* also works with reference to historical formations. The most apparent structure (other than those already made explicit in *Dogville*) centres on the cinematic representation of the civil rights movement in the US and on the question of the role played by black men and women in the emergent cinematic industry (this is further explored below).

The implicit 'historicisation' at play within these films is also indicative of von Trier's play with the Brechtian aesthetic. For Brecht, the depiction of contemporary events in drama distracted from its potential political effect. To this end, he advocated employing historical figures and events around which to frame the narrative in order to signal the parallels with issues more contemporaneous to the viewer's consumption of the drama. Von Trier elects to stage his narratives in the context of the 1930s, a period which saw the rise of cinema as an industry, but also the rise of fascism across Europe.

Reading these films in terms of their allegorical function highlights the dangers at stake in the context of contemporary global politics. The press coverage of these films makes frequent reference to the political conflicts surrounding the 'war on terror' and the 'democratisation' project of George W. Bush's administration, highlighting von Trier's explicit critique of these events.[4] The closing credit sequences of each film also make use of historical and contemporary photographs accompanied by David Bowie's 'Young Americans' on the soundtrack: in *Dogville*, contemporary images of alcoholics and the underclass are inter-cut with black-and-white images from the Depression era drawing attention to the timelessness of the failure of the US government to address issues of poverty and the implicit failure of moral consciousness symbolised in this fact; in *Manderlay*, contemporary images of African-Americans (including images of black soldiers stationed in the desert in Iraq and CCTV screens depicting the notorious scenes of Rodney King being beaten by the LAPD) are intercut with stills depicting the demonstrations and riots that were staged during the campaign for civil rights, together with images of the Ku Klux Klan and their victims, and the abject failure of anti-racist agendas in the US focus is brought sharply into focus here.

In addition, by tying this implicit critique of the contemporary geopolitical scene to a critique of the form of cultural hegemony perpetuated through patterns of industry and commerce in relation to the media, von Trier signals the importance of capital and highlights the significance of the geopolitical agenda and its deployment of commerce to promote the consumption of its values. This is achieved in relation to these films through the complex interplay of cinema history, referentiality, inter-textuality, allegory and the explicit exploitation of the very mechanisms under critique to draw attention to the critical commentary the work attempts to elicit. This is von Trier's provocative media machine in full flight, juxtaposing the foregrounding of artifice with notions of reality, setting fiction against history and using alienation as a strategy through which to explore the postmodern impossibility of authenticity and its expression in the contemporary hegemonic setting.

At the level of meta-discourse, then, von Trier cleverly integrates multiple levels of media practice and processes of mediatisation that characterise the contemporary scene of global visual culture. However, each of these films also explores in more depth themes familiar to us from earlier work in von Trier's *oeuvre*, returning again to cultural constructions of difference and themes of sacrifice and redemption.

As we have already seen, the symbolisation at play in these films is structured through baldly mythological sign systems. The naming of 'Grace' is to be understood as a 'sign' (in the fullest semiotic sense). Many critics have commented on the overt signification of von Trier's choice of name for his female protagonist, drawing attention to the inherent religious associations and the classical connotations of feminine archetypes (Hoberman 2004; Chiesa forthcoming). The idea of 'grace' connotes innate goodness and a boundless capacity for unconditional love and absolute devotion and there are distinct biblical overtones to the word, leading several critics to expound on the parallels between Grace and the figure of Jesus.

However, Grace's femininity is also important here – as we have already seen, von Trier has a tendency to align goodness and the capacity for martyrdom with femininity. However, in both *Dogville* and *Manderlay*, Grace's role seems to move beyond the formula of the 'Gold Heart' trilogy heroines, tackling the question of transgression and its relationship to borders, idealism and liberal morality. Grace is the channel through which these ideas are explored in each film, which suggests that, for von Trier, grace is best conceptualised through the scrutiny of difference and the dynamic underpinning the relationship of the idealist to the other.

In *Dogville*, Grace arrives in town as an outsider. She is situated from the outset as vulnerable and her immediate fate is dependant upon Tom's (Paul Bettany) indulgence in shielding her from the gangsters in her pursuit. This structures the terms by which her relationship with both Tom and the broader population of Dogville will unfold in the course of the narrative. As an outsider, Grace is the embodiment of otherness in this film. Her status as 'other' is determined at a number of levels. Firstly, she is an outsider, a stranger whose back story is never made entirely clear. Secondly, she is a woman – the fact of her sexed identity marks her out as different, especially as she is a lone figure and one who becomes steadily more subjected and oppressed as the narrative unfolds. Lastly, she is in hiding which suggests that she is a transgressor of some sort – the narrative never makes clear exactly what it is that Grace is fleeing (although the ending reveals that it is her father); however, as the story develops, the police list her as 'missing' and, later, 'wanted'. She is marginalised and set outside the boundaries of the everyday.

In this context, it is interesting to consider the position of Grace as an object of power play and manipulation in this film. Her status as an outsider, an other/transgressor, marks her out as dependent on the good will of those with whom she seeks haven. The effect of this is to configure her as a signifier of the potential downward spiral of charity into oppression. The figure of the other is always simultaneously seductive and repellent and courts a sense of ambivalence deemed to be central to the formation of identity. In the psychoanalytic account, the subject is always a split subject, one who requires an other against whom to forge a sense of self and with whom to identify as well as idealise. In *Dogville*, Grace becomes a cipher for the exposition of the place of the other. The film foregrounds the effects of 'othering' and its role in the formation of community, morality and power. As a stranger in the midst of a community that seeks 'moral re-armament', Grace becomes a symbol of the way in which the other is simultaneously idealised and denigrated. She is both good and bad object for the townsfolk of Dogville, illustrating the importance of 'the other' in the formation of community. Zygmunt Bauman has suggested that

> the ability to live with differences, let alone to enjoy such living and to benefit from it, does not come easily and certainly not under its own impetus. This ability is an art which, like all arts, requires study and exercise. The inability to face up to the vexing plurality of human beings and the ambivalence of all classifying/filing decisions are, on the contrary, self-perpetuating and self-reinforcing: the more effective the drive to homogeneity and the efforts to eliminate the difference, the more difficult it is to feel at home in the face of strangers, the more threatening the difference appears and the deeper and more intense is the anxiety it breeds ... As the drive to uniformity grows more intense, so does the perceived horror of the dangers presented by the 'strangers at the gate'. The danger presented by the company of strangers is a classic self-fulfilling prophecy. (2000: 106)

What is interesting here in relation to *Dogville* is the way in which the 'ability to live with differences' is also seen to entail a projection of the internal guilt felt as a result of feeling the threat of difference. The inhabitants of Dogville come to mistrust Grace because her willingness to suffer increasing levels of degradation and suffering in order to repay them for their 'kindness' in tolerating her presence in the town acts as a constant reminder of their manipulation of her 'goodness'. The masochism of Grace's ability to bear the ever more unacceptable behaviour to which she is subjected is important here. As a woman, Grace is positioned by patriarchal values as having the capacity and forbearance for such masochism (a theme explored in von Trier's earlier work in the 'Gold Heart' trilogy). However, her unspoken acceptance of this position works in tandem with her continuing efforts to be 'good' to constitute her as a marker of the abuse of power at play in the town. In a 'properly' feminine way, Grace allows herself to be subjected to the abuses of the townsfolk and thereby allows herself to be still further 'othered'. Grace's behaviour is bound up with her relationship to her father, who, as it turns out later at the end of the film, is the gangster chasing her. Psychoanalytically, then, Grace's masochistic behaviour is allied with her Oedipal trajectory.

According to Freud, masochism is 'the expression of feminine essence' (1991e: 415). Like sadism, masochism is a means of survival for the subject; it emerges in the context of transferring feelings of desire and attachment from one parent to another, and is thus linked to the Oedipus complex. The fantasies of punishment at play in the formation of masochistic tendencies enable the subject to preserve fantasies of a child-like state of helplessness (Freud 1955) and to negotiate the threat of death and destruction (Freud 1991c). It is this threat that produces the apparent passivity of masochism – Freud suggests that the passive state is a construct designed to mask the fear of destruction it covers. The guilt and inherent sexuality of the masochistic position highlights its Oedipal origins.

Grace is a case in point: her horror at the sadistic and terrorising impulses of her gangster father, to whom (according to patriarchal symbolic law) she must eventually transfer her desire in the Oedipal triangle, induces a fear of destruction and reprisal and produces the masochistic state of helplessness she takes on in an effort to ward off the threat to her innocence. However, by the end of the film, Grace has been subjected to manifold experiences of gratuitous abuse and sexual torture, and this presents her position as one that is ultimately doomed in its intentions. At the climax of the film, Grace is returned to her father (James Caan), who, in a parable tale of arrogance and misplaced infantile narcissism, forces Grace out of her masochistic position and into its opposite: sadism. This culminates in the violent recriminations that make up the ending of this film, and Grace's return to her father's worldview turns her into the phallic woman associated with the law of the father that characterises patriarchy. In order to escape her passivity and transcend the boundaries of patriarchal notions of femininity, Grace embraces symbolic and literal violence.

Once again, Grace is left no room in which to exist as a subject on her own terms – her choice in the ending of *Dogville* is a stark one: she must either bear the brunt of rejection by the father or inflict punishment on those who have treated her so badly in order to properly enter into the symbolic domain of paternal law and take up her properly feminised position. Grace's decision at the end of the film is arguably as much about survival as the one she makes at the beginning. *Dogville* becomes a first instalment of Grace's Oedipal narrative, and, as patriarchal law dictates, her attempts to transgress boundaries must always be reined in.

The moral fable underpinning this narrative is one that seems to be written with reference to the Old Testament sensibility of 'an eye for an eye' rather than in relation to the New Testament ethos of 'turn the other cheek'. Commenting on this ethical dilemma and its representation in the film, Bo Fibiger suggests that Grace is 'stretched out between her father's merciless attitudes and her own more humanistic preference for grace and understanding', but, nevertheless, 'the sins of the father' prevail (2003). For Fibiger, 'the film may be seen as presenting the ethical dilemma of good and evil, and thus the terribly violent scene at the end is meant to call into question the Old Testament' (ibid.). The film foregrounds the relationship and difference between 'good' and 'evil' and attempts to ask how human subjects seek to resolve the tension between these poles. As suggested above, this links to von Trier's rather crude attempt to stage a critique of contemporary global politics, but it is also connected to the scrutiny of gender and it is interesting to observe how this unfolds in the tension between Grace's burgeoning feminine sexuality and the hyper-masculinity embodied by her father.

Grace's Oedipal trajectory continues in *Manderlay*, a narrative that opens shortly after the massacre at Dogville, when Grace (now played by Bryce Dallas Howard) and her father (now played by Willem Dafoe) happen upon Manderlay, a forgotten plantation where slavery is still in effect some seventy years after its legal dismantling. The Oedipal tussle between Grace and her father has still not been resolved and she is determined to manifest her independence from him and to prove to him the importance of her pursuit of liberalist ideals. Nevertheless, Grace's independence from her father relies upon the provision of his guns: she maintains her phallic status as a kind of guarantor for her pursuit of these ideals. Thus she also maintains the fantasy that she might somehow have access to a modality of symbolic authority that might allow the ideals for which she stands to become attainable. Nevertheless, as the film unfolds, Grace finds herself compromised by her liberal politics and she falls into the trap of desire, fetishising Timothy (Isaach de Bankolé) as her object of desire, and thereby forcing herself into a relationship to the other less premised in fantasy and therefore more compromised by structures of power that emerge from the Oedipal agenda.

Throughout *Manderlay*, the Oedipal scenario is made to appear ever more inevitable, and it is rather unsurprising at the end when Grace responds to her father's note and turns up to meet him at the gate, having succumbed to the power structures at play and the apparent inevitability of the hegemonic formation she had earlier sought to resist. However, Grace's faith in the protective potential of her relationship with her father is undercut in the final scenes as she is exposed for her double standards and her father misinterprets her actions in whipping Timothy as a phallic display of power and control. As a woman, of course, Grace cannot be permitted to escape unpunished for such a phallic display and her punishment comes in the form of her misinterpretation of the time and her subsequent failure to meet her father. We see her staggering blindly across a symbolic map of the US as the narrative comes to an end, but there is a sense that the Oedipal drama will only be completed with the third instalment of the trilogy. The 'rescue' narrative familiar to us from many Hollywood depictions of the Oedipal myth is suspended at the end of this film. However, the narrative's meditation on otherness does undergo some closure at least with regard to the politics of race depicted in the film, as the next section will explore.

Fig. 32 The phallic display of Grace (Bryce Dallas Howard) whipping Timothy (Isaach de Bankolé) at the end of *Manderlay*

As we have seen, the question of power runs through the narratives of both *Dogville* and *Manderlay* and is, at one level, explored in relation to gender relations. However, the latter film makes the dynamics of power much more explicitly felt in its problematic depiction of the encounter between Grace and the former group of slaves at Manderlay, raising the spectre of the socio-historical construction of subjugation and oppression and foregrounding the on-going silences of power and its abuse in both the conservative and neoliberal contexts.

In his analysis of power, Michel Foucault highlights the fact that power is not constructed through any straightforward binary opposition between rulers and the ruled. Instead, power emanates from below and is dispersed through the network of discourse, flowing through the matrix of social relations. There is an important relationship, then, between power and freedom, as the notion of resistance is implicit in the Foucauldian understanding of the operation of power. For Foucault, 'power is not simply repressive; it is also productive' (Sheridan 1980: 217). Power is also aligned with knowledge and it constitutes the site of an unequal relationship between those who are perceived to have power and those who are not. Knowledge is deployed in this context through the construction of discourse (Foucault 1978).

This dynamic of power is clearly seen in *Manderlay*, as Grace invokes her liberalist sensibility by which she feels herself to be empowered enough to know how the relationship of power at stake in the master/slave relationship is one of oppression. She thereby unwittingly establishes yet another regime of power, reifying her position to that of 'the one who knows'. The film exposes the hypocrisy of this situation in its ending, when Willem (Danny Glover) reveals to Grace the fact that the former slaves' apparently silent acceptance of her imposition of 'democratic' processes within the community at Manderlay did not equate to a lack of insight into her arrogant assumption that they might not know better. On the contrary, Willem reveals that it was *he* who wrote 'Mam's Law' and that he did so in order to provide a structure in which the day-to-day life of the community might continue to be functional.

Grace's horror at this revelation is important in constructing the discursive relationship between her and the former slaves she attempts to 'liberate' and 'educate'. This is predicated on Grace's assumption that she occupies a morally superior position by virtue of the fact of her whiteness on the one hand and her liberalist agenda on the other, both of which apparently furnish her with 'knowledge' of what constitutes 'justice'. The discursive inscription of her position is such that she is not able to see its limits. Knowledge is always a form of power, according to Foucault, but power is also at play in the forces that determine whether knowledge can be applied or not and how particular sets of circumstances impact on such a decision. In his discussion of how white people are apparently 'non-raced', Richard Dyer suggests that

> there is no more powerful position than that of being 'just' human. The claim to power is the claim to speak for the commonality of humanity. Raced people can't do that – they can only speak for their race. Non-raced people can, for

they do not represent the interests of a race. The point of seeing the racing of whites is to dislodge them/us from the position of power, with all the inequities, oppression, privileges and sufferings in its train, dislodging them/us by undercutting the authority with which they/we speak and act in and on the world. (1997: 539–40)

It is possible to read the ending of *Manderlay* as an enactment of this position and to suggest that von Trier's films foreground the sense in which white, elite liberal values are self-deluding. As Jason Harsin argues,

Manderlay is a trap for the so-called educated liberal elite (forget about the conservatives: they will never see this film). Their do-goodism is seen in this film and its predecessor to be naïve and undertheorised. Uninterested in playing policymaker, von Trier leaves his different audiences to argue about his depiction of the problem and, hopefully, about some new solution that has not been widely recognised so far. (2006)

According to this logic, the film's strategies of alienation are crucial to the production of such a position. Nevertheless, von Trier's position is not without its problems, as many critics have suggested. There is much in this film that can be read as reproducing the very racist assumptions that the film simultaneously sets out to expose. How is this dilemma to be understood?

Von Trier's depiction of many of the black characters in this film re-deploys a series of familiar stereotypes. In particular, we see images familiar to us from Hollywood cinema including those of the Uncle Tom, the mammy and the sexually fetishised black man, and this raises questions about the role of cinema in the production of racism at one level. As Dyer has suggested,

stereotyping – complex and contradictory though it is – does characterise the representation of subordinated social groups and is one of the means by which they are categorised and kept in their place, whereas white people in white culture are given the illusion of their own infinite variety (1997: 543–4).

However, the moral of von Trier's own fable, that 'the road to hell is paved with good intentions', is one that seems shot through his own approach to the making of the film, and this makes for uncomfortable viewing. In order to produce the alienated observation of the construction of black American ethnicity in this film, von Trier takes on the means of its production. A generous reading of this strategy allows room for its analysis as the adoption of essentialism as a means of exposing the production of its discursive formation. The politics of this can be seen as dubious, although such an approach does draw attention to the unconscious mechanisms at play in the representation of otherness and its embodiment.

Psychoanalytically speaking, difference is managed and formulated through the relationship to the other which underpins the formation of the self. In order for the unconscious mechanisms at play in the production of racism to be understood, it is important to acknowledge the role of the other in the formation of cultural myths and counter-myths that centre on the apparent threat to subjectivity that is posed by the existence of the other. Michael Rustin has argued that unconscious mechanisms such as splitting, projection, projective identification and idealisation are all at play in the formulation of the meaning of the other. For example, the attribution to the other of a capacity to inflict danger can be understood as a result of the subject's desire to rid her/himself of 'bad' components of identity; they become split off and projected onto the other who comes to embody the badness, enabling the subject to feel justified in condemning the other and expressing anxiety in relation to it (1991: 57–85). In this context, the endemic re-production of racism within society must be understood psychically as the inability to tolerate difference and the anxiety that it produces.

However, as Frantz Fanon (1952) suggests, racism generates important psychological constructs that work to blind black subjects to their subjection to the universalised white norm. Black subjectivity, therefore, is always marked by this experience and the concomitant cultural values are harmfully internalised by black people as a result. In some ways, the plot of von Trier's narrative alludes to the cultural complexities of such a position. By the end of the film, the shock of Willem's confession that it is *he* who wrote 'Mam's Law' partly stems from the realisation that, in order to undertake such a thing, he must necessarily have internalised the deeply offensive cultural and social mores underpinning the organisation of slavery, thereby 'naturalising' them as a way of being within a hegemonic system premised on the assumption of whiteness as the basis for 'proper' subjectivity and freedom. Von Trier's text, then, can be read as somehow performative (albeit rather clumsily) of this. Homi Bhabha has argued that

> the sign of history does not consist in an essence of the event itself, nor exclusively in the *immediate consciousness* of its agents and actors, but in its form as a spectacle; spectacle that signifies *because of* the distanciation and displacement between the event and those who are its spectators. (1994: 360)

It is as though the alienation strategies at play in von Trier's film construct a space in which to explore the history of the othering of black identity and experience in the context of white, western hegemonic formations and that the strategy of estrangement employed in the text helps to underscore the need for this to be performed *because of* the apparent impossibility of its proper articulation within dominant systems of representational practice. To cite Bhabha again, it is as though the film can be read as

> staging the past as *symbol*, myth, memory, history, the ancestral – but a past whose iterative *value as a sign* reinscribes the 'lessons of the past' into the very textuality of the present that determines both the identification with, and the interrogation of, modernity: what is the 'we' that defines the prerogative of my present? (1994: 363)

It is a risky strategy for von Trier, who cannot escape the fact of his own whiteness as a director and whose approach to such a strategy has rightfully been criticised in the press as heavy-handed and ripe for misinterpretation. Nevertheless, as a strategy, it does wield an important political message, as Harsin suggests:

> Von Trier is using extremely exaggerated irony in order to make a larger point about the dangers and hardships 'free' African-Americans faced in the society at large. Here he intervenes in the conservative view that African-Americans just need to exercise the freedom that was granted them in the Fourteenth Amendment. Likewise, he interrupts the liberal view that all African-Americans need is polite recognition, civil rights, and the legal franchise ... The film's biggest problem is not that it is racist but that it does not go beyond alienation. The audience is left to choose between the perspectives of the self-hating, frustrated liberal social worker, the accommodating African-American survivalist, or the conservative gangster-social Darwinist. Like many fashionable contemporary philosophies and stories, *Manderlay* depicts the complexity of the problem and leaves solutions for the audience to debate. (2006)

The familiar spectacle of von Trier as provocateur is to be detected here once again. The 'U-S-A – Land of Opportunities' trilogy in the making is deeply inflected with signifiers of irony and postmodern play with what might be otherwise contrived as properly political issues. The enunciative position of both films in this partially-completed trilogy positions the spectator as god-like: the sparse set designs and the lack of solid doors and walls mean that all characters are perpetually on show and open to observation throughout each film; in addition, the camera-work frequently swoops down from 'on high', extending the sense of the all-seeing and all-powerful gaze that is spoken by the narrator to the spectator in the audience. As spectators, then, we are aligned with von Trier as director – we are interpellated as though we are in his place. The effect of this is to underscore the question of political and ethical responsibility that cuts through each of the narratives. This marks yet a further shift in von Trier's cinematic posturing: not content with aligning himself with the position of omniscience, he places the audience in the very same position, thereby extrapolating himself from this dynamic and situating himself as a puppeteer. This shift informs the most recent turn in von Trier's work which marks a further stage in the exploration of control and its abdication, as the closing chapter will signal.

CHAPTER NINE

From Provocateur to Puppeteer:
The Five Obstructions, The Boss of It All and the Advance Party

On the occasion of his fiftieth birthday, Lars von Trier issued a 'Statement of Revitality' in which he announced his determination to reschedule his professional activities in order to be able to rediscover his 'original enthusiasm for film'.[1] Setting out a number of intentions to scale back his visibility in relation to the promotion of his films, the statement indicates that he sees his films as taking on a more 'ascetic' quality aimed at his 'core' audience. All of this is cast in terms of von Trier's desire to meet his 'own needs in terms of curiosity and play' and he promises that this will result in the production of more films and their promotion through greater exploration in the quality press rather than through launches at 'prestigious, exotic festivals'. This statement seems to be an abandonment of sorts – it is as though von Trier is attempting to shake off his reputation as the *agent-provocateur* of European cinema and to establish himself as someone who no longer wishes to court controversy in relation to his work. Instead, the message is that he wishes to be taken seriously, to be given room to be the artist he wishes to be and to produce work for a fan-base that appreciates this.

In this context, it is interesting to consider the sidebar of projects associated with von Trier's name during the past few years. Such projects include the collaborative live TV film, *D-Dag* (Lars von Trier, Thomas Vinterberg, Søren Kragh-Jacobsen and Kristian Levring, 2000), his collaborative documentary experiment with Jørgen Leth in *The Five Obstructions* (2003), the realisation of his script in Thomas Vinterberg's *Dear*

Wendy (2005) and, more recently, the establishment of the Advance Party project, a collaborative filmmaking venture organised between von Trier's production company, Zentropa, and Sigma Films based in Scotland. A common theme running across these projects is the idea of game-playing and the exploration of the effects of rules on the production of films. Increasingly, von Trier is committed to constructing the rules by which others are required to deliver rather than imposing them upon himself. The familiar trope of control becomes apparent here and this closing chapter sets out to scrutinise the significance of this for an understanding of the director's work more broadly.

Rules of the Game

As we saw in chapter five, rules have played a central role in the formation of von Trier's *oeuvre*. From the outset, his engagement with cinema has entailed an engagement with the 'language of filmmaking': in the early films made at film school in Denmark and in the 'Europa' trilogy, von Trier pushed received knowledge about the construction of cinema to its limits, exposing the technical and formal constraints associated with cinema as 'art'. Subsequently, from the inception of Dogme 95 onward, von Trier has produced rules for himself and others, articulating new constraints and exploring the effects of limitation on the production of meaningful, affective and effective films. Von Trier describes the effect of this as a form of 'liberation from aesthetics' (Björkman 2003: 215) and he frequently alludes to the importance of playing games as part of his preferred mode of leisure (Bunbury 2003). Indeed, the 'Statement of Revitality' foregrounds the director's desire to play. This is also seen in his most recent development, the 'lookey'. The 'lookey' is described as a 'basic mind game, played with movies as game boards' designed to address film's 'great flaw – it's a one-way media [sic] with a passive audience' (Mitchell 2006).[2]

In the psychoanalytic account, play is a fundamental means of grappling with unconscious anxieties and fantasies, allowing the subject to explore them in the 'safe' domain of 'make-believe', externalising that which is harmful and enabling the subject to explore the terrain of unconscious desires as a consequence. Much has been written on the propensity of cinema in particular to provide space for the spectator to explore unconscious mechanisms of desire and identification and this is a well-known tenet of screen theory (see Mulvey 1975; Neale 1983, amongst others). However, in von Trier's meta-cinematic work, it becomes clear that the process of creativity is also about exploring just such anxieties and fantasies, and he makes this clear through his emphasis on the importance of play. While at one level, this is consistent with a mode of postmodern irony and self-scrutiny, it is also contingent on the ways in which contemporary culture deploys its media to explore emotional life and its resonance for the fragmented subject. Arguably, von Trier's meta-cinematic foregrounding of play as central to the production of his films signals something about creativity and its therapeutic symbolism.

The importance of cinema as a game for von Trier is also significant in understanding his pursuit of authenticity through the display of artifice. At various stages throughout his career to date, von Trier has courted controversy and sensation through a frequently elaborate masquerade of rather contrived expressions of opinion – he is the master of the 'sound bite' and has used this to his advantage in the promotion of his work. Nevertheless, his recent choices have been anchored in a concrete desire to be in control of what he does. Control for him appears to be the key to attaining a sense of authenticity around the work he produces. As he comments in an interview with Stig Björkman,

> When I'm doing something I know I can do – it might be one of several things, filmmaking, for instance – I don't feel frightened. There I'm in control. … I'm scared of things I can't control. But I don't feel the slightest bit anxious about things I know I can control. (2003: 185–6)

For von Trier, then, the dialectic between play and control is fundamental to managing anxiety and to producing his work. In the very contradictions between these apparently exclusive terms, the question of authenticity is what is at stake. This is the theme underpinning von Trier's recent projects and his play with rules and limitations.

In *The Five Obstructions*, for example, von Trier sets down a challenge to Jørgen Leth, a much respected Danish director of some repute and a former mentor to von Trier. The challenge centres on Leth's film, *The Perfect Human*, a film which von Trier purports to have viewed some twenty or so times and one which represents a pinnacle of artistic achievement in his view. Von Trier's challenge to Leth is to meet with him, firstly to view the original film and later to establish 'limitations, commands or prohibitions' to be put in place by von Trier and according to which Leth would 're-make' his film five times. The 'obstructions' imposed by von Trier have as their focus an attempt to undo Leth's pursuit of 'masterful' observations of human nature and to dismantle his approach to filmmaking systematically in the hope of breaking him down. Von Trier presents this as a kind of 'therapy', suggesting that the conceptual game underpinning the documentary might have the effect of opening up access to some mode of authenticity (premised in emotion or primitive sensibilities) which seems impossible in filmmaking that does not work in this dialogical way.

Von Trier's obstructions are also premised on attributes of Leth as a filmmaker. Known for his long, meditative takes, Leth is demonstrably taken aback when the first obstruction requires him to construct the 're-make' from takes no longer than twelve frames in length. The second obstruction in designed to force Leth to 're-make' his film with reference to ethical sensibilities. The third version is made as a cartoon (a form which both directors profess to despise), while the fourth obstruction (invented as a punishment for Leth's misdemeanours) entails the imposition of no rules/obstructions at all. Lastly, von Trier prepares a letter for Leth and has him read it as the voice-over for the final 're-make' of the film, neatly illustrating the problem of where control actually lies in this process of exchange between the two filmmakers and foregrounding questions about where the authentic film lies. (In this regard, it is also interesting to note that the original film is not shown in its entirety during the course of *The Five Obstructions*. Nor are any of the 're-made' versions.)

Fig. 33 Scenes of intense dialogue between Lars von Trier and Jørgen Leth make up a substantial part of *The Five Obstructions*

Much of *The Five Obstructions* consists of images of von Trier and Leth in dialogue or in reflection on the process they have undertaken. In this regard, the film does present itself as a form of therapeutic encounter. Nevertheless, it is not clear where the power relation lies and the film confuses this as it unfurls. While, on the surface, von Trier appears to be in control, issuing the obstructions and formulating the challenges, Leth resists his adversary's attempt to re-shape his working methods and ultimately comes off more successfully at the end of the film. As Leth has commented, in his admission toward the end of the film that 'it is always the attacker who is exposed', von Trier signals the fact that it is Leth who seems to end up victorious. Moreover, the struggle did not result in Leth having a break-down as von Trier appears to have hoped – there is no exposure of the emotional 'inner scream' at the heart of Leth's film-making practice (Brooks 2003).

The Five Obstructions is a 'meta-text', one that deals with the process of film-making and exposes this process through its own rendering. Like the Dogme 95 project, it posits filmmaking as a game of sorts, as something that can be played out with reference to a set of rules, but in which the element of chance is always at play. This is central to von Trier's conception of rules and games as a route to the essence of authenticity. It is as though his work suggests that the imposition of rules will always elicit interpretations of the rules that, in turn, produce originality within their very terms. The exposure to rules encourages play with them and the result is often to be seen as centred in the struggle to make one's mark on the outcome of the rules; it is the struggle for artistic authenticity. In the Dogme movement the films produced by the brethren were not of a kind, but rather premised in the uniqueness of any given director's relation to and interpretation of the rules in place. In *The Five Obstructions*, this theme is revisited with the invention of rules as the premise for the duel that forms the film's narrative focus. The shift in this film is interesting, because it begins to stage the dynamic of the exchange of rules and their monitoring as the space of narrative, as the substance for what 'authentic' filmmaking as 'art' might be about. That the film is structured as a documentary is also important here, signalling the idea of 'truth' and its exploration through the dynamic of the film.

The dialectical relationship between von Trier and Leth in this film is a fundamental one. The meaning of the film as meta-text is produced in the exchange and parrying that takes place between the two directors and what is at stake is the locus of control. This is a fundamentally Oedipal struggle – von Trier appears to be tussling with a father-like mentor for recognition and authority. The inter-generational context of what is to be understood as specifically Danish filmmaking is important in this context too. Is it possible for Lars von Trier, a director whose initiatives are credited with single-handedly ensuring the visibility of Danish cinema in a global context, to impose his initiatives on one of the recognised artists of his homeland and thereby to assert his authority? Is authority essential to the pursuit of authenticity at all? Such are the questions raised in the context and reception of this film. The question of specifically Danish cinema is also an important one in understanding the significance of recent developments in the von Trier project, as the next section suggests.

Transnationalism and Reputation

In a forthcoming piece on the transnational significance of Danish cinema and Danish cinematic initiatives, Mette Hjort suggests that

> Danish film is more than visible today in the global landscape in the form of artistic initiatives, innovative works, star directors, competent actors and self-confident producers with a proven ability to find effective solutions to the well-known obstacles faced by minor cinemas.

This visibility is, in part, due to the extensive critical acclaim and controversy that has surrounded von Trier's work and Hjort indicates the importance of this in her discussion of von Trier's collaborative formulation of the Advance Party initiative that has recently got underway with the production and release of Andrea Arnold's *Red Road* (2006). The Advance Party project is one based in collaboration between von Trier's production company, Zentropa, and the Scottish production company, Sigma Films. Von Trier's role in the project is an enabling one: as Hjort explains, he 'came up with a three-film concept involving first-time feature filmmakers and a set of precise rules'.[3]

Here, then, von Trier steps out of his role as director and into a role as puppet-master. He displaces his play with cinema, moving it beyond the studio and into the realm of production. The basis of such a move is discernible in the idea underpinning his work on *The Five Obstructions*, but in the context of the Advance Party initiative, von Trier's role is demonstrably 'hands-off'. Instead, as Hjort argues, 'Advance Party is about making a gift of reputation to first-time feature-length filmmakers whose talents may not suffice to make them visible within the highly competitive world of international filmmaking'.

In making a 'gift of reputation', von Trier is setting himself apart from the new generation of filmmakers and constructing himself as an avuncular figure, one who is in a position to support and help to direct the future of cinema. It is interesting, in this context, that he has chosen to do this in relation to transnational cinematic initiatives. It underscores the importance he invests in the capacity of cinema to transcend national boundaries in the context of the global age and to provide an alternative to the mainstream commercial films that have dominated historically. Von Trier's commitment to the collaborative value of what Hjort calls 'meta-culture' (the use of rules to promote collaboration) must be read in terms of the on-going struggle for non-commercial cinema to find a means of sustaining itself in the face of the immense wealth of the Hollywood studio machines and their capacity to dominate the global market. In this setting, von Trier's reputation becomes highly saleable and it carries considerable cultural capital. Its visibility in the articulation of transnational projects such as the Advance Party and the subsequent success of its first production, *Red Road*, which garnered the Special Jury Prize at the 2006 Cannes Film Festival, is clear cut. However, it is also important to note that von Trier has not succumbed to the lure of the big-budget studios himself, as he so easily might have done. This signals the importance of his affinity with the small-scale cinema industry he has worked to sustain in Denmark, and it also shores up some of the overtly political criticisms he has made in relation to the vacuity of contemporary mainstream films. This demonstrates effectively Hjort's view that the Advance Party constitutes an experiment that is

> designed to produce visibility and success through leveraging, and to translate such success into a solid political enthusiasm for film, into increased support, into the kind of upbeat enthusiasm that can help to galvanise a milieu into producing a critical mass of works that achieve global attention, not because they reactively or mimetically conform to the norms of globalising transnationalism, but because they reveal the periphery to be the very locus of innovation.

Von Trier's reputation as an innovator thus becomes secured alongside a newly developing reputation as a nurturer of cinematic futures. This development in construction of his international media image helps to lend him *gravitas*, which, in turn, enables him to articulate his desire to 'revitalise' by seemingly diminishing the self-conscious mediatisation of his work by adopting a more 'ascetic' turn. Of what does such a turn consist? And how does such a turn impact on our reading of von Trier and his status as an *auteur*?

The Boss of It All: Irony and Self-Reflexivity

The first film to emerge as a manifestation of von Trier's 'revitalisation' is *Direktøren for det hele* (*The Boss of It All*, 2006), a comedy made with reference to the Dogme rules in which von Trier takes as his focus the everyday matter of life in a small Danish IT company and the efforts of the company director to maintain congenial relationships with his employees which produces the farcical situation around which the narrative coheres. Ravn (Peter Gantzler), the company director, hires Kristoffer (Jens Albinus) to play the part of the fictitious boss he invented in order to obscure his responsibility for unpopular decisions affecting the livelihood of his employees. Kristoffer is initially expected to play the role of the absent boss only as part of negotiations with an Icelandic tycoon for the purchase of the company, but events unfold which implicate him in a broader spectrum of relationships with the people who work at the company and this provides the focus of the film's scrutiny of deceit, 'actorliness', and the banality of office politics and personalities. The comedy centres on the specificity of office life and is nuanced with specific reference to the character of Danish life and the historical relationship of Denmark with Iceland. While ostensibly grounded in the specificity of Danish everyday life (the cast consists of several well-known Danish actors), the film also taps into the global appeal of comedy based on the day-to-day experience the working environment seen in television comedies such as *The Office* (BBC, 2001–03).

In the publicity surrounding the release of this film, von Trier continues to foreground rules, the question of control and game play. The film is shot according to the principles of 'Automavision', a technique implemented via a computer affecting the framing of every image in the film. Von Trier explains:

> For a long time, my films have been hand-held. That has to do with the fact that I am a control freak and that no one can master framing or images completely. It was better to skip framing altogether and go for a hand-held 'pointing' camera. With Automavision, the technique was that I would frame the picture first and then we would push a button on the computer. That would give us a lot of randomised offsets. I was not in control, the computer was in control. (McNab 2006)

Here we see a playful acknowledgement of the kind of control for which von Trier has become infamous. The construction of 'Automavision' is clearly ironic, as the control is always in the hands of the director who makes decisions about which images to include and exclude in the final cut. Von Trier's playful allusions here are reminiscent of the idea of 'automatic writing' at the heart of the Surrealist project, where the idea was that authors would attempt to access their deepest unconscious motivations and fantasies in the process of writing. Akin to the idea of 'channelling', automatism suggests an abdication of responsibility and an approach that foregrounds a desire for knowledge of the interiority of the self.

In the case of 'Automavision', then, it is as though von Trier is once again tinkering with filmmaking techniques in order to comment on perceptions of his approach to his work. The knowing and ironic tone with which he foregrounds discussion of this new 'technique' undercuts the assumption that his status as a 'control freak' is anything other than a media construct. The question of control emerges throughout this film in the context of self-reflexivity. The opening voice-over by von Trier in *The Boss of It All* suggests that the film is 'a harmless comedy' and the film frequently reverts back to the voice-over as a reminder of the fact that the film is being constructed for the viewers' entertainment. The sardonic commentary by von Trier is accompanied by shots of him wielding a camera seen in the reflective surface of office windows, thereby connoting clearly notions of self-reflexivity and highlighting his control of what is being depicted. In this respect, the film's title is also instructive: it allows for a reading of the film based on von Trier's role as a director and co-owner of the film's production company, Zentropa, and foregrounds once again the question of the *auteur* as a god-like figure, shaping the cinematic world in which he operates.

The Boss of It All can thus be read as a 'technology of the self' for von Trier. Foucault (1986) suggests that the history of how an individual acts upon himself can be seen as 'a technology of the self'. That is, a technology of the self involves the engagement with and monitoring of the relationship between the self and the externalised versions of the self that help to construct an image of who we are. In other words, a technology of the self provides a useful means of understanding the ways in which the self (and its images) are constituted. *The Boss of It All* functions as a kind of meditation on these processes, foregrounding the public persona of von Trier as a playful and controlling personality and sending up the idea of 'control'. In the context of von Trier's statement of 'revitalisation', this is meaningful as it points to the discursive failures to grapple with who the director is and for what it is that he stands. The centrality of artifice to cinema is at the heart of this dynamic, drawing attention to the process of staging involved not just at the level of the production of the film text but also in terms of the production of the *auteur* as a figure.

Peter Schepelern has commented on von Trier's knowing self-construction as an *auteur*:

> The whole of Trier's work and career could be seen as a prototype auteurist initiative. Not only is there originality and coherence in his work made entirely according to his own whims, his work is also ... designed, by himself, to be the *oeuvre* of an auteur. One could say that Lars Trier's project was not primarily to make films, but to construct Lars von Trier, the auteur filmmaker. He is not an accidental auteurist but a very deliberate one. (2005: 111)

Schepelern usefully highlights in this article the ways in which von Trier's work constitutes a self-conscious formulation of authorship built around themes such as sexual perversity, suffering and martyrdom, idealism, allegories of the past and (self-)punishment. Strains of the intentionality of von Trier's project are also seen in his working patterns around the roles of writing, producing, filming, directing and editing. In addition, as we have seen, von Trier has established both his own film production company and Filmbyen ('Film City'), a dedicated cinema-focused location built to house a number of production facilities and designed to promote the kind of collaboration and cross-fertilisation identified in Hjort's work, discussed above.

What is at stake here for von Trier is the architecture of his identity. The apparent artifice of his methods, and his playful exposure of the way his self-constructed 'reputation' is shot through with the artifice of its own staging, is indicative of an artist whose project is formulated as a mode of working through, an effort to attain some sense of authenticity through the very public exploration of his innermost motivations. For Schepelern, this is linked to the revelations made by his mother on her death-bed, relating to her wilful conception of her son with a man other than her husband in an attempt to produce a more 'artistic' sensibility in him. Schepelern comments that

> Trier, the film artist, is not only his own deliberate construction, but also a reconstruction as it were in the sense that Trier, the person, is also a project realised by his mother, Inger Høst (1915–89) ... Trier was a kind of artistic construction, a genetic project constructed by his ambitious mother. (2005: 123–4).

While this reading returns to a mode of *auteur* theory in which the biography of the individual is privileged, it is interesting to note the way in which the actions of his mother may have impacted on von Trier's unconscious formulation of his technology of the self. However, as recent developments in *auteur* theory suggest, the sign of the *auteur* depends as much for its meaning on the context of reception as on the manoeuvring of the individual concerned. In this respect, it is important to consider the significance of the role of the media more broadly in formulating the notion of what the sign of 'von Trier' connotes in terms of authorship.

As this volume has signalled a number of times, a great many critics foreground von Trier's staging of game play and the manipulation of rules as central to the responses they formulate in relation to his work. The critical readings of his work are often made through just such a lens, frequently indicating the apparently 'postmodern' sensibility of a director who likes to 'toy' as much with the medium as with his audiences.

The 'postmodern' label is an interesting one in relation to Lars von Trier. Whilst at one level, it is clear that knowing posturing and ironic self-referencing and promotion are integral to the construction of himself as an *auteur*, there is not really an attendant sense that the work is empty of meaning or cultural and ideological significance. On the contrary, much of von Trier's work grapples with often complex ideological ideas and frequently sets out the terrain of cultural responsibility in terms that foreground the role of the media in the contemporary setting. While certain elements of von Trier's work (perhaps, most notably, the Dogme 95 project) can be read directly as expressions of postmodernism, his *oeuvre* as a whole seems more modernist in style. The apparently 'overstated' artifice of von Trier's work indexes the difficulty of sustaining a sense of 'authenticity' – by elaborately 'staging' the mechanisms at play, von Trier exposes their pitfalls. This can be read as a rather modernist trait.

In her discussion of questions of authenticity in relation to modernism and architecture, Hilde Heynen suggests that

> authenticity is an important category in cultural debates, and has emerged in parallel with the notion of 'modernity'. 'Authenticity' refers to the idea that something is 'real' or 'true', that its outer appearance is in correspondence with its inner being, in contrast to things that are 'fake' or 'false' or 'dissimu-

lating'. Although the term thus seems to have a rather unequivocal meaning, its usage evokes quite some paradoxes. (2006: 287)

In the case of von Trier, the deployment of artifice and dissimulation is most frequently seen at the level of the performative. It is part of the *mise-en-scène* of his authorship. The chief concern of this project of authorship, however, seems more concerned with getting to grips with the increasing importance of locating spaces of authenticity in the postmodern context. In a world where 'real' events such as those of 9/11 in the US are discussed with reference to Hollywood films, and where 'reality' television and its elaborate staging occupy most of the mainstream media on a daily basis, raising issues of social and cultural responsibility and the authenticity of experience, von Trier's work signals the importance of art as a testing ground for what 'authenticity' might still mean. The paradox of the postmodern context of his work informs the performativity at work in his films and in his public commentary on them. The staging of artifice, however, has as its aim a fascination with the possibility of authenticity, and it is this paradoxical relationship that marks the *auteur* status of Lars von Trier.

APPENDIX: STATEMENTS AND MANIFESTOS

MANIFESTO 1 (released to accompany *The Element of Crime*)

Everything seems to be alright: filmmakers are in an unsullied relationship with their products, possibly a relationship with a hint of routine, but, nonetheless, a good and solid relationship, where everyday problems fill the time more than adequately, so that *they alone* form the content! In other words, an ideal marriage that not even the neighbours could be upset by: no noisy quarrels in the middle of the night ... no half-naked compromising episodes in the stairwells, but a union between both parties: the filmmaker and his 'film-wife', to everyone's satisfaction ... at peace with themselves ... but anyway ... We can all tell when The Great Inertia has arrived!

How has film's previously so stormy marriage shrivelled up into a marriage of convenience? What's happened to these old men? What has corrupted these old masters of sexuality? The answer is simple. Misguided coquetry, a great fear of being uncovered (what does it matter if your libido fades when your wife has already turned her back on you?) ... have made them betray the thing that once gave this relationship its sense of vitality: *Fascination*!

The filmmakers are the only ones to blame for this dull routine. Despotically, they have never given their beloved the chance to grow and develop in their love ... out of pride they have refused to see the miracle in her eyes … and have thereby crushed her … and themselves.

These hardened old men must die! We will no longer be satisfied with 'well-meaning films with a humanist message', we want more – of the real thing, fascination, experience – childish and pure, like all real art. We want to get back to the time when love between filmmaker and film was young, when you could see the joy of creation in every frame of a film!

We are no longer satisfied with surrogates. We want to see religion on the screen. We want to see 'film-lovers' sparkling with life: improbable, stupid, stubborn, ecstatic, repulsive, monstrous and *not* things that have been tamed or castrated by a moralistic, bitter old filmmaker, a dull puritan who praises the intellect-crushing virtues of niceness.

We want to see heterosexual films, made for, about and by men. We want visibility!

3 May 1984

MANIFESTO 2 (released to accompany *Epidemic*)

Everything seems fine. Young men are living in stable relationships with a new generation of films. The birth-control methods which are assumed to have contained the epidemic have only served to make birth-control more effective: no unexpected creations, no illegitimate children – the genes are intact. These young men's relationships resemble the endless stream of Grand Balls in a bygone age. There are also those who live together in rooms with no furniture. But their love is growth without soul, replication without any bite. Their 'wildness' lacks discipline and their 'discipline' lacks wildness.

LONG LIVE THE BAGATELLE!

The bagatelle is humble and all-encompassing. It reveals creativity without making a secret of eternity. Its frame is limited but magnanimous, and therefore leaves space for life. EPIDEMIC manifests itself in a well-grounded and serious relationship with these young men, as a bagatelle – because among bagatelles, the masterpieces are easy to count.

17 May 1987

MANIFESTO 3 (released to accompany *Europa*)

I confess!

Everything seems fine: the film director Lars von Trier is a scientist and an artist and a human being. Yet all the same I say that I am a human being AND an artist, AND a film director.

I am crying as I write this, because I have been so arrogant in my attitude: who am I to think that I can master anything and show people the right path? Who am I to think that I can scornfully dismiss other people's life and work? My shame keeps getting worse, because my apology – that I was seduced by the pride of science – falls to the ground like a lie! Certainly it's true that I have tried to intoxicate myself in a cloud of sophistries about the goals of art and the artist's duties, that I have worked out ingenious theories about the anatomy and nature of film, yet – and I am admitting this quite openly – I have never succeeded in suppressing my inner passions with this feeble veil of mist: MY FLESHLY DESIRES!!

Our relationship to film can be described in so many ways, and is explained in myriad different ways: We have to make films with a pedagogical purpose, we can desire to use film as a ship that can carry us off on a voyage of discovery to unknown lands, or we can claim that we want to use film to influence our audience and get it to laugh or cry – and pay. All this can sound perfectly OK, but I still don't think much of it.

There is only ONE excuse for suffering and making other people suffer the hell that the genesis of a film involves: the gratification of the fleshly desires that arise in a fraction of a second, when the cinema's loudspeakers and projector, in tandem, and inexplicably, allow the illusion of movement and light to find their way like an electron leaving its path and thereby generating the light needed to create ONE SINGLE THING: a miraculous blast of LIFE! THIS is the only reward a filmmaker gets, the only thing he hopes and longs for. This physical experience when the magic of film takes place and works its way through the body to a trembling ejaculation... NOTHING ELSE! There, now it's written down, which feels good. So forget all the excuses: 'childish fascination' and 'all-encompassing humility', because this is my confession, in black and white: LARS VON TRIER, THE TRUE ONANIST OF THE SILVER SCREEN.

And yet, in *Europa*, the third part of the trilogy, there isn't the least trace of derivative manoeuvring. At last, purity and clarity are achieved! Here there is nothing to hide reality under a suffocating layer of 'art' ... no trick is too mean, no technique too tawdry, no effect too tasteless.

JUST GIVE ME ONE SINGLE TEAR OR ONE SINGLE DROP OF SWEAT AND I WOULD WILLINGLY EXCHANGE IT FOR ALL THE 'ART' IN THE WORLD.

At last. May God alone judge me for my alchemical attempts to create life from celluloid. But one thing is certain: life outside the cinema can never find its equal, because it is His creation, and therefore divine.

29 December 1990

DOGME 95 MANIFESTO AND THE VOW OF CHASTITY

DOGME 95
…is a collective of film directors founded in Copenhagen in spring 1995.

DOGME 95 has the expressed goal of countering 'certain tendencies' in the cinema today.

DOGME 95 is a rescue action!

In 1960 enough was enough! The movie was dead and called for resurrection. The goal was correct but the means were not! The new wave proved to be a ripple that washed ashore and turned to muck.

Slogans of individualism and freedom created works for a while, but no changes. The wave was up for grabs, like the directors themselves. The wave was never stronger than the men behind it. The anti-bourgeois cinema itself became bourgeois, because the foundations upon which its theories were based was the bourgeois perception of art. The auteur concept was bourgeois romanticism from the very start and thereby … false!

To DOGME 95 cinema is not individual.

Today a technological storm is raging, the result of which will be the ultimate democratisation of the cinema. For the first time, anyone can make movies. But the more accessible the media becomes, the more important the avant-garde. It is no accident that the phrase 'avant-garde' has military connotations. Discipline is the answer … we must put our films into uniform, because the individual film will be decadent by definition!

DOGME 95 counters the individual film by the principle of presenting an indisputable set of rules known as THE VOW OF CHASTITY.

In 1960 enough was enough! The movie had been cosmeticised to death, they said; yet since then the use of cosmetics has exploded.

The 'supreme' task of the decadent filmmakers is to fool the audience. Is that what we are so proud of? Is that what the '100 years' have brought us? Illusions via which emotions can be communicated? ... By the individual artist's free choice of trickery?

Predictability (dramaturgy) has become the golden calf around which we dance. Having the characters' inner lives justify the plot is too complicated, and not 'high art'. As never before, the superficial action and the superficial movie are receiving all the praise.

The result is barren. An illusion of pathos and an illusion of love.

To DOGME 95 the movie is not illusion!

Today a technological storm is raging of which the result is the elevation of cosmetics to God. By using new technology anyone at any time can wash the last grains of truth away in the deadly embrace of sensation. The illusions are everything the movie can hide behind.

DOGME 95 counters the film of illusion by the presentation of an indisputable set of rules known as THE VOW OF CHASTITY.

13 March 1995

THE VOW OF CHASTITY[1]

'I swear to submit to the following set of rules drawn up and confirmed by DOGME 95:

1. Shooting must be done on location. Props and sets must not be brought in (if a particular prop is necessary for the story, a location must be chosen where this prop is to be found).
2. The sound must never be produced apart from the images or vice versa. (Music must not be used unless it occurs where the scene is being shot).
3. The camera must be hand-held. Any movement or immobility attainable in the hand is permitted. (The film must not take place where the camera is standing; shooting must take place where the film takes place).
4. The film must be in colour. Special lighting is not acceptable. (If there is too little light for exposure the scene must be cut or a single lamp be attached to the camera).
5. Optical work and filters are forbidden.
6. The film must not contain superficial action. (Murders, weapons, etc. must not occur.)
7. Temporal and geographical alienation are forbidden. (That is to say that the film takes place here and now.)

8. Genre movies are not acceptable.
9. The film format must be Academy 35mm.
10. The director must not be credited.

Furthermore I swear as a director to refrain from personal taste! I am no longer an artist. I swear to refrain from creating a 'work', as I regard the instant as more important than the whole. My supreme goal is to force the truth out of my characters and settings. I swear to do so by all the means available and at the cost of any good taste and any aesthetic considerations.

Thus I make my VOW OF CHASTITY.'

13 March 1995

On behalf of DOGME 95

Lars von Trier
Thomas Vinterberg

SELMA'S MANIFESTO (released to accompany *Dancer in the Dark*)

Selma comes from the east. She loves musicals. Her life is hard, but she can survive because she has a secret. When things get too much to bear she can pretend that she is in a musical ... just for a minute or two. All the *joy* that life can't give her is there. Joy isn't living ... joy is there to make it bearable for us to live.

Selma loves *The Sound of Music* and the other big song-and-dance films. And now she's got the chance to play the lead in an amateur version of *The Sound of Music* ... At the same time she is about to fulfil her life's greatest goal. It looks like dream and reality are going to melt together for Selma.

So, popular music and the famous musicals are what fill the spaces in her brain. But she isn't just a dreamer! She *is someone who loves all of life!* She can feel intensely about the miracles that every corner of her (fairly grim) life offers. And she can see all the details ... every single one. Strange things that only she can see or hear. She is a genuine watcher ... with a photographic memory. And it is this double-sided nature that makes her an artist: her love and enthusiasm for the artificial world of music, song and dance, and her keen fascination for the real world ... her humanity. Her art consists of the musical interludes that she takes refuge in when she needs to ... fragments of Selma's own musical ... like no other musical ... it's a collision of splinters of melodies, folk songs, noises, instruments, texts and dances that she has experienced in the cinema and in real life, using the components that she – because of her gift – can find there.

This isn't pure escapism! It's much, much more ... it's art! It stems from a genuine inner need to play with life and incorporate it into her own private world.

A situation might be incredibly painful, but it can always provide the starting point for even a tiny manifestation of Selma's art. It can be incorporated into the little world that she can control.

About the film

In order to tell Selma's story, the film must be able to give concrete form to her world. All the scenes that don't contain her musical-fantasies must be as realistic as possible as far as acting, décor and so on are concerned, because the scenes from Selma's daily life are the models for what she adds to her musical numbers ... and these have to be true to life. What she sees at the cinema is flawless ... painless ... in other words, entirely at odds with real life ... where it is the flaws and the pain that make it shine. The intimation of humanity ... of nature ... of life!

So the events that form part of the story will partly be expressed by the finest, most beautiful music, recorded according to unambiguous methods – and mixed with all the muddles and mistakes that reality can contribute.

This is also the principal for Selma's musical. Punk is the word I would use to underline the whole thing: as I see it, punk is a collision between tradition and nature. It isn't destructive ... it isn't solemn, because it's trying to get back to basics ... by confronting the system with a modern, more honest view of life ... and forcing life into something that has become stale and enclosed ... using violent means! This is probably the only violence Selma participates in?

The Music

The musical elements that include instruments and melodies come from the musicals that she loves. They might be fragments that are incorporated into different contexts ... or instrumental sounds that are used in unusual ways. Selma loves the cheapest musical effects: riffs and other clichés ... and she uses them in ways that have nothing whatever to do with good taste ... but these elements are mixed with the sounds of life and through this she becomes far from banal. She loves the simple sounds of living expression ... hands, feet, voices, and so on ... (the sighs caused by hard work?) ... the noise from machines and other mechanical things ... the sounds of nature ... and above all the little sounds caused by chance ... the creak of a floor when a floorboard develops a defect. Her music extols dream on the one hand, life on the other. She uses her own daily life to create music. Mostly to use this positively ... but occasionally to sing out her pain ... It's important that the artificial is allowed to remain and sound articificial ... we have to be aware of where things come from ... the clichés from musicals ... and even more important: the sounds from the real world ... they should never be 'refined' ... the closer to reality the better ... we prefer a rhythm created by hand using a rattling window than a smpled version of the same thing ... if sampling is to be used here, then it must take place on the artificial side. The music should sway from one side to the other ... let there be occasions when only natural noises reign (stomp).

In any case, there will be an explosion of feelings and above all a celebration of joy that fantasy can bring. The sounds of reality do not only come from machines and daily routine ... they also come from creative people like Selma who can use anything and everything in every scene as an instrument! This is an area where Selma is superior. She can weave gold from mud. She can hear music in noise ... and when she shows it to us ... we can also hear ... that the noise contains life and it is as beautiful as any traditional, celebrated masterpiece from the stage. Both sides are there ... alike and not alike.

The Dancing

The principle is the same: Selma exploits and loves grand effects: poses, homogeneity ... glamour ... but she combines all this with real people... with real movements and faults. With the chaos of life. With acting. Efficiency and inefficiency. Her use of effects is a challenge to good taste ... and her consideration of life vicissitudes is immense. Every arena is utilised. She can see possibilities in every unexpected thing. The dancers can use whatever they like in their dance and their music. She has worked in the factory for a long time and takes pleasure in the slightest human gesture. She knows what a body can do ... when it does its best to attain perfection in dance, like in the big films, and she knows how the joy and pain of everyday life can be expressed in movement. Selma dances like a child ... for herself ... in ecstasy ... it might look terrible ... but suddenly, in a fraction of a second, the whole room is in harmony ... and she is its queen.

The dance has no façade ... it faces every direction ... it has no boundaries ... a fingertip touching a surface is dance! (If we should need explanations or preparations for a shift from reality ... we can show it in the non-musical episodes.)

The Songs

The songs from the musicals provide the bass ... and they've got rhythm! They're primitive ... they're Selma's naïve way of telling a story through a song ... but sometimes her fascination with sounds, rhythms, words and rhymes fights through ... then she starts to play with it and forgets everything. The songs are Selma's dialogue with herself ... even if sometimes they are put in other characters' mouths, who express her words, her doubts, fears, joys and so on. They are naïve songs, with all the well-used words from popular music ... but often things don't work for her ... and certain deeper truths seep out ... When that happens Selma is quick to turn it all into a game again

... playing with words ... or fragments of words ... like a child! ... sheer astonishment at letting sounds come out of her mouth!

And remember she enjoys mimicry ... she can sound like a machine or a violin. A mistake can suddenly also be used as an effect ... a mispronounced word can gain its own meaning when thirty people pronounce it the same way!

The Décor

Super-realism! Neither more nor less! No one should be able to say that this is a film that wasn't made on location ... and that these places have never been documented by a camera before. Everything in these places and that is used in dance and music ... must be there *because of the story or the location or the characters*. We are working against the principle of musicals entirely here ... there are NOT suddenly ten identical things to use in a dance. The same applies to costume ... there shouldn't be a troupe of dancers wearing the same clothes. The costumes are also an expression of realism, and they say something about the person wearing them.

And, as usual, it's the sudden gaps in logic that make things credible and alive! That make everything human! And this all has its origin in Selma ... She is the person seeing and speaking!

2000

STATEMENT OF REVITALITY (released on Lars von Trier's fiftieth birthday)

In conjunction with the departure of Vibeke Windeløv, who has been my producer for ten years, and the arrival of Meta Louise Foldager in her place, I intend to reschedule my professional activities in order to rediscover my original enthusiasm for film.

Over the last few years I have felt increasingly burdened by barren habits and expectations (my own and other people's) and I feel the urge to tidy up.

In regards to product development this will mean more time on freer terms; i.e. projects will be allowed to undergo true development and not merely be required to meet preconceived demands. This is partly to liberate me from routine, and in particular from scriptual structures inherited from film to film.

I will aim to reduce the scope of my productions in regards to funding, technology, the size of the crew, and particularly casting, but I should like to expand the time spent shooting them.

I want to launch my products on a scale which matches the more ascetic nature of the films, and aimed at my core audience: i.e. my films will be promoted considerably less glamorously than at present, which also means without World Premieres at prestigious, exotic festivals.

With regard to PR, my intention is for a heavy reduction in quantity, compensated for by more thorough exploration in the quality press.

In short, in my fiftieth year I feel I have earned the privilege of narrowing down. I hope that this attempt at personal revitalisation will bear fruit, enabling me to meet my own needs in terms of curiosity and play, and to contribute with more films.

11 February 2006

THE LOOKEY

1. Lookey is a mind-game, played with movies as a board.
2. A 'Lookey' is a visual element out of context that is added to a movie.
3. A feature film includes between five and seven Lookeys.
4. All Lookeys in a movie can be decoded by a system that is unique for the movie. To decipher the system is part of the challenge.
5. The superior observer is awarded.

6 December 2006

NOTES

1   Bowie's music is used on the soundtracks for *Breaking the Waves* and *Dogville*.

2   For an explanation of the links between German Expressionism and the *film noir* movement that emerged from Hollywood in the post-war period, see Krutnik 1991; Silver & Ursini 1999; Dickos 2002.

3   See, for example, the films of G. W. Pabst. *The Joyless Street* (1925) explicitly focuses on the downfall of middle-class families who embody bourgeois cultural values and is illustrative of the cultural shifts taking place in this period.

4   Good examples of the way in which this nightmarish sensibility was captured on film can be seen in Robert Wiene's *The Cabinet of Dr Caligari* (1920), F. W. Murnau's *Nosferatu* (1922) and Fritz Lang's *Metropolis* (1927).

5   Von Trier's mother had been part of the resistance movement in Denmark publishing illegal periodicals. This led to her name being included on a list of people to be executed and led to her flight to Sweden, where she met Ulf Trier. They returned to Denmark only after Liberation Day in 1945. Stevenson documents this neatly in his account of von Trier's upbringing and early life (2002: 6).

6   Stig Björkman has noted that this film seemed to be 'haunted by cinema history' (1996b: 11), while Gavin Smith describes von Trier as 'constructing a kind of pastiche authoritarian aesthetic out of his oppressive mastery of stylish artifice and defiant art cinema rhetoric' (2000: 22).

7   *Zentropa* is the US title for *Europa*. This title echoes the name of the train company within the film and also provides the name of von Trier's production company (see http://www.zentropa.dk).

8   Hitchcock's interest in the Freudian unconscious and in the formation of the ego is well-documented. For an interesting set of readings of his work in relation to psychoanalysis, see Modleski 1988.

9   Most of von Trier's in-depth interviews have now been collected together (in translation where necessary) in Lumholdt 2003. See also Björkman 2003 for an extended series of interviews between

the editor and the director on the genesis of von Trier's work.

10   This trilogy consists of *Dogville* and *Manderlay* and will be completed with *Wasington*, which is currently in production.

11   See MacKenzie 2003 on the relationship between the Dogme 95 and the future of film manifestos.

12   Key examples include Alfred Hitchcock, John Ford, Jean Vigo and Jean Renoir.

13   The Dogme 95 manifesto is published online at www.dogme95.dk and is reprinted in Stevenson 2002, and Hjort & MacKenzie 2003. It is also reprinted in the appendix at the back of this volume.

14   See, for example, *A Hard Day's Night* (Richard Lester, 1964), *Darling* (John Schlesinger, 1965), *Alfie* (Lewis Gilbert, 1966) and *Blow Up* (Michelangelo Antonioni, 1966).

15   On 6 May 2000 von Trier launched the 'Dogumentary' movement as a follow-up to and a generically-focused reworking of the mechanics of the Dogme 95 Vow of Chastity. The various manifestos and the Dogumentary Vow of Chastity are re-printed in Stevenson 2003.

16   For an interesting discussion of the origins of melodrama, see the work of Thomas Elsaesser (1987) and Christine Gledhill (1987). See also John Mercer and Martin Shingler's (2004) useful introduction to the genre.

17   *The Life and Adventures of Nicholas Nickleby* was adapted for Broadway by Nelle Nugent in 1980 and performed by the Royal Shakespeare Company. The production became very famous as its staging lasted for more than ten hours including intervals and breaks for dinner. The stage version was eventually recorded for television in the UK (Channel 4, 1982).

18   In an interview with Stig Björkman, von Trier explains that he does not have any difficulty with his films being attributed to him, even in the case of *The Idiots*, his film that follows the Dogme 95 manifesto in which the director is famously not supposed to be credited. He claims that credit for a work is an important aspect of the relationship between an artist and the public.

CHAPTER TWO

1   For interesting commentaries on *film noir*'s treatment of masculinity, see Krutnik 1991; Abbott 2002; Chopra-Gant 2006. Many classic examples of *film noir* foreground the ways in which masculinity was seen as undergoing a 'crisis' of sorts after World War II. For example, films such as *Double Indemnity* (Billy Wilder, 1944), *The Big Sleep* (Howard Hawks, 1946), *Out of the Past* (Jacques Tourneur, 1947) and *Kiss Me, Deadly* (Robert Aldrich, 1955) signal the fragility of male desire, uncertainty around masculine roles and psychological states of confusion and duplicity. Many films made in the *film noir* style draw attention to the anxieties associated with the social and political climate and its effect of masculine subjectivity.

2   For further discussion of the alienating effect of this critical distance, see chapters one and eight for their discussion of the work of Bertolt Brecht and his influence on von Trier's style and approach.

3   Questions of inter-textuality and authenticity are often linked to postmodernism and understood in terms of pastiche. I will return to these debates in chapter five.

4   Galt's article provides a very useful analysis of the debt owed by von Trier in the making of *Europa* to these ruin films. It also provides a very useful reading of the relationship between the technical elements of the film and the context of the emergent European Union.

5   Galt provides a very useful analysis of von Trier's use of technical effects, reading the text in relation to work done on superimposition by Marc Vernet. In addition, Galt makes a number of important links between the style of the film, its form and its deployment of historicity. Her reading is particularly useful in terms of its analysis of the configuration of contemporary European politics in relation to this film.

6   See Romney 1992.

7   This further signals the links between von Trier and *la nouvelle vague*.

8   Von Trier specifies hypnosis as a unifying thematic across these films. As Niels Vørsel explains, 'In *The Element of Crime* the hypnosis theme is present as an obvious element, as theatre, make-believe. In *Epidemic* it becomes a real, documented organic expression. And in *Europa* ... the thought/idea was that the audience would be hypnotized' (Björkman 2003: 96).

9   See Laplanche & Pontalis 1988: 111–14 for a detailed overview of the concept of deferred action in psychoanalysis. The importance of this concept in relation to von Trier's work will be further explored in the next chapter.

10   For a detailed overview of the contexts of reception and distribution of these films, see Stevenson 2002.

CHAPTER THREE

1   For detailed discussion of von Trier's childhood and upbringing, see Stevenson, 2002: 6-32.

2   See Hjort & Bondebjerg 2001. The cultural and political context of the work done under the umbrella of Dogme 95 is explored further in chapter five.

3   Whilst at film school, von Trier was a member of the Danish Youth Communist Party, but this interest was not one that found its way into the substance of his work. Rather, as von Trier himself has suggested, the radical liberalism of his family life made the step into membership of the party rather inevitable and politics came to be something that von Trier toyed with as a way of relating to and rebelling against his parents.

4   In many ways, *Epidemic* is a forerunner of the Dogme 95 project. It contains the seeds of many of the ideas sketched out in the Dogme manifesto including the prescription for hand-held camera work and an overt commentary on status of film as art as opposed to entertainment. See chapter five for a full discussion of the motivations of the Dogme project.

5   The individual is most certainly inscribed as masculine in this trilogy of films. Women exist in these narratives only as objects of lust or agents of betrayal. This, of course, is in line with the trilogy's homage to *film noir* but it also helps to illuminate the gendered inscription of ethics as this chapter will go on to discuss.

6   There are parallels here with the work of the 'apparatus theorists' in cinema which draws explicitly on the post-Marxist position of Althusser and suggests that cinema is by its nature ideological because its mechanics of representation are inherently ideological. See Mulvey 1975; Metz 1981; Baudry 1985.

7   Von Trier has stated that he is 'extremely afraid to get into a cinema. I don't want to be seduced. It's like that with hypnosis, asking you to relax – then when it has you in its grip, when you don't have any resistance, it can open things up in you' (Romney 1992: 85).

8   Von Trier comments that 'the railway track looks a lot like a reel of film' (Björkman 2003: 129).

9   See, for example, Elsaesser 2001; Kaplan 2001; Radstone 2001; Turim 2001; Bainbridge *et al.* 2004a and 2004b.

10   The 'Gold Heart' trilogy of films will be discussed further in chapters five, six and seven.

11   Antigone is an important figure in Greek mythology. She was the daughter of Oedipus and Jocasta and accompanied Oedipus during his period of exile on discovering that Jocasta, the mother of his children, was also his own mother. In order to go into exile, Oedipus had to step down as King of Thebes and he charged his sons, Eteocles and Polyneices, with control of the kingdom, demanding that they alternate the role of leader between them. When Oedipus died, Antigone returned to Thebes and fell in love the Haemon, the son of Creon. After a year of reigning over Thebes, Eteocles refused to stand down and Polyneices became very angry, attacking Thebes with his supporters. Both brothers died in battle, and Creon ascended to the throne. He declared that Polyneices should not be entitled to burial but should rather be left to be eaten by birds and animals as a symbol of the shame of taking arms against one's countrymen. He threatened anyone who tried to bury his body with certain death. Antigone was horrified and defied Creon in order to give her brother the burial she thought he merited. Creon followed up on his word and, despite her betrothal to his son, ordered that Antigone should be walled up alive inside a cave and left to die. Under protest from the soothsayer, Tiresias, and his son, Haemon, Creon decided that his actions had been too harsh. He went to the cave inside which Antigone was imprisoned only to find that she had hanged herself rather than live out the pain of being buried alive. When Haemon arrived at the cave, he was so distraught that he killed himself. Subsequently, Creon's wife, Eurydice, would also take her own life when she heard what had happened to her son. The myth of Antigone has long symbolised philosophical debates around ethical principles and Irigaray's work brings this into focus with particular emphasis on the gendered subjectivities at stake in the tale.

12   This is, of course, highly evocative of the Antigone myth.

13   The phenomenology of such a state is arguably mirrored in the structure of trauma, according to the psychoanalytic account. Freud conjectures that the psychological experience of trauma is structured through two stages or moments: the first (originary) moment of trauma is the moment at which

the trauma itself takes place. At this point, however, the psyche does not recognise the traumatic impact of the causative event, relying on the defence mechanisms of repression and disavowal in order to protect the ego from the effects of the traumatic incident. However, at a later moment, the psychological trauma is evoked by the experience of a trigger moment or event (which sets in motion a *nachträglich*, or deferred, response) in which the overwhelming tide of realisation that trauma has been undergone becomes intricately bound up with the need to deal with the experience of the trauma itself. Freud suggests that the repetition compulsion is one means by which the psyche asserts its struggle for mastery over the traumatic event and that this struggle is essential to the avoidance of psychosis. The second moment of trauma, then, is essential to the ability to overcome trauma through the retrospective re-working of events in order to gain mastery over them. In a sense, the experience of dereliction is similar to this second moment, in that it has the power to become all-consuming and unbearable, potentially culminating in a deathly abyss. This parallels the development of Freud's notion of the death drive which he further explores in *Beyond the Pleasure Principle*, first published in 1920.

14   Von Trier gives the name 'Hartmann' to the family in *Europa*, suggesting that he is somehow struggling with the revelations made to him by his mother on her death bed as he conceptualises this film and the interpersonal relationships depicted in it.

CHAPTER FOUR

1   In Denmark, *The Kingdom* was broadcast in four episodes, each of which closes with a to-camera address by von Trier who, dressed in Carl Theodor Dreyer's tuxedo, provides a few moments of rather arch commentary on the thematic content of the episode that is drawing to a close. Each of these epilogues ends with an exhortation to the viewer: 'Should you want to spend more time with us at the Kingdom, be prepared to take the good with the evil.' In Germany, France and the UK, *The Kingdom* was broadcast in five episodes. However, the series in its entirety was also released as a film (with extensive global distribution) in which the episodic structure and the closing epilogue scenes are omitted. The same principle was applied to the television and cinematic releases of *The Kingdom II*. The importance of this for the reception of the text will be considered later in this chapter.

2   The blurring of reality and fiction is a key marker of the turn in von Trier's work towards approaches to cinema that help to formulate the Dogme 95 project, as the next chapter explores.

3   Interestingly, 'gothic' was often aligned with a 'Teutonic' sensibility, a fact which no doubt has significance for von Trier with his interest in all things German.

4   This quotation from Shakespeare's *Hamlet* is frequently referenced by critics and commentators on von Trier's work in *The Kingdom*.

5   The quotation here is based on the English-language subtitles of the DVD version of *The Kingdom II* (Zentropa Entertainments, 1997).

6   In this context, it is interesting to note that von Trier's work on *The Kingdom* provided inspiration for Stephen King's *Kingdom Hospital* (ABC, 2004). The US series can be seen as a re-working of the original but with greater televisual specificity.

7   Tangherlini elaborates on this connection in his article on *The Kingdom* (2001: 12). While these issues may appear to be overtly of domestic interest, there have been a number of similar scandals in nations other than Denmark. For example, controversies around an illicit trade in organs for transplantation have circulated globally with reference to China and India. In the UK, a number of local scandals have also arisen in the context of hospitals such as Alder Hey Children's Hospital in Liverpool.

8   It is interesting to note the ways in which technologies of surveillance and medical investigation provide spaces for the manifestation of the uncanny throughout *The Kingdom*. Creeber comments that technologies in *The Kingdom* constitute a kind of 'fog': 'The grainy images of hearing scans, brain scans, ultrascans and x-ray images also continue to foreground the presence of a dark "subterranean" world, as if the doctors are literally peering into unknown realms through a dense and impenetrable (albeit technological) mist' (2002: 392).

9   There have been a number of popular cultural texts emerging in the latter years of the twentieth century and the first decade of the twenty-first that signal what might be seen as a turn toward a discourse of the spiritual. Examples include *The X Files* (Fox, 1993–2002); *The Others* (Alejandro Amenàbar, 2001); *Sea of Souls* (BBC, 2004–); *Forbrydelser* (*In Your Hands*, Annette K. Olesen, 2004); *Medium* (NBC, 2005); and the surge of interest in television programmes premised on mediumship

and the pursuit of 'phantoms' of all kinds (for example, *Most Haunted* (Living TV, 2002–)).

CHAPTER FIVE

1   The 'Dogme 95 manifesto' and the 'Vow of Chastity' are published online at www.dogme 95.dk and are also reproduced in the appendix to this volume.

2   Academy 35mm is 'the original film format'. The term describes the basic film gauge that has been in use since the inception of cinema. All cinemas have 35mm projection facilities, which means that this is the only film format that can be projected in every cinema around the world.

3   The manifestos are collected together and published in Björkman 2003 and also in the appendix to this volume.

4   For an interesting overview of Vertov's work, see Dawson 2003.

5   For a useful overview of the content of the manifestos that influenced von Trier, see Schepelern n.d.; MacKenzie 2003.

6   It is interesting to note that the drive toward 'authenticity' is seen across a range of media formats during the late 1980s and early 1990s, which saw the beginning of 'unplugged' performances of pop and rock music, for example, and the move toward more live television and 'phone-in' radio programmes.

7   See the appendix for the manifestos and statements published by von Trier.

8   This film was in post-production at the time of von Trier's announcement of Dogme 95. There are several interesting discussions of the trope of religion in this film. See Heath 1998; Keefer & Linafelt 1998; Makarushka 1998; Watkins 1999; Mercadente 2001; Bekkenkamp & Sherwood 2003; Penner & Stichele Vander 2003.

9   In fact, there were six screenings in total which took place between 1956 and 1959. The screenings combined work by these directors with films made under the umbrella of *la nouvelle vague* and included *O Dreamland* (Lindsay Anderson, 1956), *Momma Don't Allow* (Karel Reisz & Tony Richardson, 1956), and *Together* (Lorenza Mazzetti, 1956). The British Film Institute has a useful online resource for those interested in reading more about this movement: http://www.bfi.org.uk/features/freecinema.

10   This was also a factor at play in the development of *la nouvelle vague* in France, of course.

11   For an interesting commentary on this, see Biressi & Nunn 2005: 42–7.

12   In psychoanalysis, the primal scene is defined as a scene of fantasy in which the infant re-stages the idea of the sexual relationship between its parents and imagines interrupting such a scene, becoming a voyeur in the process. Laplanche and Pontalis suggest that such a scene is perceived as an act of violence perpetrated by the father and illustrate how the scene becomes to basis for castration anxiety in the little boy (1988: 335).

13   For a more detailed discussion of these ideas, see Bainbridge 2004a.

14   Of course, the Dogme 95 manifesto explicitly rejects the construction of 'illusion films' and so Kracauer's work seems particularly apposite here.

15   This is seen in a number of ideological domains, but perhaps most clearly in the context of ecological protests which make use of the internet to disseminate information to protestors and to establish spaces of political expression and community.

CHAPTER SIX

1   For a useful overview of the debates, see Ryall 1998.

2   For example, Robert Stam comments that 'A number of perennial doubts plague genre theory. Are genres really "out there" in the world, or are they merely the constructions of analysts? Is there a finite taxonomy of genres or are they in principle infinite? Are genres timeless Platonic essences or ephemeral, time-bound entities? Are genres culture-bound or transcultural? ... Should genre analysis be descriptive or proscriptive? ... While some genres are based on story content (the war film), others are borrowed from literature (comedy, melodrama) or from other media (the musical). Some are performer-based (the Astaire-Rogers films) or budget-based (blockbusters), while others are based on artistic status (the art film), racial identity (black cinema), locate (the western) or sexual orientation (Queer cinema). Some, like documentary and satire, might better be seen as "transgenres"' (2000: 14).

3   Further discussion of the 'femininity' of these films follows later in this chapter and in chapter seven.

4   For an overview of the history of melodrama, see Gledhill 1987.

5   For commentary on the Brechtian style of Douglas Sirk, who directed films such as *Magnificent Obsession* (1954), *All That Heaven Allows* (1955), *Written on the Wind* (1956) and *Imitation of Life* (1959), see Willemen 1972/73 and 1991.

6   In this respect, it is interesting that the term 'melodrama' derives etymologically from *melos* (music) and *drama*. The generic blending at play in *Dancer in the Dark* therefore seems appropriate.

7   The chapter headings are: 'Bess Gets Married'; 'Life with Jan'; 'Life Alone'; 'Jan's Illness'; 'Doubt'; 'Faith'; and 'Bess's Sacrifice'. The epilogue is entitled 'The Funeral'. Each chapter heading is accompanied by a digitally-enhanced, 'painterly' and long-held static shot of the Scottish landscape, rendered by Per Kirkeby, who describes them as based on romantic paintings 'from history which lurk somewhere in the subconscious, on museum visits, and in any kitsch painting ... Their effect lies primarily in the symbolic power of changes in the light. It's an ancient, banal, quite unverbalised message' (1996: 12).

8   Key examples of Romantic art and literature include Johann Wolfgang von Goethe's *The Sorrows of Young Werther* (1774); E. T. A. Hoffmann's *The Sandman* (1817), which would later inform Freud's work on 'The Uncanny' (1925); the poetry of William Wordsworth, Samuel Taylor Coleridge, Lord Byron, Percy Bysshe Shelley, John Keats and Mary Shelley; the paintings of J. M. W. Turner and, later, the Pre-Raphaelites. For a useful introduction to Romanticism across the arts, see Prickett 1981.

9   Further discussion of Bess and her heroic status which is often inscribed in terms of 'transcendent goodness' follows later in this chapter.

10 The songs used are: 'All the Way From Memphis' composed by Ian Hunter and performed by Mott the Hoople; 'In a Broken Dream' written and performed by Python Lee Jackson and featuring Rod Stewart; 'Cross-Eyed Mary' written by Ian Anderson and performed by Jethro Tull; 'Whiter Shade of Pale' written by Keith Reid and Gary Brooker and performed by Procul Harum; 'Suzanne' composed and performed by Leonard Cohen; 'Goodbye Yellow Brick Road' composed and performed by Elton John; 'Time' composed by Jon Lord, Ritchie Blackmore, Ian Gillian, Roger Glover and Ian Paice and performed by Deep Purple; and 'Your Song' composed and performed by Elton John.

11 Describing the look of the film in terms of its 'subdued, death-row-drab palette', Gavin Smith suggests that *Dancer in the Dark* 'is a profoundly interiorised reworking of the most exhibitionistic of movie genres (the melodrama)' (2000: 23).

12 Alessandro Ago has suggested that this film should be regarded as a 'sadistic melodrama' (2003: 39).

13 For example, in reviewing *Breaking the Waves*, several critics commented on the dizzying camera-work so seemingly at odds with the narrative content.

14 There is a substantial body of critical work emerging around the themes of testimony and trauma in the formation of contemporary subjectivities. For an insight into how this is deployed in relation to film theory and criticism, see Radstone 2001; Hammond *et al.* 2003; Bainbridge *et al.* 2004b.

15 This re-visioning of the musical as operatic is echoed in von Trier's decision to open the film with an 'overture'. In opera, the overture often foreshadows the key events of the story that follows, setting up themes of tragedy etc from the outset of the work.

16 See Björkman 2003 for an interesting comment on how we also have to work as active spectators in order to work out the relationship between different characters in von Trier's work.

17 While it is clear that the epilogue here is, in one way, intended as a playful reminder of the film's general attack on dogmatic religious belief and practice, the recourse to fantasy arguably underscores the commitment to the ideal of transcendence and this can be understood as a desire to maintain a relation to God or to the divine despite the overt critique of religious practices. In this, von Trier is heavily influenced by Carl Theodor Dreyer (see Björkman 2003: 168).

18 As José Arroyo has remarked, this is, indeed, the best way to upset an audience (2000: 16).

19 These themes of love and trauma are further explored in the next chapter.

CHAPTER SEVEN

1   'When I was little, I had a children's book called *Guldhjerte* ('Gold Heart'), which I had very clear and happy memories of. It was a picture book about a little girl who goes into the forest with some slices of bread and other stuff in her pockets. But at the end of the book, when she's got through the forest, she's standing there naked and with nothing left. And the last line of the book was: "'Well, at least I'm okay', said Gold Heart"' (von Trier in Björkman 2003: 164). Other commentators have signalled the

fact that the little girl, in fact, gives away all her possessions until she has none left (Smith 2000: 22) and that von Trier's version of the picture book was missing its ending in which a boy helped by Gold Heart turns out to be a prince. She finally gives him her heart and they marry and live happily ever after (Stevenson 2002: 101).

2   There are five manifestos written to accompany von Trier's films in the 'Europa' and 'Gold Heart' trilogies. See the appendix at the end of this book.

3   Of course, *The Kingdom* also deploys discourses around disability in its sensitive use of Downs Syndrome actors as the Chorus.

4   As Stephen Heath has pointed out, various characters in the film describe Bess as 'susceptible', 'not right in the head' and as 'prone to hysterics'. He also highlights the fact that Bess was said to be sectioned under the terms of the Mental Health Act shortly after the death of her brother and this becomes a means of getting Bess treated properly toward the end of the film. See Heath 1998: 94.

5   *The Idiots* in particular garnered an array of brickbats. Alexander Walker, for example, commented that 'a more repugnant piece of drivel it would (thankfully) be hard to find' (1999: 30), while Nigel Cliff stated 'I cannot decide whether this film is courageous, offensive or plain idiotic' (1999). In the *Guardian*, Peter Bradshaw described *Dancer in the Dark* as a 'middlebrow dumbfest', remarking that it was 'the most sensationally silly film of the year – as well as the most shallow and crudely manipulative' (2000). *Dancer in the Dark* received so many negative reviews, that Film Four offered a money back guarantee in the week of its release, publicising this in the major British press (Anon. 2000).

6   It is interesting that Bess explicitly signals that the oil rig workers have more cultural capital than the inhabitants of the community in her conversation with the Chairman of the Council of Elders at the Kirk:

Chairman: We seldom consent to these mixed marriages. I have to say that none has ever proved a happy one. Can you think of anything of real value that the outsiders have brought with them?

Bess (smiles):   Their music?
The chairman looks at her angrily. She beams up at him. He cannot break her smile. He shrugs his shoulders. (von Trier 1996: 25)

7   For a discussion of the critical responses to von Trier's depiction of Bess as a martyr, see chapter six. It is interesting that in response to questions about the apparent misogyny of the film in which the director is accused of making the heroine suffer, von Trier comments 'But, for God's sake, most American films follow that advice!' (Björkman 2003: 179).

8   Galt's discussion of nation in this article is an interesting one, signalling how which von Trier's representation of Germany can be read in terms of a broader context of what might be understood as 'New European' identity developing out of the European Union.

9   For further discussion of the American Dream in cinema, see Rosen 1973; Charyn 1989; Maltby 1995.

10   In this respect, I am thinking of the claims to the political set out in the work of thinkers such as Diana Fuss (1989), where essentialism is read as a strategic tool to be used in the opening up of spaces for newly politicised thinking.

CHAPTER EIGHT

1   This remark is widely quoted in the press coverage of von Trier's work in this trilogy. It is extracted from the press conference interview following the launch of *Manderlay* in 2005 (www.festival-cannes.fr/perso/index.php?langue=6002&personne=2139). Interestingly, on the official website for *Manderlay* (www.manderlaythefilm.com), in a short film interview with the director entitled 'On freedom and democracy', von Trier draws a direct parallel between the plot of the film and George W. Bush's project in attempting to 'bring democracy' to Iraq. The geopolitical context of the films in this trilogy is not something from which von Trier wishes to shy away. Rather, he seems deliberately to court the attention the films garner in this regard, signalling that the provocations he makes in interviews around these films should be read in terms of the allegorical qualities of the films and with full knowledge of his interventions and commentaries on his motivations.

2   Props consist, for example, of self-standing window frames, the occasional bedstead, Hessian sacks and fence posts. In *Dogville*, even the town's dog is symbolised through a chalk drawing on the floor, only

coming to life as a 'real' dog in the closing sequence of the film.

3   See the production notes for *Dogville* published on the official website for the film, www.dogville.dk. This film was purportedly inspired by a song from Brecht's *Threepenny Opera* (co-written with Kurt Weill) entitled 'Pirate Jenny'. Pirate Jenny's song anticipates her collusion in ensuring that the town in which she feels herself to have been betrayed be razed to the ground in an act of vengeance and retribution. See http://www.kore.it/caffe/poesia/pirate.html for the lyric of the song translated into English.

4   At the press conference for *Manderlay*, von Trier called Bush 'an asshole', making no bones about his own perspective on geopolitical events and their allegorical representation in his work. See n.1 above.

CHAPTER NINE

1   The full text of the statement is included in the appendix to this book, together with the various other manifestos released by von Trier during the course of his career.

2   The dedicated website (www.lookey.dk) explains that the 'lookey' is a visual element out of context that is added to a movie and that there are between five and seven 'lookeys' in any given film. They can be decoded according to a system unique to the movie concerned. Von Trier offers a prize of 30,000 Danish Kroner to the first Dane to spot the 'lookeys' in his latest film, *The Boss of It All* (2006), as well as the opportunity to appear in von Trier's next film.

3   The rules for this project were that each filmmaker should work with the same cast of actors and the same selection of characters and that each film must be shot using digital technology on location in Scotland. Hjort usefully observes that the rules are not merely limitations in this context, but are (like the Dogme 95 rules before them) designed to elicit collaboration and innovation.

APPENDIX

1   See http://www.dogme95.dk/menu/menuset.htm for the original source of both this manifesto and the 'Vow of Chastity'.

FILMOGRAPHY

For details of the films made by Lars von Trier during his childhood and whilst studying film at Copenhagen University, see Jack Stevenson (2002) *Lars von Trier*. London: British Film Institute, 204–5. The following details include the key works of cinema and television since his time at the Danish film school in 1980.

Short Films

Nocturne (1980)

Format: 16mm
Running Time: 8 minutes
Language: Danish
Colour and Black & White
Director: Lars von Trier
Production: Danske Filmskole
Screenplay: Lars von Trier
Photography: Tom Elling
Editor: Tómas Gislason
Cast: Yvette, Solbjerg Højfeldt, Annelise Gabold

Den sidste detalje (*The Last Detail*, 1981)

Format: 35mm
Running Time: 31 minutes
Language: Danish
Black &White

Director: Lars von Trier
Production: Danish Film School
Screenplay: Rumle Hammerich
Photography: Tom Elling
Editor: Tómas Gislason
Cast: Otto Brandenburg (Danny); Torben Zeller (Frank); Gitte Pelle (The Woman); Ib Hansen (The Gangster Boss); Michael Simpson (The Assistant)

Befrielsesbilleder (*Images of a Relief*, 1982)

Format: 35mm
Running Time: 57 minutes
Language: Danish and German
Colour
Director: Lars von Trier
Production: Danske Filmstudie for Danske Filmskole
Producer: Per Årman
Photography: Tom Elling
Editor: Tómas Gislason
Music: Københavns Strygekvartet, Vokalgruppen Ars Nova
Sound: Morten Degnbol, Iben Haahr
Cast: Edward Fleming, Kirsten Olesen

Feature Films

The Europa Trilogy

Forbrydelsens element (*The Element of Crime*, 1984)

Format: 35mm widescreen
Running Time: 103 minutes
Language: English
Colour
Director: Lars von Trier
Production: Per Holst in collaboration with the Danish Film Institute
Screenplay: Lars von Trier and Niels Vørsel
Photography: Tom Elling
Editor: Tómas Gislason
Cast: Michael Elphick (Fisher); Esmond Knight (Osbourne); Me Me Lai (Kim); Jerold Wells (Police Chief Kramer); Ahmed El Shenawi (Therapist); Lars von Trier (Receptionist)

Epidemic (1987)

Format: 16mm and 35mm
Running Time: 106 minutes
Language: Danish and English
Colour and Black & White
Director: Lars von Trier
Production: Element Film in collaboration with the Danish Film Institute
Screenplay: Lars von Trier and Niels Vørsel
Photography: Henning Bendtsen
Editor: Lars von Trier and Thomas Kragh
Cast: Ole Ernst; Michael Getting; Colin Gilder; Svend Ali Haman; Claes Kastholm Hansen; Gitte Lind; Susanne Ottesen; Allan de Wall

Europa (1991; released in the USA as *Zentropa*)

Format: 35mm CinemaScope
Running Time: 113 minutes
Language: English and German
Colour and Black & White
Director: Lars von Trier
Assistant Director: Tómas Gislason
Production: Nordisk Film in collaboration with the Danish Film Institute, the Swedish Film Institute, PCC,
        Telefil GMBH; Gunnar Obel, WMG and Gérard Mital Productions
Screenplay: Lars von Trier and Niels Vørsel
Photography: Henning Bendtsen
Editor: Hervé Schneid
Cast: Jean-Marc Barr (Leopold Kessler); Barbara Sukowa (Katharina Hartmann); Udo Kier (Lawrence
        Hartmann); Ernst-Hugo Jåregård (Uncle Kessler); Erik Mørk (priest)

The Gold Heart Trilogy

Breaking the Waves (1996)

Format: 35mm and digital video – for projection in 35mm and CinemaScope
Running Time: 158 minutes
Language: English
Colour
Director: Lars von Trier
Assistant Director: Morten Arnfred
Production: Zentropa Entertainments
Screenplay: Lars von Trier (co-written by Peter Asmussen and David Pirie)
Photography: Robby Müller
Editor: Anders Refn
Cast: Emily Watson (Bess); Stellan Skarsgård (Jan); Katrin Cartlidge (Dodo); Jean-Marc Barr (Terry);
        Adrian Rawlins (Dr Richardson); Jonathan Hackett (the minister)

Idioterne (*The Idiots*, 1998)

Format: Digital video for projection on 35mm
Running Time: 111 minutes
Language: Danish
Colour
Director: Lars von Trier
Production: Zentropa Entertainments
Screenplay: Lars von Trier
Photography: Lars von Trier with assistance from Kristoffer Nyholm, Jesper Jargil and Casper Holm
Editor: Lars von Trier and Molly Malene Stensgaard
Cast: Bodil Jørgensen (Karen); Jens Albinus (Stoffer); Anne Louise Hassing (Susanne); Troels Lyby (Henrik);
        Nikolai Lie Kaas (Jeppe); Louise Mieritz (Josephine); Henrik Prip (Ped); Luis Mesonero (Miguel);
        Knud Romer Jørgensen (Axel); Trine Michelsen (Nana); Anne-Grethe Bjarup Riis (Katrine)

Dancer in the Dark (2000)

Format: 35mm and digital video
Running Time: 139 minutes
Language: English
Colour

Director: Lars von Trier
Screenplay: Lars von Trier
Production: Zentropa Entertainments
Photography: Robby Müller
Editor: Molly Malene Stensgaard and François Gédigier
Cast: Björk (Selma); Catherine Deneuve (Kathy); David Morse (Bill); Vladica Kostic (Gene); Peter Stormare (Jeff); Joel Grey (Oldrich Novy); Vincent Patterson (Samuel)

The U-S-A – Land of Opportunities Trilogy

Dogville (2003)

Format: Digital video for projection in 35mm
Running Time: 178 minutes
Language: English
Colour
Director: Lars von Trier
Production: Zentropa Entertainments
Screenplay: Lars von Trier
Photography: Anthony Dod Mantle
Editor: Molly Malene Stensgaard
Cast: Nicole Kidman (Grace); Harriet Andersson (Gloria); Lauren Bacall (Ma Ginger); Jean-Marc Barr (The Man with the Big Hat); Paul Bettany (Tom Edison); Blair Brown (Mrs. Henson); James Caan (The Big Man); Patricia Clarkson (Vera); Jeremy Davies (Bill Henson); Ben Gazzara (Jack McKay); Philip Baker Hall (Tom Edison Sr.); Thom Hoffman (Gangster); Siobhan Fallon (Martha): John Hurt (Narrator); Zeljko Ivanek (Ben); John Randolph Jones (Gangster); Udo Kier (The Man in the Coat); Cleo King (Olivia); Miles Purinton (Jason); Bill Raymond (Mr. Henson); Chloë Sevigny (Liz Henson); Shauna Shim (June); Stellan Skarsgård (Chuck); Evelina Brinkemo (Athena); Anna Brobeck (Olympia); Tilde Lindgren (Pandora); Evelina Lundqvist (Diana); Helga Olofsson (Dahlia)

Manderlay (2005)

Format: Digital video for projection in 35mm
Running Time: 139 minutes
Language: English
Colour
Director: Lars von Trier
Production: Zentropa Entertainments
Screenplay: Lars von Trier
Photography: Anthony Dod Mantle
Editor: Bodil Kjærhauge and Molly Malene Stensgaard
Cast: Bryce Dallas Howard (Grace); Isaach De Bankolé (Timothy); Danny Glover (Wilhelm); Willem Dafoe (Grace's Father); Michaël Abiteboul (Thomas); Lauren Bacall (Mam); Jean-Marc Barr (Mr. Robinsson); Geoffrey Bateman (Bertie); Virgile Bramly (Edward); Ruben Brinkmann (Bingo); Doña Croll (Venus); Jeremy Davies (Niels); Llewella Gideon (Victoria); Mona Hammond (Old Wilma); Ginny Holder (Elisabeth); John Hurt (Narrator); Emmanuel Idowu (Jim); Zeljko Ivanek (Dr. Hector); Teddy Kempner (Joseph); Udo Kier (Mr. Kirspe); Rik Launspach (Stanley Mays); Suzette Llewellyn (Flora); Charles Maquignon (Bruno); Joseph Mydell (Mark); Javone Prince (Jack); Clive Rowe (Sammy); Chloë Sevigny (Philomena); Nina Sosanya (Rose); Wendy Juel (Claire); Seth Mpundu (Ed); Derrick Odhiambo-Widell (Willie); Alemayehu Wakijra (Milton); Fredric Gildea (Gangster); Andrew Hardiman (Truck Driver); Aki Hirvonen (Gangster); Mikael Johansson (Gangster); Hans Karlsson (Gangster); Ian Matthews (Mr. Miller); Maudo Sey (Burt); Erich Silva (Viggo); Ross Taylor (Gangster); Eric Voge (Gangster); Nick Wolf (Gangster)

Wasington (announced as forthcoming)

De fem benspænd (*The Five Obstructions*, 2003)

Format: 35mm
Running Time: 90 minutes
Language: Danish, English, French and Spanish
Colour and Black & White
Directors: Jørgen Leth and Lars von Trier
Production: Zentropa Real; Wajnbrosse Productions; Almaz Film Production; Panic Productions
Writers: Jørgen Leth and Lars von Trier with Sophie Destin and Asger Leth
Photography: Kim Hattesen and Dan Holmberg
Editor: Daniel Dencik, Morten Højbjerg and Camilla Skousen
Cast: Claus Nissen (The Perfect Man – from *Det perfekte menneske* (*The Perfect Human*, 1967) (archive footage)); Majken Algren Nielsen (The Perfect Woman, from *Det perfekte menneske*, 1967 (archive footage)); Jørgen Leth (Speaker – from *Det perfekte menneske*, 1967/Himself as Director (segments 'The Conversations')/Speaker (segment 'Obstruction #1 – The Perfect Human: Cuba')/The Perfect Man/ Speaker (segment 'Obstruction #2 – The Perfect Human: Bombay')/Speaker (segment 'Obstruction #4 – The Perfect Human: Cartoon')/Jørgen Leth/The Perfect Human/Speaker (segment 'Obstruction #5 – The Perfect Human: Avedøre, Denmark'));Lars von Trier (Himself – Obstructor (segments 'The Conversations')/Lars von Trier (segment 'Obstruction #5 – The Perfect Human: Avedøre, Denmark')); Daniel Hernandez Rodriguez (The Perfect Man (segment 'Obstruction #1 – The Perfect Human: Cuba')); Jacqueline Arenal (The Perfect Woman (segment 'Obstruction #1 – The Perfect Human: Cuba'));Vivian Rosa; Alexandra Vandernoot (The Perfect Woman (segment 'Obstruction #3 – The Perfect Human: Brussels')); Patrick Bauchau (The Perfect Man/Speaker (segment 'Obstruction #3 – The Perfect Human: Brussels')/Speaker (segment 'Obstruction #4 – The Perfect Human: Cartoon')); Marie Dejaer (Maid (segment 'Obstruction #3 – The Perfect Human: Brussels')); Pascal Perez (Couple (Man) (segment 'Obstruction #3 – The Perfect Human: Brussels')); Meschell Perez (Couple (Woman) (segment 'Obstruction #3 – The Perfect Human: Brussels')); Bent Christensen (Gangster from *Det gode og det onde* (*Good and Evil*, 1975) featured in segment 'Obstruction #4 – The Perfect Human: Cartoon' (archive footage)); Anders Hove (Naked Man, from *Notater om kærligheden* (*Notes on Love*, 1989) featured in segment 'Obstruction #4 – The Perfect Human: Cartoon' (archive footage)); Charlotte Sieling (Naked Woman – from *Notater om kærligheden* featured in segment 'Obstruction #4 – The Perfect Human: Cartoon' (archive footage)); Jan Nowicki (Man with jacket, from *Notater om kærligheden* featured in segment 'Obstruction #4 – The Perfect Human (archive footage)); Stina Ekblad (Woman with money, from Notater om kærligheden featured in segment 'Obstruction #4 – The Perfect Human (archive footage)); Bob Sabiston (Himself)

Dear Wendy (2005)

Format: Digital video form projection in 35mm
Running Time: 105 minutes
Language: English
Colour
Director: Thomas Vinterberg
Production: Lucky Punch, Nimbus Film, Zentropa Entertainments and TV2 Danmark
Screenplay: Lars von Trier
Photography: Anthony Dod Mantle
Editor: Mikkel E.G. Nielsen
Cast: Jamie Bell (Dick Dandelion); Bill Pullman (Krugsby); Michael Angarano (Freddie); Danso Gordon (Sebastian); Novella Nelson (Clarabelle); Chris Owen (Huey); Alison Pill (Susan); Mark Webber (Stevie); Trevor Cooper (Dick's Dad); Matthew Geczy (Young Officer); William Hootkins (Marshall Walker); Teddy Kempner (Mr. Salomon); Thomas Bo Larsen (Customer)

Direktøren for det hele (*The Boss of it All*, 2006)

Format: 35mm
Running Time: 99 minutes
Language: Danish, Icelandic, English, Russian
Colour
Automavision*
Director: Lars von Trier
Production: Zentropa Productions
Screenplay: Lars von Trier
Editor: Molly Malene Stensgaard
Cast: Jens Albinus (Direktøren for det hele/Kristoffer/Svend E.); Peter Gantzler (Ravn); Benedikt Erlingsson (Tolk); Iben Hjejle (Lise); Henrik Prip (Nalle); Mia Lyhne (Heidi A.); Casper Christensen (Gorm); Louise Mieritz (Mette); Jean-Marc Barr (Spencer); Sofie Gråbøl (Kisser); Anders Hove (Jokumsen); Friðrik Þór Friðriksson (Finnur); Lars von Trier (Narrator)

TV Productions

Medea (1988)

Format: Video, transferred to film and then copied back to video
Running Time: 75 minutes
Language: Danish
Colour
Director: Lars von Trier
Production: Danmarks Radio TV
Screenplay: Carl Theodor Dreyer and Proben Thomsen
Editor: Finnur Sveinsson
Cast: Udo Kier (Jason); Kirsten Olsen (Medea); Henning Jensen (Kreon); Solbjerg Højfeldt (nurse); Baard Owe (Aigeus); Preben Lerdorff Rye (teacher); Ludmilla Glinska (Glauce)

Riget (*The Kingdom*, 1994)

Format: 16mm and video (blown up to 35mm for theatrical release)
Running Time: 280 minutes
Language: Danish
Colour
Director: Lars von Trier
Production: Zentropa Entertainments and Danmarks Radio TV
Writers: Lars von Trier and Niels Vørsel
Photography: Eric Kress and Henrik Harpelund
Editors: Molly Malene Stensgaard and Jacob Thuesen
Cast: Ernst-Hugo Jåregård (Stig G. Helmer); Kirsten Rolffes (Mrs Sigrid Drusse); Ghita Nørby (Rigmer); Søren Pilmark (Krogshøj); Otto Brandenburg (Hansen); Jens Okking (Bulder); Holger Juul Hansen (Dr Einar Moesgaard); Annevig Schelde Ebbe (Mary); Baard Owe (Bondo); Birgitte Raaberg (Judith); Peter Mygind (Mogge); Vita Jensen (Dishwasher 1); Morten Rotne Leffers (Dishwasher 2); Solbjørg Højfeldt (Camilla); Udo Kier (Aage Krüger)

Lærerværelset (*The Teacher's Room*, 1994)

Concept: Lars von Trier
Running Time: 6 episodes of 25 minutes (experimental talk show)
Language: Danish
Directors: Lars von Trier and Rumle Hammerich

Production: Zentropa Entertainments for TV2
Cast: Søren Gericke; Lotte Heise; Jacob Ludvigsen; Arne Melchior; Klaus Rifbjerg

Marathon (1996)

Concept: Lars von Trier
Running Time: 24 hours edited into 8 chat shows (experimental talk show blending fiction and reality)
Language: Danish
Director: Lars von Trier
Production: Zentropa Entertainments for Danmarks Radio TV
Cast: Peter Øvig Knudsen

Riget II (*The Kingdom II*, 1997)

Format: 16mm and video (blown up to 35mm for theatrical release)
Running Time: 286 minutes
Language: Danish
Colour
Directors: Lars von Trier and Morten Arnfred
Production: Zentropa Entertainment and Danmarks Radio TV
Writers: Lars von Trier and Niels Vørsel
Photography: Eric Kress and Henrik Harpelund
Editors: Molly Malene Stensgaard and Pernille Bech Christensen
Cast: Ernst-Hugo Järegård (Stig Helmer); Peter Mygind (Mogge); Kirsten Rolffes (Sigrid Drusse); Holger
    Juul Hansen (Dr. Moesgaard); Søren Pilmark (Krogshøj); Ghita Nørby (Rigmor Mortensen); Jens
    Okking (Bulder); Ole Boisen (Christian); Birthe Neumann (Mrs. Svendsen); Otto Brandenburg
    (Hansen); Erik Wedersøe (Ole); Baard Owe (Bondo); Birgitte Raaberg (Judith); Henning Jensen
    (Bob); Nis Bank-Mikkelsen (Priest #1); Michelle Bjørn-Andersen (Pediatrician); Laura Christensen
    (Mona); Ulrik Cold (Narrator); Annevig Schelde Ebbe (Mary); Jannie Faurschou (Orthopaedist);
    Henrik Fiig (Car Crash Victim); Claus Flygare (Detective Nielsen); Louise Fribo (Susanne Jeppesen);
    Vera Gebuhr (Gerda); Peter Gilsfort (Dishwasher 2); John Hahn-Petersen (Nivesen); Mette Hald
    (Cross Girl); Peter Hartmann (Removal Man); Solbjørg Højfeldt (Camilla); Anders Hove (Celebrant);
    Paul Hüttel (Dr. Steenbaek); Kim Jansson (Detective Jensen); Birger Jensen (Rengøringsmand); Søren
    Elung Jensen (Man in Top Hat); Vita Jensen (Dish washer 1); Ruth Junker (Dishwasher 1); Annette
    Ketscher (Casualty Nurse); Udo Kier (Lillebror/Aage Krüger); Thomas Bo Larsen (Falken); Morten
    Rotne Leffers (Dish Washer 2); Britta Lillesøe (Woman in Bed); Hanne Løvendahl (Patient); Lars
    Lunøe (Minister of Health); Timm Mehrens (Doctor in Operating Theatre); Tine Miehe-Renard
    (Night Nurse); Bjarne G. Nielsen (Hospital Pastor); Claus Nissen (Madsen); Klaus Pagh (Bailiff);
    Holger Perfort (Professor Ulrich); Dorit Stender Petersen (Assisting nurse); Mette Munk Plum (Mona's
    Mother); Lise Schrøder (Nurse 2); Fash Shodeinde (Philip Marco); Michael Simpson (Man from
    Haiti); Stellan Skarsgård (Stig Helmer's lawyer); Jens Jørn Spottag (Attorney Bisgaard); Tomas Stender
    (Student); Steen Svare (Man in Overalls); Birte Tove (Nurse 1); Helle Virkner (Fru Mortensen); Lars
    von Trier (Himself); Klaus Wegener (Casualty Doctor); Julie Wieth (Paediatric Nurse); Philip Zandén
    (Dr. Jönsson); Torben Zeller (Crematorium Functionary)

D-Dag (*D-Day*, 2000)

Format: Digital video
Running Time: 70 minutes (experimental TV show made at the millennium)
Language: Danish
Colour
Directors: Søren Kragh-Jacobsen, Kristian Levring, Thomas Vinterberg and Lars von Trier
Production: Nimbus Film, Zentropa Entertainments, Danmarks Radio TV, TV 2, TV3, TV Danmark
Photography: Anthony Dod Mantle, Jesper Jargil, Eric Kress, Henrik Lundø and Jens Schlosser

Editor: Valdís Óskarsdóttir

Cast: Nicolaj Kopernikus (Niels-Henning); Charlotte Sachs Bostrup (Lise); Dejan Cukic (Boris); Bjarne Henriksen (Carl); Jesper Asholt (Jørgen); Helle Dolleris (Carl's wife); Louise Mieritz (Lise's sister); Klaus Bondam (Receptionist); Therese Glahn; Thomas Bo Larsen; Lasse Lunderskov; Stellan Skarsgård (Lise's husband); Alexander Skarsgård; Tommy Kenter

Klown – It's A Jungle Down There (2005)

Format: Digital video
Running Time: 25 minutes (sitcom)
Language: Danish
Colour
Directors: Mikkel Nørgaard
Production: Zentropa Episode and Nutmeg Movies for TV 2
Writers: Casper Christensen and Lars von Trier
Photography: Jacob Banke Olesen
Editor: Nicolaj Monberg

Cast: Frank Hvam (Frank); Casper Christensen (Casper); Iben Hjejle (Iben); Mia Lyhne (Mia); Michael Carøe (Michael Carøe); Dya Josefine Hauch (Susan); Pernille Højmark (Pernille Højmark)

BIBLIOGRAPHY

Abbott, M. E. (2002) *The Street Was Mine: White Masculinity in Hard-Boiled Fiction and Film Noir*. New York: Palgrave.

Abraham, N. (1987) 'Notes on the Phantom: A Complement to Freud's Metapsychology', in N. Abraham and M. Torok (eds) *The Shell and the Kernel: Renewals of Psychoanalysis Volume 1*. Chicago: University of Chicago Press, 171–6.

Ago, A. (2003) 'Once Upon a Time in Amerika: *Dancer in the Dark* and Contemporary European Cinema', *Spectator – The University of Southern California Journal of Film and Television*, 23, 2, 32–43.

Alderman, H. (1977) *Nietzsche's Gift*. Athens: Ohio University Press.

Althusser, L. (1969) *For Marx*. London: Allen Lane.

Andersen, L. K. (2003 [1994]) 'A Stone-Turner from Lyngby', in J. Lumholdt (ed.) *Lars von Trier: Interviews*. Jackson: University Press of Mississippi, 88–99.

Anderson, B. (1983) *Imagined Communities: Reflections on the Origin and Spread of Nationalism*. London: Verso.

Anderson, J. (2003) 'September 11 Revisited', *Guardian*, 23 May, 10.

Anderson, L., L. Mazzetti, K. Reisz and T. Richardson (1956) 'Free Cinema Programme'; available at: www. bfi.org.uk/features/freecinema/programme/prog2.html [accessed 19 August 2001].

Andrews, N. (2003a [1991]) 'Maniacal Iconoclast of Film Convention', in J. Lumholdt (ed.) *Lars von Trier: Interviews*. Jackson: University Press of Mississippi, 81–3.

____ (2003b) 'Dogville', *Financial Times*, 23 May, 17.

Anon. (n.d.) 'Lars von Trier'; available at: http://www.filmreference.com/Directors-Ve-Y/von-Trier-Lars. html [accessed 19 January 2005].

____ (2000) 'Money Back Guarantee for *Dancer in the Dark*', *Guardian*, 26 September; available at: http:// www.film.guardian.co.uk/News_Story/Exclusive/0,373566,00.html [accessed 31 October 2000].

Arnheim, R. (1957) *Film as Art*. Berkeley: University of California Press.

Arroyo, J. (2000) 'How Do You Solve a Problem like Lars von Trier?', *Sight and Sound*, 10, 9, 14–16.

Audé, F. (1991) 'Le point de vue du noyé', *Positif*, 369, 39–40.

Badt, K. (2005) 'At War With Myself: A Word with Lars von Trier at Cannes 2005', *Bright Lights Film Journal*, 49, 49; available at: http://www.brightlightsfilm.com/49/trieriv.htm [accessed 14 January 2006].

Bainbridge, C. (2002) 'Feminine Enunciation in Cinema', *Paragraph: A Journal of Modern Critical Theory*, 25, 3, 129–42.

____ (2004a) 'Just Looking? Traumatic Affect, Film Form and Spectatorship in the Work of Lars von Trier', *Screen*, 45, 4, 391–400.

____ (2004b) 'Making Waves: Trauma and Ethics in the Work of Lars von Trier', *Journal for Cultural Research*, 8, 3, 353–69.

Bainbridge, C., A. Biressi and H. Nunn (eds) (2004a) 'Special Edition: Trauma and Ethics in the Field of Vision', *Journal for Cultural Research*, 8, 3.

____ (2004b) 'The Trauma Debate Continued', *Screen*, 45, 4, 391–422.

Bakhtin, M. (1982 [1924]) 'Forms of Time and of the Chronotope in the Novel: Notes Towards a Historical Poetics', in M. Holquist (ed.) *The Dialogic Imagination: Four Essays*. Austin: University of Texas Press, 84–258.

____ (1984) *Rabelais and His World*. Bloomington: Indiana University Press.

____ (1986) *Speech Genres and Other Late Essays*. Austin: University of Texas Press.

Barthes, R. (1972) *Mythologies*. London: Vintage.

Baudry, J.-L. (1985 [1970]) 'Ideological Effects of the Basic Cinematic Apparatus', in B. Nichols (ed.) *Movies and Methods: An Anthology Volume 2*. Berkeley: University of California Press, 531–43.

Bauman, Z. (2000) *Liquid Modernity*. Cambridge: Polity Press.

Bazin, A. (1967) *What is Cinema? Volume 1*. Berkeley: University of California Press.

Bekkenkamp, J. (1998) '*Breaking the Waves*: Corporeality and Religion in a Modern Melodrama', in J. Bekkenkamp and M. de Haardt (eds) *Begin with the Body: Corporeality, Religion and Gender*. Leuven: Uitgeverij Peeters, 134–56.

Bekkenkamp, J. and Y. Sherwood (2003) *Sanctified Aggression: Legacies of Biblical and Post Biblical Vocabularies of Violence*. London: T & T Clark International.

Bell, E. (2005) 'Lars von Trier: Anti-American? Me?', *Independent*, 21 October 2005; available at: http://enjoyment.independent.co.uk/film/features/article321010.ece [accessed 12 January 2006].

Bell, J. (2005) 'Gun Crazy', *Sight and Sound*, 15, 9, 20–2.

Beltzer, T. (2005) 'Lars von Trier', *Senses of Cinema*; available at: http://www.sensesofcinema.com/contents/directors/02/vontrier.html [accessed 17 April 2006].

Berthelius, M. and R. Narbonne (2003 [1987]) 'A Conversation with Lars von Trier', in J. Lumholdt (ed.) *Lars von Trier: Interviews*. Jackson: University Press of Mississippi, 47–58.

Bhabha, H. K. (1994) 'Race, Time and the Revision of Modernity', in L. Back and J. Solomos (eds) (2000) *Theories of Race and Racism*. London: Routledge, 354–68.

Billen, A. (2006) 'Shout? No, I Just Tease a Lot', *Times*, 21 February, 8.

Biressi, A. and H. Nunn (2005) *Reality TV: Realism and Revelation*. London: Wallflower Press.

Björkman, S. (1996a) *I am curious, film*. London: Channel 4 Television.

____ (1996b) 'Naked Miracles', *Sight and Sound*, 6, 10, 11–14.

____ (1999) 'Juggling in the Dark', *Sight and Sound*, 9, 12, 8–10.

____ (ed.) (2003) *Trier on von Trier*. London: Faber and Faber.

Björkman, S. and L. Nyman (2003 [1995]) 'I am Curious, Film: Lars von Trier', in J. Lumholdt (ed.) *Lars von Trier: Interviews*. Jackson: University Press of Mississippi, 100–2.

Bondebjerg, I. (2003) 'Dogma 95 and the New Danish Cinema', in M. Hjort and S. MacKenzie (eds) *Purity and Provocation: Dogma 95*. London: British Film Institute, 70–85.

Bourdieu, P. (1977) *Outline of a Theory of Practice*. Cambridge: Cambridge University Press.

____ (1984) *Distinction: A Social Critique of the Judgement of Taste*. Cambridge, MA: Harvard University Press.

____ (1986) 'The Forms of Capital', in J. G. Richardson (ed.) *Handbook of Theory and Research for the Sociology of Education*. New York: Greenwood Press, 241–58.

Bradshaw, P. (2000) '*Dancer in the Dark*', *Guardian*, 15 September; available at: http://film.guardian.co.uk/

News_Story/Critic_Review/Guardian_Film_of_the_week/0,4267,368401,00.html [accessed 21 July 2001].

____ (2001) 'All Roads Lead to Rome', *Guardian*, 15 February, microfiche.

Brecher, J., T. Costello and B. Smith (2000) *Globalization From Below: The Power of Solidarity* Cambridge, MA.: South End Press.

British Film Institute (n.d.) *Europa* Press Pack and Microjacket. London: British Film Institute.

Brooker, C. and R. North (2005a) *The Great Deception: Can the European Union Survive?* London: Continuum.

____ (2005b) *The Great Deception: The Secret History of the European Union*. London: Continuum.

Brooks, X. (1999) 'The Idiots', *Sight and Sound*, 9, 5, 34–5.

____ (2003) 'The Pupil's Revenge', *Guardian*, 7 November; available at: http://film.guardian.co.uk/interview/interviewpages/0,6737,1080386,00.html [accessed 21 April 2004].

Bruzzi, S. (2000) *New Documentary: A Critical Introduction*. London: Routledge.

Bunbury, S. (2003) 'The Dogged Dane', *The Age*, 14 December; available at: http://www.theage.com.au/articles/2003/12/13/1071125713337.html?from=storyrhs&oneclick=true [accessed 19 April 2004].

Buscombe, E. (1986) 'The Idea of Genre in the American Cinema', in B. K. Grant (ed.) *Film Genre Reader*. Austin: University of Texas Press, 14–24.

Calhoun, D. (2005) 'Mission to Lars', *Time Out*, 1823, 22–4.

Cavell, S. (1979) *The World Viewed: Reflections on the Ontology of Film*. Cambridge, MA: Harvard University Press.

Chanter, T. (2004) 'The Picture of Abjection: Thomas Vinterberg's *The Celebration*', *Parallax*, 10, 1, 30–9.

Charyn, J. (1989) *Movieland: Hollywood and the Great American Dream Culture*. New York: New York University Press.

Chiesa, L. (2006) 'Tragic Transgression and Symbolic Re-Inscription: Lacan With Lars von Trier', *Angelaki: Journal of the Theoretical Humanities*, 11, 2, 49–62.

____ (forthcoming) 'What is the Gift of Grace? An Essay in Sixteen Sections and Three Epigraphs', *Film Philosophy*.

Chopra-Gant, M. (2006) *Hollywood Genres and Postwar America: Masculinity, Family and Nation in Popular Movies and Film Noir*. London: I. B. Tauris.

Christensen, C. (2003) 'Documentary Gets the Dogma Treatment', in M. Hjort and S. MacKenzie (eds) *Purity and Provocation: Dogma 95*. London: British Film Institute, 183–8.

Christensen, O. (2000a) 'Authentic Illusions: The Aesthetics of Dogma 95', *p.o.v.: A Danish Journal of Film Studies*, 10; available at: http://imv.au.dk/publikationer/pov/Issue_10/section_4/artc2A.html [accessed 24 May 2002].

____ (2000b) 'Spastic aesthetics – *The Idiots*', *p.o.v.: A Danish Journal of Film Studies*, 10, 35–45; available at: http://imv.au.dk/publikationer/pov/Issue_10/section_2/artc4A.html [accessed 24 April 2004].

Ciment, M. and P. Rouyer (2003 [1988]) 'A Conversation with Lars von Trier', in J. Lumholdt (ed.) *Lars von Trier: Interviews*. Jackson: University Press of Mississippi, 59–63.

Clark, J. (2004) '*Dogville*: Or How Not to Discover America', *Bright Lights Film Journal*, Vol., 45; available at: http://www.brightlightsfilm.com/45/dog2.htm [accessed 31 January 2006].

Cliff, N. (1999) 'New Movies', *The Times*, 13 May, microfiche.

Combs, R. (2000) 'Rules of the Game', *Film Comment*, 36, 5, 28–32.

Conrich, I. and E. Tincknell (2000) 'Film Purity, the Neo-Bazinian Ideal and Humanism in Dogma 95', *p.o.v.: A Danish Journal of Film Studies*, 10; available at: http://pov.imv.au.dk/Issue_10/section_4/artc7A.html [accessed 24 May 2002].

Cooper, D. (2000) 'Flailing Vision', *Artforum International*, 39, 2, 29.

Corliss, R. (1996) 'Breaking the Waves', *Time Magazine*, 148, 25, 81.

Corner, J. (1996) *The Art of Record: A Critical Introduction to Documentary*. Manchester: Manchester University Press.

Cowie, P. (1973) *A Ribbon of Dreams: The Cinema of Orson Welles*. London: Tantivy Press.

Craib, I. (1994) *The Importance of Disappointment*. London: Routledge.

Creeber, G. (2002) 'Surveying *The Kingdom*: Explorations of medicine, memory and modernity in Lars von Trier's *The Kingdom* (1994)', *European Journal of Cultural Studies*, 5, 4, 387–407.

Crofts, S. (1998) 'Concepts of National Cinema', in J. Hill and P. Church Gibson (eds) *The Oxford Guide* to Film Studies. Oxford: Oxford University Press, 385–94.

Dalton, S. (2004) 'Lars Attacks!', The Times, 14 February; available at: http://www.thetimesonline.co.uk/article/0,,7943-1000325,00.html [accessed 21 April 2004].

Darke, P. A. (2001) 'A Masterpiece of Normalcy'; available at: http://www.outside-centre.com/darke/mycv/writings/televis/idiots.html [accessed 18 November 2005].

Dawson, J. (2003) 'Dziga Vertov', Senses of Cinema, 25 (March–April); available at: http://www.sensesofcinema.com/contents/directors/03/vertov.html [accessed 16 July 2003].

De Sade, M. (1797) Justine. London: Wordsworth Press.

De Walle, M. (1996) 'Heaven's Weight', Artforum International, 35, 6, 82–8.

Dickos, A. (2002) Street With No Name: A History of the Classic American Film Noir. Lexington: University of Kentucky Press.

Donald, J. (1989) 'The Fantastic, the Sublime and the Popular, Or, What's at Stake in Vampire Films?', in J. Donald (ed.) Fantasy and the Cinema. London: British Film Institute, 233–51.

Dutton, D. (2003) 'Authenticity in Art', in J. Levinson (ed.) The Oxford Handbook of Aesthetics. Oxford: Oxford University Press; available at: http://www.denisdutton.com/authenticity.htm [accessed 2 January 2007].

Dyer, R. (1997) 'The Matter of Whiteness', in L. Back and J. Solomos (eds) (2000) Theories of Race and Racism. London: Routledge, 539–48.

Eisner, L. (1973) The Haunted Screen. London: Secker and Warburg.

Elliott, A. (1996) Subject to Ourselves: Social Theory, Psychoanalysis and Postmodernity. Cambridge: Polity Press.

Ellis, J. (1977) 'Free Cinema', 1951–1976: British Film Institute Productions; available at: http://www.bfi.org.uk/features/freecinema/archive/ellis-freecinema.html [accessed 19 August 2001].

Elsaesser, T. (1987 [1972]) 'Tales of Sound and Fury: Observations on the Family Melodrama', in C. Gledhill (ed.) Home is Where the Heart Is: Studies in Melodrama and the Woman's Film. London: British Film Institute, 43–69.

____ (1989) 'Social Mobility and the Fantastic: German Silent Cinema', in J. Donald (ed.) Fantasy and the Cinema. London: British Film Institute, 23–38.

____ (2001) 'Postmodernism as Mourning Work', Screen, 42, 2, 193–201.

Esslin, M. (1974) Brecht: The Man and His Work. New York: Norton.

Faber, A. (2003) 'Redeeming Sexual Violence?: A Feminist Reading of Breaking the Waves', Literature and Theology, 17, 1, 59–75.

Fanon, F. (1986 [1952]) Black Skin, White Masks. London: Pluto Press.

Feuer, J. (1992) 'Genre Study and Television', in R. C. Allen (ed.) Channels of Discourse Reassembled: Television and Contemporary Criticism. London: Routledge, 138–60.

Fibiger, B. (2003) 'A Dog Not Yet Buried: On Dogville as a Political Manifesto', p.o.v.: A Danish Journal of Film Studies, 16, December; available at: http://pov.imv.au.dk/Issue_16/section_1/artc7A.html [accessed 19 April 2004].

Fiske, J. (1982) Introduction to Communication Studies. London: Routledge.

Foucault, M. (1978) The History of Sexuality Volume I: An Introduction. London: Penguin.

____ (1986) The History of Sexuality Volume III: The Care of the Self. New York: Pantheon.

Frampton, D. (1993) 'Lars von Trier x 6', Filmosophy, June; available at http://www.filmosophy.org/articles/vontrier [accessed 15 April 2004].

Fraser, N. (1991) 'Rethinking the Public Sphere: A Contribution to the Critique of Actually Existing Democracy', in C. Calhoun (Ed.) Habermas and the Public Sphere. Boston, MA: MIT Press.

French, P. (1985) 'The Element of Crime', The Observer, 9 June, 21.

Freud, S. (1955 [1919]) 'A Child is Being Beaten', in J. Strachey (ed.) The Standard Edition of the Complete Psychological Works of Sigmund Freud, Volume 17. London: The Hogarth Press, 175–204.

____ (1968 [1937]) 'Analysis Terminable and Interminable', in J. Strachey (ed.), The Standard Edition of the Complete Psychological Works of Sigmund Freud, Volume 23. London: The Hogarth Press, 209–54.

____ (1991a [1905]) 'Three Essays on Sexuality' (Ed.), On Sexuality, Penguin Freud Library Volume 7. London: Penguin.

____ (1991b [1919]) 'The Uncanny', in Art and Literature, Penguin Freud Library Volume 14. London: Penguin, 339–76.

_____ (1991c [1920]) 'Beyond the Pleasure Principle', in *On Metapsychology, Penguin Freud Library Volume 11*. London: Penguin, 269-338.

_____ (1991d [1921]) 'Group Psychology and the Analysis of the Ego' (Ed.), *Civilization, Society and Religion, Penguin Freud Library Volume 12*. London: Penguin, 91–178.

_____ (1991e [1924]) 'The Economic Problem of Masochism', in *On Metapsychology, Penguin Freud Library Volume 11*. London: Penguin, 411–26.

Freud, S. and J. Breuer (1991 [1893]) *Studies on Hysteria: Penguin Freud Library Volume 3*. London: Penguin.

Frosh, S. (1991) *Identity Crisis: Modernity, Psychoanalysis and the Self*. London: Macmillan.

Fuller, G. (1992) 'Shots in the Dark', *Interview*, 22, 1, 29.

Fuss, D. (1989) *Essentially Speaking: Feminism, Nature, Difference*. London: Routledge.

Galt, R. (2005) 'Back Projection: Visualizing Past and Present Europe in *Zentropa*', *Cinema Journal*, 45, 1, 3–21.

Garrett, G. (1999) 'Hitchcock's Women on Hitchcock: A panel discussion with Janet Leigh, Tippi Hedren, Karen Black, Suzanne Pleshette, and Eva Marie Saint', *Literature Film Quarterly*, 27, 2, 78–89; available at: http://www.findarticles.com/p/articles/mi_qa3768/is_199901/ai_n8846083/pg_2 [accessed 21 April 2004].

Gaut, B. (2003) 'Naked Film: Dogma and its Limits', in M. Hjort and S. MacKenzie (eds) *Purity and Provocation: Dogma 95*. London: British Film Institute, 89-101.

Geijerstam, E. A. (2003 [1990]) 'A Conversation with Lars von Trier, Henning Bendtsen and Ernst-Hugo Järegård', in J. Lumholdt (ed.) *Lars von Trier: Interviews*. Jackson: University Press of Mississippi, 64-70.

Gibbons, F. (2003) 'Kidman says it's time to quit', *Guardian*, 20 May, 5.

Giddens, A. (1991) *Modernity and Self-Identity: Self and Society in the Late Modern Age*. Cambridge: Polity Press.

_____ (1992) *The Transformation of Intimacy: Sexuality, Love and Eroticism in Modern Societies*. Cambridge: Polity Press.

Gilbey, R. (2002) 'Dogme is Dead. Long Live Dogme', *Guardian*, 19 April; available at: http://film.guardian.co.uk/features/featurepages/0,,686645,00.html [accessed 12 January 2006].

Gledhill, C. (1987) 'The Melodramatic Field: An Investigation', in C. Gledhill (ed.) *Home is Where the Heart Is: Studies in Melodrama and the Woman's Film*. London: British Film Institute, 5–39.

Gordon, S. (2004) '*Breaking the Waves* and the Negativity of Melanie Klein: Rethinking "the female spectator"', *Screen*, 45, 3, 206–25.

Gramsci, A. (1971) *Selections from the Prison Notebooks of Antonio Gramsci*. London: Lawrence & Wishart.

Groves, T. (2003) 'Cinema/Affect/Writing', *Senses of Cinema*, 25, March-April; available at: http://www.sensesofcinema.com/contents/03/25/writing_cinema_affecthtml [accessed 21 April 2004].

Gruzinski, S. (1997) '*Europa*: Journey to the End of History', in C. David and J. F. Chevrier (eds) *Documenta X – The Book: Politics, Poetics*. Ostfildern: Cantz-Verl, 508-13.

Halsall, P. (1998) 'The Black Death and the Jews 1348-1349 CE', *Jewish History Sourcebook*; available at: http://www.fordham.edu/halsall/jewish/1348-jewsblackdeath.html [accessed 17 September 2005].

Hammond, M., D. Humphrey, K. Randell and P. Thomas (2003) 'The Trauma Debate Continued', *Screen*, 44, 2, 200-28.

Hampton, H. (1995) 'Wetlands: *The Kingdom* of Lars von Trier', *Film Comment*, 31, 40-3.

Harsin, J. (2006) 'Von Trier's Brechtian Gamble: On *Manderlay*', *Bright Lights Film Journal*, 51; available at: http://www.brightlightsfilm.com/51/manderlay.htm [accessed 14 April 2006].

Heath, S. (1998) 'God, Faith and Film: *Breaking the Waves*', *Literature and Theology*, 12, 1, 93–107.

Heynen, H. (2006) 'Questioning Authenticity', *National Identites*, 8, 3, 287–300.

Hjort, M. (2003a) 'Dogma 95: A Small Nation's Response to Globalisation', in M. Hjort and S. MacKenzie (eds) *Purity and Provocation: Dogma 95*. London: British Film Institute, 31–47.

_____ (2003b) 'The Globalisation of Dogma: The Dynamics of Metaculture and Counter-Publicity', in M. Hjort and S. MacKenzie (eds) *Purity and Provocation: Dogma 95*. London: British Film Institute, 133-57.

_____ (2003c) '*Lars von Trier* by Jack Stevenson, Book Review', *Senses of Cinema*, 24 (Jan-Feb); available at: http://www.sensesofcinema.com/contents/books/03/24/von_trier.html [accessed 16 July 2003].

_____ (forthcoming) 'Affinitive and Experimental Transnationalism: The "Advance Party" Initiative', in D. Iordanova, D. Martin-Jones and B. Vidal (eds) *Cinema at the Periphery*. Detroit, MI: Wayne State University Press.

Hjort, M. and I. Bondebjerg (2001) *The Danish Directors: Dialogues on a Contemporary National Cinema*. Bristol: Intellect Books.

Hjort, M. and S. MacKenzie (eds) (2003) *Purity and Provocation: Dogma 95*. London: British Film Institute.

Hoberman, J. (2004) 'The Grace of Wrath: Failed Christian charity, Old Testament payback: A Danish director's American tragedy', *Village Voice*; available at: http://www.villagevoice.com/film/0412,hoberman,52001,20.html [accessed 16 June 2004].

Holden, S. (2006) 'An America Where Gangsters Free Slaves Not Keen for Liberation', *New York Times*, 27 January; available at: http://movies2.nytimes.com/2006/01/27/movies/27mand.html?n=Top%2fReference%2fTimes%20Topics%2fPeople%2fV%2fVon%20Trier%2c%20Lars [accessed 21 February 2006].

Irigaray, L. (1985a) *Speculum of the Other Woman*. New York: Columbia University Press.

_____ (1985b) *This Sex Which Is Not One*. New York: Columbia University Press.

_____ (1993a) *An Ethics of Sexual Difference*. London: The Athlone Press.

_____ (1993b) *Sexes and Genealogies*. New York: Columbia University Press.

_____ (1996) *I Love To You: Sketch for a Felicity Within History*. New York and London: Routledge.

Johnson, B. D. (1996) '*Breaking the Waves*', *Maclean's*, 109, 49, 94.

Johnson, C. (2005) *Telefantasy*. London: British Film Institute.

Kapla, M. (2003 [2001]) 'Lars von Trier in *Dogville*', in J. Lumholdt (ed.) *Lars von Trier: Interviews*. Jackson: University Press of Mississippi, 205–12.

Kaplan, E. A. (2001) 'Melodrama, Cinema and Trauma', *Screen*, 42, 2, 201–5.

Kaufmann, S. (1996) '*Breaking the Waves*', *New Republic*, 215, 24, 26–8.

_____ (2004) 'Town Limits', *New Republic*, 24–5.

Keefer, K. and T. Linafelt (1998) 'The End of Desire: Theologies of Eros in *The Song of Songs* and *Breaking the Waves*', *Journal of Religion and Film*, 2, 1; available at: www.unomaha.edu/jrf/endofdes.htm [accessed 31 October 2000].

Kennedy, H. (1991) 'Go Deeper: To *Europa*, with love', *Film Comment*, 27, 4, 68–71.

_____ (1996) 'Orbiting Sublimity', *Film Comment*, 32, 4, 6–8.

King Heyraud, J. (2001) '*Dancer in the Dark*', *Psychological Perspectives*, Vol., 42, 145–9.

Kirkeby, P. (1996) 'The Pictures Between the Chapters in *Breaking the Waves*', in L. von Trier (ed.) *Breaking the Waves*. London: Faber and Faber, 12–14.

Klein, M. (1988) *Love, Guilt, Reparation and Other Works 1921–1945*. London: Vintage.

Knudsen, P. Ø. (2003 [1998]) 'The Man Who Would Give Up Control', in J. Lumholdt (ed.) *Lars von Trier: Interviews*. Jackson: University Press of Mississippi, 117–24.

Koplev, K. (2003 [2000]) '9 A.M., Thursday, September 7, 2000: Lars von Trier', in J. Lumholdt (ed.) *Lars von Trier: Interviews*. Jackson: University Press of Mississippi, 170–204.

Kracauer, S. (1960) *Theory of Film: The Redemption of Physical Reality*. Oxford: Oxford University Press.

_____ (2004 [1967]) *From Caligari to Hitler: A Psychological History of the German Film*. Princeton: Princeton University Press.

Kristeva, J. (1982) *Powers of Horror: An Essay on Abjection*. New York: Columbia University Press.

Krutnik, F. (1991) *In a Lonely Street: Film Noir, Genre, Masculinity*. London: Routledge.

Lacan, J. (1993) *The Seminar of Jacques Lacan Book III: The Psychoses 1955–56*. London: W. W. Norton.

Laplanche, J. and J.-B. Pontalis (1988) *The Language of Psychoanalysis*. London: Karnac Books.

Larsen, J. K. (1984) 'A Conversation between Jan Kornum Larsen and Lars von Trier', *Kosmorama*, 167, 9–17.

Lasch, C. (1978) *The Culture of Narcissism*. New York: W. W. Norton.

Lash, S. (1990) *Sociology of Postmodernism*. London: Routledge.

Le Fanu, M. (1987) *The Cinema of Andrei Tarkovsky*. London: British Film Institute.

Luckhurst, R. (2003) 'Trauma Culture', *New Formations*, 50, 28–47.

Lumholdt, J. (2003) *Lars von Trier: Interviews*. Jackson: University Press of Mississippi.

MacKenzie, S. (2000) 'Direct Dogma: Film manifestos and the *fin de siècle*', *p.o.v.: A Danish Journal of Film*

Studies, 10; available at: http://imv.au.dk/publikationer/pov/Issue_10/section_4/artc6A.html [accessed 24 May 2002].

_____ (2003) 'Manifest Destinies: Dogma 95 and the Future of the Film Manifesto', in M. Hjort and S. MacKenzie (eds) *Purity and Provocation: Dogma 95*. London: British Film Institute, 48–57.

Mairs, G. (1998) '*The Idiots*'; available at: http://www.culturevulture.net/Movies/Idiots.html [accessed 21 April 2004].

Makarushka, I. S. M. (1998) 'Transgressing Goodness in *Breaking the Waves*', *Journal of Religion and Film*, 2, 1; available at: www.unomaha.edu/jrf/breaking.htm [accessed 31 October 2000].

Maltby, R. (1995) *Hollywood Cinema: An Introduction*. Oxford: Blackwell.

Matheou, D. (2004) 'Lars von Trier: No sets or props, but we do get Nicole in chains', *Independent*, 1 February; available at: http://enjoyment.independent.co.uk/low_res/story.jsp?story=486833&host=5&dir=213 [accessed 21 April 2004].

Matheson, N. (1985) 'The Lars Frontier', *New Musical Express*, 22 June, 19.

Matthews, P. (1998) '*Kingdom II*', *Sight and Sound*, 8, 8, 46–7.

_____ (2000) '*Dancer in the Dark*', *Sight and Sound*, 10, 10, 41–2.

McNab, G. (2006) 'Interview with Lars von Trier', *The Boss of It All* Press Book; available at: http://www.trust-film.dk/download/direktoeren_presseb_engelsk2.pdf [accessed 1 December 2006].

Mercadante, L. (2001) 'Bess the Christ Figure? Theological Interpretations of *Breaking the Waves*', *Journal of Religion and Film*, 5, 1; available at: http://www.unomaha.edu/~wwwjrf/bessthe.htm [accessed 5 November 2003].

Mercer, J. and M. Shingler (2004) *Melodrama: Genre, Style, Sensibility*. London: Wallflower Press.

Metz, C. (1981) *The Imaginary Signifier: Psychoanalysis and the Cinema*. Bloomington: Indiana University Press.

Michelsen, O. (2003 [1982]) 'Passion is the Lifeblood of Cinema', in J. Lumholdt (ed.) *Lars von Trier: Interviews*. Jackson: University Press of Mississippi, 5–12.

Milne, T. (1971) *The Cinema of Carl Dreyer*. London: Zwemmer Books.

Mitchell, W. (2006) 'Lars von Trier unveils Lookey concept', *Screen Daily*, 6 December; available at: http://www.screendaily.com/story.asp?storyid=28856&st=lookey&s=3 [accessed 9 December 2006].

Modleski, T. (1988) *The Women Who Knew Too Much*. London: Routledge.

Morrow, F. (2004) 'The Dogmatic Great Dane', *Independent*, 30 January, 8–9.

Mulvey, L. (1975) 'Visual Pleasure and Narrative Cinema', *Screen*, 16, 3, 6–18.

Neale, S. (1980) *Genre*. London: British Film Institute.

_____ (1983) 'Masculinity and Spectacle: Reflections on Men and Mainstream Cinema', *Screen*, 24, 6, 2–16.

_____ (2001) 'Genre and Television', in G. Creeber (ed.) *The Television Genre Book*. London: British Film Institute, 1–4.

Nelson, V. (1997) 'The New Expressionism: Why the Bells Ring in *Breaking the Waves*', *Salmagundi*, 116/17, 228–38.

Nichols, B. (2001) *Introduction to Documentary*. Bloomington: Indiana University Press.

Norman, N. (2003) 'The Odd Couple', *Evening Standard*, 22 April, 23.

Nunn, H. (2002) *Thatcher, Politics and Fantasy: The Political Culture of Gender and Nation*. London: Lawrence & Wishart.

Oppenheimer, J. and D. E. Williams (1996) 'Von Trier and Muller's Ascetic Aesthetic on *Breaking the Waves*', *American Cinematographer*, 77, December, 18–22.

Orr, J. (2002) 'Out of Dreyer's Shadow? The Quandary of Dogme95', *New Cinemas: Journal of Contemporary Film*, 1, 2, 69–77.

Parkinson, D. (1995) *History of Film*. London: Thames and Hudson.

Pence, J. (2004) 'Cinema of the Sublime: Theorizing the Ineffable', *Poetics Today*, 25, 1, 29–67.

Penner, T. and C. Stichele Vander (2003) 'The Tyranny of the Martyr: Violence and Victimization in Martyrdom Discourse and the Movies of Lars von Trier', in J. Bekkenkamp and Y. Sherwood (eds) *Sanctified Aggression: Legacies of Biblical and Post-Biblical Vocabularies of Violence*. New York: T & T Clark International, 175–92.

Pinder, J. (2001) *The European Union: A Very Short Introduction*. Oxford: Oxford University Press.

Prendergast, T. and S. Prendergast (2000) *International Dictionary of Films and Filmmakers Volume 2:*

Directors. London: St James Press.

Prickett, S. (ed.) (1981) *The Romantics*. London: Methuen.

Radstone, S. (2001) 'Trauma and *Screen* Studies: Opening the Debate', *Screen*, 42, 2, 188–92.

Reid, T. R. (2004) *The United States of Europe: The New Superpower and the End of American Supremacy*. London: Penguin.

Restuccia, F. L. (2001) 'Impossible Love in *Breaking the Waves*: Mystifying Hysteria', *Literature and Psychology*, 47, 1/2, 34–54.

Richards, B. (1994) *Disciplines of Delight: The Psychoanalysis of Popular Culture*. London: Free Association Books.

Richolson, J. M. (1992) '*Zentropa*', *Cinéaste*, 19, 2/3, 62–3.

Roberts, J. (1999) 'Dogme 95', *New Left Review*, 238, 141–9.

Rockwell, J. (2001) 'Von Trier and Wagner, A Bond Sealed in Emotion', *New York Times*, 8 April; available at: http://query.nytimes.com/gst/fullpage.html?sec=health&res=9F0DE3D61E3FF93BA35757C0A9 679C8B63 [accessed 29 December 2002].

____ (2002) 'Lars von Trier, Bayreuth and The Ring: The Danish film director stages Wagner's tetralogy in 2006', *Opera*, 43, 1, 30–4.

____ (2003) *The Idiots*. London: British Film Institute.

Roman, S. (2003 [1999]) 'Lars von Trier: The Man Who Would Be Dogme', in J. Lumholdt (ed.) *Lars von Trier: Interviews*. Jackson: University Press of Mississippi, 133–43.

Romney, J. (1992) 'Euro Paean', in J. Humboldt (ed.) *Lars von Trier: Interviews*. Jackson: University Press of Mississippi, 84–5.

____ (2004) 'Return of the Provocateur', *Independent*, 15 February, 9.

Rosen, M. (1973) *Popcorn Venus: Women, Movies and the American Dream*. New York: Coward, McCann & Geoghegan.

Royle, N. (2003) *The Uncanny*. Manchester: Manchester University Press.

Rundle, P. (1999) 'We Are All Sinners'; available at: http://www.dogme95.dk/menu/menuset.htm [accessed 15 March 2000].

Rustin, M. (1991) *The Good Society and the Inner World*. London: Verso.

Ryall, T. (1998) 'Genre and Hollywood', in J. Hill and P. Church Gibson (eds) *The Oxford Guide to Film Studies*. Oxford: Oxford University Press, 327–41.

Scallan, A. D. and V. Garin (1997) 'Leave Her to Heaven: Lars von Trier's *Breaking the Waves* as Neo-Melodrama', *Film West*, 27; available at: http://www.iol.ie/~galfilm/filmwest/27larsvon.htm [accessed 31 January 2006].

Schatz, T. (1981) *Hollywood Genres: Formulas, Film-Making and the Studio System*. Philadelphia: Temple University Press.

Schepelern, P. (n.d.) 'Film According the Dogma: Restrictions, Obstructions and Liberations'; available at: http://www.dogme95.dk/news/interview/schepelern.htm [accessed 24 May 2002].

____ (2003) '"Kill Your Darlings": Lars von Trier and the Origin of Dogma 95', in M. Hjort and S. MacKenzie (eds) *Purity and Provocation: Dogma 95*. London: British Film Institute, 58–69.

____ (2005) 'The Making of an Auteur: Notes on the Auteur Theory and Lars von Trier', *Visual Authorship: Creativity and Intentionality in Media. Northern Lights Film and Media Studies Yearbook 2004*, 3, 103–28; available at: http://www.mtp.hum.ku.dk/cgibin/userdownload/1885ljb111220061602/u/ The_Making_of_an_Au.pdf [accessed 15 March 2006].

Schwander, L. (2003 [1983]) 'We Need More Intoxicants in Danish Cinema', in J. Lumholdt (ed.) *Lars von Trier: Interviews*. Jackson: University Press of Mississippi, 13–23.

Scott, A. O. (2000) 'Universe Without Happy Endings', *New York Times*, 22 September; available at: http:// movies2.nytimes.com/mem/movies/review.html?_r=1&title1=Dancer%20in%20the%20Dark%20 (Movie)%20%20 [accessed 28 December 2002].

Sheridan, A. (1980) *Michel Foucault: The Will to Truth*. London: Routledge.

Silver, A. and J. Ursini (eds) (1999) *Film Noir Reader*. New York: Limelight Editions.

Sjödin, C. (2003) 'The Significance of Belief for Psychoanalysis', *International Forum of Psychoanalysis*, 12, 1, 44–52.

Smith, G. (2000) 'Imitation of Life', *Film Comment*, 36, 5, 22–6.

Smith, P. J. (2003) 'Social Activism and the Internet', *Labour/Le Travail*, 51; available at: http://www.

historycooperative.org/journals/llt/51/smith.html [accessed 2 June 2006].

Sobchack, V. (1996) 'History Happens', in V. Sobchack (ed.) *The Persistence of History: Cinema, Television and the Modern Event*. London: Routledge, 1–14.

Stam, R. (1989) *Subversive Pleasures: Bakhtin, Cultural Criticism and Film*. Baltimore and London: John Hopkins University Press.

_____ (2000) *Film Theory: An Introduction*. Oxford: Blackwell.

Sterrit, D. (2000) '*Idioterne*', *Film Comment*, 36, 2, 75–6.

Stevenson, J. (2002) *Lars von Trier*. London: British Film Institute.

_____ (2003) *Dogme Uncut : Lars von Trier, Thomas Vinterberg, and the Gang that took on Hollywood*. Santa Monica, CA: Santa Monica Press.

Strick, P. (1991) '*Europa*', *Sight and Sound*, 2, 5, 47–8.

Tangherlini, T. R. (2001) 'Ghost in the Machine: Supernatural Threat and the State in Lars von Trier's *Riget*', *Scandinavian Studies*, 73, 1, 1–25.

Tanner, M. (1995) *Wagner*. Princeton: Princeton University Press.

Tapper, M. (2003 [1990]) 'A Romance in Decomposition', in J. Lumholdt (ed.) *Lars von Trier: Interviews*. Jackson: University Press of Mississippi, 71–80.

Taylor, E. (2001) 'Dancing in Denmark', *Creative Screenwriting*, 8, 1, 32–6.

Thomas, D. (2004) 'Meet the Punisher: Lars von Trier Devastates Audiences – and Actresses', *Newsweek*, 5 April; available at: http://msnbc.msn.com/id/4608844 [accessed 21 April 2004].

Thomsen, C. B. (2003 [1996]) 'Control and Chaos', in J. Lumholdt (ed.) *Lars von Trier: Interviews*. Jackson: University Press of Mississippi, 106–16.

Thomson, P. (1998) 'Rechristening *The Kingdom*', *American Cinematographer*, 79, 6, 24.

_____ (2000) '*The Idiots* Play by von Trier's Rules', *American Cinematographer*, 81, 1, 19–20.

Tirard, L. (2002) *Moviemakers' Master Class: Private Lessons from the World's Foremost Directors*. New York: Faber and Faber.

Todorov, T. (1973) *The Fantastic: A Structural Approach to Literary Genre*. Ithaca: Cornell University Press.

Truffaut, F. (1976 [1954]) 'Auteur Criticism: A Certain Tendency of the French Cinema', in B. Nichols (ed.) *Movies and Methods: An Anthology Volume 1*. Berkeley: University of California Press, 224–37.

Turim, M. (2001) 'The Trauma of History: Flashbacks upon Flashbacks', *Screen*, 42, 2, 205–10.

Turner, G. (2001) 'Genre, Format and "Live" Television', in G. Creeber (ed.) *The Television Genre Book*. London: British Film Institute: 4–7.

US Council of Catholic Bishops (2004) '*Dogville* – Review'; available at: http://www.usccb.org/movies/d/dogville.htm [accessed 21 April 2004].

Van der Walle, M. (1996) 'Heaven's Weight – Film Director, Lars von Trier', *Art Forum*, 35, 3.

Vestergaard Kau, E. (2000) 'Auteurs in Style: The heresy or indulgence of the Dogma brothers', *p.o.v.: A Danish Journal of Film Studies*, 10; available at: http://pov.imv.au.dk/Issue_10/section_4/artc4A.html [accessed 24 April 2004].

Vice, S. (1997) *Introducing Bakhtin*. Manchester: Manchester University Press.

von Trier, L. (1995a) 'Dogme95 Manifesto'; available at: http://www.dogme95.dk/menu/menuset.htm [accessed 26 July 1999].

_____ (1995b) 'Vow of Chastity'; available at: http://www.dogme95.dk/menu/menuset.htm [accessed 26 July 1999].

_____ (1996) *Breaking the Waves*. London: Faber and Faber.

_____ (2000) *Dancer in the Dark*. London: FilmFour Books.

_____ (2003) 'Dogville Official Website'; available at: http://www.dogville.dk [accessed 17 January 2004].

Walker, A. (1999) '*The Idiots*', *Evening Standard*, 13 May, 30.

Wall, J., M. (1997) '*Breaking the Waves*', *The Christian Century*, 114, 5, 115–17.

Walters, T. (2004) 'Reconsidering *The Idiots*: Dogme95, Lars von Trier and the Cinema of Subversion?', *Velvet Light Trap*, 53, 40–55.

White, H. (1996) 'The Modernist Event', in V. Sobchack (ed.) *The Persistence of History: Cinema, Television and the Modern Event*. London: Routledge, 17–37.

White, J. (2001) 'Fear of Togetherness? Community in the Films of Lars von Trier', *Parachute: Contemporary Art Magazine*, 102, 73–80.

Whitford, M. (1991) *Luce Irigaray: Philosophy in the Feminine*. London: Routledge.

Willemen, P. (1972/73) 'Towards an Analysis of the Sirkian System', *Screen*, 13, 4, 128–34.

_____ (1991) 'Distanctiation and Douglas Sirk', in L. Fischer (ed.) *Imitation of Life*. New Brunswick: Rutgers University Press, 268–72.

_____ (1994) *Looks and Frictions*. London: British Film Institute.

Williams, L. (2001) 'Cinema and the Sex Act', *Cinéaste*, 27, 1, 20–5.

Winston, B. (1995) *Claiming the Real: The Documentary Film Re-Visited*. London: British Film Institute.

Winters, L. (1996) 'Hot Danish: *Breaking the Waves*' director, Lars von Trier, may be as strange as his mysterious film', *Washington Post*, 24 November, 6.

Wise, D. (2003) 'No Dane, No Gain', *Observer*, 12 October; available at: http://film.guardian.co.uk/interview/interviewpages/0,,1061059,00.html [accessed 20 May 2004].

Wollen, P. (1998) *Signs and Meaning in the Cinema*. London: British Film Institute.

Wood, R. (1969) *Ingmar Bergman*. London: Studio Vista Ltd.

_____ (1998) 'Humble Guests at the Celebration: An Interview with Thomas Vinterberg and Ulrich Thomsen', *Cinéaction*, 48, No., 47–54.

Woodward, R. B. (2004) 'Hauteur Theory', *The American Prospect*, 15, 6, 41–3.

Wright, E. (ed.) (1992) *Feminism and Psychoanalysis: A Critical Dictionary*. Oxford: Blackwell.

INDEX